THE ASCENT

Sean Kelly, Stephen Roche and the
Rise of Irish Cycling's Golden Generation

Barry Ryan

Gill Books

Gill Books

Hume Avenue

Park West

Dublin 12

www.gillbooks.ie

Gill Books is an imprint of M.H. Gill and Co.

© Barry Ryan 2017

978 07171 7550 5

Design and print origination by O'K Graphic Design, Dublin

Edited by Neil Burkey

Photo on endpaper © Alamy

Printed by TJ International, Cornwall

This book is typeset in 12/18 pt Minion with headings in Monoton.

The paper used in this book comes from the wood pulp of managed forests. For every tree felled, at least one tree is planted, thereby renewing natural resources.

A CIP catalogue record for this book is available from the British Library.

5 4 3 2 1

ACKNOWLEDGEMENTS

This book would never have come to pass had Alasdair Fotheringham not pointed me in the direction of actually writing it after several years of procrastination. Alasdair's advice was invaluable throughout the process, and he continued to save me from myself after submission by doing virtually all the driving in southern Italy on the Giro d'Italia. Thanks Al (and Naomi and Mar).

I count myself very fortunate to have spent the last seven years at *Cyclingnews* working with and learning from Dan Benson and Stephen Farrand, two fine role models and even better friends (and thanks to Steve for doing virtually all the driving in northern Italy on the Giro). Thanks to Pierre Carrey, the Eric Cantona of cycling journalism (there is no higher compliment), for his friendship and help.

I am very grateful to everybody at Gill Books for their help and support, especially Conor Nagle, whose enthusiasm for the project from the very outset and guidance throughout were so important to me. Thanks to Sheila Armstrong for her organisation and keeping everything on schedule, to Jane Rogers and Neil Burkey for their copyediting, to Jen Patton for sourcing photographs, and to Ellen Monnelly, Grainne O'Reilly and Paul Neilan. Thanks to my agent Mark Stanton (Stan) for all his help.

From Killorglin to Calpe to Muscat, the people I interviewed for this book were extremely generous with their time and their memories. Thanks to Sean Kelly, Stephen Roche, Paul Kimmage, Martin Earley, Pat McQuaid, Alan McCormack, Laurence Roche, John Mangan, Roger Legeay, Frank Quinn, Eddy Schepers, Kieron McQuaid, David Walsh, Marcel Tinazzi, Noël Converset, Damien Long, John Mangan, Patrick Valcke, Brian Holm, Floyd Landis, Philippa York, Giuseppe Martinelli, Jean-François Rodriguez, Valerio Piva, Davide Boifava, Bernard Bourreau, Jock Boyer, Philippe Bouvet and Roberto Visentini. I was also very glad to have had the opportunity to interview the late Christy Kimmage in 2014, long before this book was commissioned but while the idea was taking shape.

Thanks to Brecht Decaluwé, Sadhbh O'Shea, Patrick Fletcher, Zeb Woodpower, Susan Westemeyer and all *Cyclingnews* colleagues past and present for their company and support over the years. Thanks to Sam Dansie and Ed Pickering at *Procycling*. Thanks to friends and colleagues in the press room, including Peter Cossins, Marco Pastonesi, Ciro Scognamiglio, Jean-François Quenet, Claudio Gregori, Rupert Guinness, Gregor Brown, Phil Sheehan, Rose Manley, William Fotheringham, Jeremy Whittle and Laura Fletcher. Thanks to John Pierce, who went far beyond the call of duty in sourcing photographs and sharing his vast knowledge of the era with me.

I am immensely grateful to the staff of the Bibliothèque Nationale de France in Paris for their assistance in sourcing archive materials, and to everybody at the National Library of Ireland in Dublin.

Special thanks to Siobhán Condon and Jason Dowling for their friendship and encouragement all the way from

Vancouver, and to John O'Farrell and Roz Flynn for putting a roof over my head in leafy South Dublin. Thanks to Shane Baker for helping to form ideas over medialunas. Thanks to James Roche, Richard Kelleher and all William Barry Bowl team owners. Thanks to Eoin Mulholland and Eimear Finnegan, to Liam Burke, Paddy Foley, Brendan Foley, Juan Mata, Martin O'Neill, Liam Cotter, Ciaran Cotter and Stefano Baschiera. Thanks to Giulia De Lorenzi for her constant support.

Thanks to everybody in Glanworth GAA Club. Thanks to Jim and Michael Hennessy for keeping me on the road. Thanks to Mark Jones and everybody in the sports department of the *Sunday Tribune* for their kindness in the summer of 2003. Thanks to Cecily O'Toole for her support then, and her kindness to my family ever since. Thanks to Dermot Coakley and the late Dick Henchion for their encouragement in St. Colman's, Fermoy.

I am especially grateful to my family for their understanding and support as I gradually withdrew from polite society to write this book. Love and thanks to my sister Catherine and my brother Terence for far too many things to mention, to my sister-in-law Sarah and to my niece Kate. Special thanks to my nephew Ollie for allowing his room to be converted into an office for a few months. Above all, love and thanks to my mother Mary for her example, her patience and her encouragement. This would not have been possible without her.

This book is dedicated to the memory of my late father Ollie, whose inspiration is present on every page and in every day.

CONTENTS

PROLOGUE

Cork city in September and a grey sky so low it might drown in the Lee. The crowds are sparser than in the years of plenty, but the diehards are padded out by weekend shoppers, hemmed in by the barriers as they make their way home from Roche's Stores or the Queen's Old Castle. They pause, having no alternative, to watch the spectacle.

They see the boys of summer, not in their ruin, but inclining towards their rest. It is nearly time. Sean Kelly and Stephen Roche are autumn's men now, and the 1992 Nissan Classic is almost certainly the last.

A mass of bodies and bikes and embrocation and swear words whizzes past, and sweeps onto St Patrick's Hill, and all eyes are strained for a sight of one of the lads. A young Lance Armstrong is somewhere in this peloton, in the red and blue of Motorola, and nobody notices. Men like Phil Anderson, Adrie van der Poel and Andrei Tchmil are mere accoutrements.

From the bottom of St Patrick's Hill, the crowds watch the cyclists weave against the gradient, then grow smaller and fainter as they melt into the gloom towards the summit. A figure in white moves ahead, and a man leaning across a barrier hazards that it might be Roche, but nobody is sure. Ten minutes later, the cyclists hurtle past the same spot, and the man realises it wasn't.

Twice more the scene repeats itself. Generous applause follows the riders all the way up the ascent, but for those viewing from the bottom of the hill, the cheers fade gently as they grind towards that impalpable greyness at the top. Twice more, the man draped over the barrier says that Roche is off the front, and on the final occasion, he turns out to be right.

One last lap around the houses. Roche leads a breakaway with Anderson and Raúl Alcalá down the hillside and back to the river. Kelly is poised among the chasers behind. For a moment, it is yesterday.

The finish line is a couple of hundred yards to the right, and the sound of the public address system doesn't carry. After the race ends, riders freewheel as far as the crowds at the bottom of the hill, and murmurs of the result travel by induction along the St Patrick's Quay: 'Twasn't Kelly or Roche who won anyway.'

Roche has placed 4th on the stage, and his aggression has earned him an invitation to the podium, to swap his Carrera jersey for the polka dots of the King of the Mountains. He wanted yellow. In eight years, he's never worn yellow here, but this is one way of saying goodbye. He smiles and waves from the dais.

There are no bouquets for Kelly, who comes home in 10th place and wheels to a halt in the middle of the road. He is older now, but the long face and stoical expression are immutable. He is always and instantly recognisable as *Kelly*. As if confirmation were needed, Cidona has, for the week that's in it, joined Festina among the sponsors on his blue jersey.

A soigneur hands Kelly a towel, and he wipes down his face, before accepting a bottle and pedalling away gingerly. Rather than cheer him off, the crowds hush as though viewing a Marian apparition. Nobody is so crass as to call out his name. Instead, fathers nudge sons: 'There's Kelly there, look.' And they do. They watch in quiet reverence until he glides out of sight.

The following day, the Nissan Classic will conclude in Dublin. Roche will have one last year in the peloton before he calls it a day, and Kelly will linger on for two, but it will be a flickering existence. Whether they realise it or not, the era ends here.

From the early 1980s, Kelly and Roche were at the summit of their art. Between them, they swept up almost every prize in cycling that was worth claiming. Roche won the Tour de France, Giro d'Italia and World Championships, and Kelly won nearly everything else, including the Vuelta a España, seven editions of Paris-Nice and nine monument classics. He was number one in the world rankings for five unbroken years.

At a time of mass emigration, they were Ireland's most beloved ambassadors on the Continent. In an often-grey decade back home, they provided colour. And yet, though often used as props by politicians, they espoused no ideology. It was, it seems, only ever about the bike, and the life to be made from it.

Martin Earley and Paul Kimmage joined them in the peloton as the decade progressed, and Pat McQuaid's Nissan Classic brought them back home for an annual lap of honour. For a time, Ireland seemed to number among the great cycling nations of the world. It was a stunning and perhaps inexplicable ascent, especially considering just how far down the mountain the journey began.

THE MUNICH BOTHER

The flush of youth and the thrill of competition have a way of distracting the mind from the big words that make the world so unhappy. As a mark of respect for the 11 members of the Israeli delegation killed by Palestinian terrorists, the Olympic Games were suspended for 24 hours, but now, barely two days after the atrocity, the spectacle has resumed. The police presence is more obtrusive than before, but like most on the start line, 21-year-old Kieron McQuaid has eyes only for the race ahead. He lines up alongside his Irish teammates Peter Doyle, Liam Horner and Noel Teggart, and in his own excitement, he doesn't even see the four riders in white jerseys with green and orange hoops who move through the crowd distributing leaflets minutes before the start, nor does he notice when the police discreetly lead them away shortly before the flag drops.

Once the race begins, there is an immediate injection of pace, and the peloton is stretched in the opening kilometres.

There is precious little respite as they tackle the lower slopes of the circuit's climb in the forested park around Grünwald, a suburb 10 miles or so south of Munich. Up ahead, McQuaid sees three figures in white emerge from some shrubs on the roadside, mount their bikes and infiltrate the peloton. 'Some locals acting the mess, trying to ride along with the Olympics,' he shrugs to himself.

A couple of miles later, having crossed the summit, McQuaid works his way forward in the bunch and finds that one of the men in white is still up there and pedalling smoothly. As he draws closer, he squints for a better look and sees that the rider's jersey has green and orange hoops. There is something familiar, too, about his bike. It's a Carlton, just like McQuaid's. The penny drops. The interloper is John Mangan, a fellow Irishman, albeit from a rival, outlawed federation.

McQuaid drops back to alert his teammates, happening first upon Horner. 'There's NCA lads in this group. Mind yourself, there could be trouble,' he warns him. Horner nods and seeks out Mangan for a parley. The conversation is heated but brief, and though each man rides on, the truce will not be a lasting one. Shortly afterwards, Mangan attacks from the front of the group. His lack of a race number marks him out as an intruder and causes some consternation among the race marshals. A police motorbike promptly tries to remove him from the race altogether, but succeeds only in balking him, and Mangan melts back into the peloton.

As he drops backwards, Mangan now finds himself side by side with Teggart, a truck driver from Banbridge in County Down riding in his final international race. Heavy words are lightly thrown. Mangan first leans across into Teggart, and then grabs his jersey and forces him to a standstill at the roadside. Each man clasps at the other's jersey as they step from their bikes, and voices rise. A couple of ill-directed jabs are exchanged. As the rest of the world sweeps past, they stand in a gutter fighting out a local row that is not of their own making.

This is Irish cycling in 1972.

For first half of the 20th century, Irish cycling was a largely domestic affair, despite the exploits of Harry Reynolds, the so-called 'Balbriggan Flyer', who won the sprint at the Track World Championships in Copenhagen in 1896. Grass track racing was the most popular discipline, and relatively few Irish riders ventured to compete internationally on the road. At first overseen by the GAA, cycling fell under the remit of the newly founded National Athletics and Cycling Association (NACA) on the establishment of the Irish Free State in 1922, before governance was divested to the National Cycling Association (NCA) in 1938. Long after leaving the GAA umbrella, grass track cycling and athletics meets continued to be held in tandem with hurling and Gaelic football games around the country. Despite the partition of Ireland in 1922, cycling was organised on a 32-county basis, and seemed to operate in something of a vacuum, far removed from the sport's heartland in mainland Europe.

For almost half a century, the Union Cycliste Internationale (UCI) saw no need to concern itself with the Irish question, even when a separate Northern Irish federation, which operated under the auspices of the British National Cyclists' Union (BNCU), was set up in 1928. The status quo was disrupted at the UCI congress in 1947, however, when the BNCU, in anticipation of the following year's Republic of Ireland Act, proposed the NCA restrict its jurisdiction to the 26 counties south of the border. The motion was carried, and the NCA was expelled from the UCI and excluded from international competition.

Two years later, a group of primarily Dublin-based clubs broke away from the NCA to establish a new, 26-county body called the Cumann Rothaíochta na hÉireann (CRE), which was granted international recognition by the UCI at the urging of the BNCU. Despite the brisk progress of the CRE, the NCA had no intention of retreating quietly into the background, far less ceasing operations altogether. With its riders unable to compete internationally, it compensated by establishing an ambitious national tour, the Rás Tailteann, in 1953. The driving force behind the Rás and the NCA was the staunchly republican Joe Christle, a protagonist of the IRA's Border Campaign of 1956–62, and consequently both the race and federation espoused an avowedly nationalist ethos, a contrast with the apolitical CRE.

Even so, joining the NCA or CRE was largely a matter of chance rather than any overt ideological leanings: in rural Ireland, NCA clubs were simply more common, whereas the CRE was the dominant force in Dublin. At official level, however, there was considerable enmity between the two bodies, with the NCA regularly looking to disrupt CRE events in the 1950s. 'They were very violent in some of their methods: cutting down trees during the Coast to Coast, setting fire to the road or putting down tacks and changing arrows on the road,

4

all that kind of stuff,' the late Christy Kimmage, a CRE rider, recalled in 2014.

In 1955, the NCA registered its opposition to the CRE at international level by sending a team to the World Championships in Frascati, much like the Munich Olympics 17 years later. In 1959, meanwhile, NCA men were widely suspected of the bombing of the newly installed track at Morton Stadium, on the eve of the inaugural, CRE-organised event, which featured Fausto Coppi and Shay Elliott, Ireland's first Continental professional.

Elliott is labelled nowadays as a pioneer, but in the early 1970s he was an historical aberration. While back home Irish cycling seemed unable to awake from a dreary, repeated nightmare of Civil War politics, Elliott operated in a different realm on the Continent. His story had no precedent in Irish cycling. In 1954, he had won the King of the Mountains prize at the CRE-organised Tour of Ireland, and his prize was to attend a training camp in Monte Carlo for Europe's top amateur riders the following spring. After a spell with the ACBB club in Paris, he turned professional in 1956 with the Helyett team, thus beginning a 12-year career.

Elliott became the first non-Belgian winner of the Omloop Het Volk classic in 1959, after which he won a stage of the Giro d'Italia in 1960, and then led the Vuelta a España for nine days in 1962, eventually placing third overall. In 1963, he soloed to stage victory in the Tour de France at Roubaix, and wore the yellow jersey for three days. At the velodrome in Roubaix, the band was so unprepared for an Irish victor that they played 'God Save the Queen' in lieu of 'Amhrán na bhFiann'.

A year earlier, Elliott had missed out on hearing his national anthem in rather more contentious circumstances, when he was in the winning break of four at the World Championships in Salò in the company of his trade teammate Jean Stablinski of France. 'Stab' was Elliott's closest friend in cycling and godfather to his son Pascal, but that apparently did not prevent him paying the other members of the move to chase down the Irishman's late attack. Stablinski slipped away to win the rainbow jersey, and Elliott had to settle for the silver medal. The peloton was a cutthroat kind of a place, and one contemporary, Jean Bobet, later maintained Elliott was penalised by his decency. 'Loyalty and naïvety prevented him from fulfilling his true potential,' Bobet said, quoted in Graham Healy's 2011 biography of Elliot. Even so, Elliott had the strength of personality to survive more than a decade in the peloton, riding as a trusted lieutenant of five-time Tour winner Jacques Anquetil, and later in the service of his rival, Raymond Poulidor.

Those nights in Morton Stadium in 1959 aside, when the crowds cheered him even more heartily than they did Coppi, Elliott's gifts were never properly appreciated in his home country, at least outside the small, cloven cycling community. After cycling, he would know only sadness. His foray into the hotel business in Loctudy, Brittany failed, and he had separated from his wife Marguerite even before the Hotel d'Irlande shut its doors. Elliott returned to Ireland alone. He died from a self-inflicted gunshot wound on 4 May 1971, in the living quarters above his panel-beating business in Dublin. He was

36 years old. In death, Elliott is commemorated by the one-day race that carries his name, and by a small monument atop the Glenmalure climb in County Wicklow, where the inscription is simple: 'In Memory of Shay Elliott, Irish international racing cyclist.'

Young amateur cyclists in Ireland may have aspired to emulating Elliott's exploits on the Continent, but those who dared to follow his template quickly realised just how exceptional his talent and character had been. Shortly after lining up in the amateur undercard at Morton Stadium with Coppi and Elliott, Christy Kimmage travelled to Paris to ride for ACBB, but lasted barely two weeks in a Montparnasse still bearing the scars of World War II. 'I realised that it was all about the mental approach, which I didn't have and Shay had,' Kimmage said. 'He just wanted it more than anything, whereas I didn't.' Others, like Peter Doyle, would spend longer as amateurs in France, but the next step eluded them. Peter Crinnion, a friend of Elliott's and later a mentor to Stephen Roche, went furthest. He raced on the Continent as an independent professional in the 1960s, winning the prestigious Route de France in 1962 and a stage of the Volta a Catalunya in 1963.

The NCA men, barred from international competition, looked on in frustration as riders from the Irish Cycling Federation (ICF) – as the CRE was renamed in the late 1960s – tried their luck on the Continent. Only certain foreign races, such as the Grand Prix de l'Humanité, run by France's communist sports body, the Fédération Sportive et Gymnique du Travail (FSGT), offered outlets to their more ambitious riders. When, in 1972, attempts were made at official level to prevent NCA riders from competing abroad, Joe Christle was incandescent.

The beginning of the Troubles in Northern Ireland in the late 1960s had already renewed the radicalism within the body. It was decided to send an NCA team to Munich in protest.

Armed with little more than a taste for racing beyond Ireland, John Mangan caught a ferry from Rosslare to Le Havre in August 1971. 'I was driving down through Normandy and I stopped two cyclists who were out on the road. They said Brittany was the best place to go, around Rennes, so I went there,' Mangan says. 'When I got there, I asked a policeman on the street and he brought me to a bicycle shop. It was closed for lunch but I came back later and it turned out that the fella in the shop raced, so that's how that I started out there.'

Though he returned to Ireland to complete his apprenticeship as an electrician that winter, Mangan was back in France full-time by the spring of 1972, racing in Nice early in the year before migrating to Brittany as the evenings lengthened. In Nice, an FSGT stronghold, Mangan's NCA racing licence had not been an issue. In Brittany, his documentation was queried, but he managed to compete, and after returning to Ireland to win the Rás early in the summer, he was joined in Rennes by fellow Kerry men Batty Flynn and Pat Healy for the remainder of the campaign.

By that point, plans for the Munich expedition had already been floated, and in early September, the trio drove to Ostend to meet with the rest of the NCA delegation, which had travelled by ferry. The group of 10 included seven riders – Mangan, Flynn, Healy, Meathmen Gabriel Howard and TP Reilly, and northerners Brian Holmes and Joe McAloon – and was led by Benny Donnelly, who acted as 'coach' and spokesman. On arriving in Munich, they were accommodated at a house on 49 Implerstrasse in the south of the city.

Unable to speak German and with no television in the house, the NCA party was oblivious to the drama unfolding in the Olympic village on the night of Tuesday 5 September, the eve of the men's road race. The following dawn, as they rode through sombre streets towards the race circuit and took up their stations for the protest, they assumed the early hour accounted for the eerie silence, but as the morning progressed, it gradually became apparent that something was awry. Mangan, Flynn and McAloon spent the bones of three hours lying in a thicket, their bikes camouflaged amid the shrubs, before they elected to emerge from their hiding place. In broken English, a passer-by told them the Olympic Games had been suspended for 24 hours due to the Black September terrorist group's killing of 11 Israeli athletes and coaches, but the scale of what had happened seemed to be lost in translation. While 80,000 spectators and 3,000 athletes gathered in the Olympic Stadium to commemorate the dead, the NCA men returned to Implerstrasse ready to start all over the following morning.

The official Irish team, which was housed in the very complex where the hostage crisis had taken place, was scarcely more informed than their NCA counterparts. Although word of the atrocity had reached them the previous evening, they had no idea of its magnitude. 'We'd never have thought to turn the telly on even if we'd had one, and we went to bed that night not knowing whether the Games were going to be postponed or cancelled,' says Kieron McQuaid. 'We got into our race gear the following morning and eventually we were told that everything had been put back by 24 hours.'

The NCA delegation, largely – but by no means completely – ignorant of the changed context, proceeded with its protest when the race eventually took place on the morning of 7 September. Of the four on the start line, only Healy succeeded in infiltrating the peloton, though in any case, their main purpose was the distribution of multilingual leaflets which bore the slogan, 'England: Evacuate Our Sports Fields and Our Nation'. Holmes, a republican who would be interned in Long Kesh shortly after his return from Munich, later claimed to have severed the wires of the PA system at the start in a bid to sow confusion, but Mangan insists the riders hiding on the course were making a primarily sporting demonstration, protesting their inability to compete internationally. 'The leaflets were more of a political thing to get the Eastern Bloc countries to give us a hand, because they would have wanted to get back at England and those,' he says.

This version of events is flatly dismissed by McQuaid. 'The Olympic road race is 120 miles long and all they had in their back pockets were leaflets protesting about British occupation of Northern Ireland. They had no food or anything to be handed up to them, either,' he says. 'They weren't there to ride the race, that's bullshit. They were there to protest the British occupation of Northern Ireland.'

Perhaps the saddest irony of the NCA protest in Munich is that the official Irish team was, in many respects, a model of peaceful coexistence. Noel Teggart was a Protestant from

Northern Ireland, while McQuaid, though born in Dublin, was the son of a Catholic father and Protestant mother, both from County Tyrone. ICF riders regularly traversed the border to compete in Northern Ireland Cycling Federation (NICF) races, and vice versa, just as riders north and south crossed the Irish Sea to race in Britain, and British riders lined out every year at the Tour of Ireland.

After the race, Donnelly insisted that the NCA riders had been instructed not to interfere with any competitors, far less the legitimate Irish team, but it was hardly coincidental that Teggart was the one man to be obstructed. Mangan claims that Teggart, who died in 1997, greeted him by commenting, 'There's a lot of southern bastards around this morning,' an accusation vehemently denied by McQuaid, who recalls that Mangan had already taken issue with Teggart's presence in an Irish jersey during his conversation with Horner. 'I believe the powers that be in the NCA got inside his head and filled it with shit, and he became all fervently nationalistic.'

Mangan's clash with Teggart brought both his own protest and the Northerner's race to a halt. A distraught Teggart abandoned the race, the only Irishman not to finish. Despite the heightened state of alert in the wake of the Black September attack, Mangan's political protest was policed softly. Although his bike, like all the NCA machines, was sequestered until the end of the race, he was not placed in handcuffs. 'In fairness, they knew well that we were no terrorists. It was the police who arrested me and they handed me over to the army. They brought me into the compound where the army were and after one or two laps, I got talking to one of the lads and said I wanted to see the race,' Mangan says. 'They let me go and watch it on the side of the road.'

The reaction from Mangan's fellow countrymen was not as benign. After the race, the manager of the official Irish team, Liam King, called for charges to be pressed, while his riders wanted to administer their own brand of justice. 'We went into Munich that night and the purpose of the exercise was to see if we could find them,' McQuaid says. 'We'd have killed them.'

Official condemnation was swift. Taoiseach Jack Lynch was in Munich, where he had met with British prime minister Ted Heath to discuss the situation in Northern Ireland. 'The interference was a travesty of sportsmanship, reflecting no credit on the country,' he told reporters at a reception at the Irish consulate. The sense of embarrassment was only amplified by the fact that the British Olympic team, shaken by the Israeli massacre, had already seen fit to take measures to protect itself from a possible IRA attack. All union flags were removed from the team's apartment block in the Olympic village – 'A degree of anonymity might be advisable,' said chef de mission Sandy Duncan – while pentathlon winner Mary Peters, a Northern Irish woman competing for Great Britain, was brought to the airport under armed guard.

Following the Games, Irishman Lord Killanin took up office as president of the IOC and privately lobbied for Mangan to serve a suspension for his part in disrupting the road race. 'He tried his level best to get onto the federation in France and get me fucked up,' Mangan says. 'I never forgave him for it.'

Despite the Munich bother and the questions of the legality of his licence, Mangan remained in France until 1982, making a living from the prize money he won on the amateur scene as part of what he smilingly calls the mafia, a combine of experienced riders who raced together across team lines. In the early years, his NCA membership would likely have precluded a professional career, but he never countenanced switching to the ICF. 'I said I wouldn't sell my soul for 30 pieces of silver,' he says. By the late 1970s, he realised that his winnings on the amateur scene likely surpassed what he might earn as a professional. He continued to revel in the nickname of the 'French Locomotive' in Brittany, racing against – and beating – men like Jean-René Bernaudeau and Bernard Hinault as they progressed to the professional ranks.

It is tempting to say that the embarrassment of the Munich protest was the moment that shocked sense into the Irish cycling community and brought the factions together, but it was to be a drawn-out process. There was a metaphorical breaking of bread in January 1973, when future Rás organiser Dermot Dignam and four-time Rás winner Shay O'Hanlon were among the NCA men to join Kieron McQuaid and an ICF group on a training ride and propose informal talks, thus beginning the slow but ineluctable course that would eventually bring the three federations on the island of Ireland – the ICF, NICF and NCA – together into one body. The formation of the so-called Tripartite Committee in 1979, which allowed riders to compete in each federation's events, regardless of affiliation, was the key moment in the unification of Irish cycling, though many of the old fault lines would remain in place even as the factions formally merged into the Federation of Irish Cyclists (now Cycling Ireland) in 1987. The governance of cycling in

Northern Ireland, meanwhile, would remain sensitive into the 21st century.

The dissolution of the dividing lines in the late 1970s would, in time, raise standards across the board, but it would be fanciful to suggest that the golden generation of Irish talent of the 1980s owes its providence to the cessation of hostilities between the federations. By the mid-1970s, the arc of Irish cycling history may have been bending towards unity, but those events were already being overtaken by the remarkable exploits of an introverted young man from Carrick-on-Suir.

2

Mamore and All That

It was perhaps fortunate that a series of early mechanical mishaps ruined Sean Kelly's chances at the 1975 Tour of Ireland. It meant that while Pat McQuaid's overall victory was consigned soberly to the record books, descriptions of Kelly's exploits that week have taken shape in the more fluid confines of folklore. It is an article of faith in Irish cycling, for instance, that Kelly went over the Gap of Mamore using a monstrous gear – an 18-tooth sprocket, according to most variations of the gospel – during that Tour of Ireland. It is an article of faith because there were precious few on hand to bear witness to the momentous occasion in person. There were certainly no bike riders, as Kelly was already more than a minute and a half clear of the bunch by the time he reached the base of the short but viciously steep climb on the Inishowen Peninsula. There won't have been many spectators on the roadside, either – not in rural Donegal for an amateur bike race in the mid-1970s. No, for all bar the happy few in the race marshal's car, Sean Kelly's greatest exploit as a teenage bike rider on Irish roads only ever existed in the imagination. And yet the shared memory endures.

It's certainly not difficult to conjure the image of Kelly, all strength and sinew, pushing his mammoth gear against the 22 per cent slopes of the Gap of Mamore. It's easy to picture him snorting like a racehorse as he approaches the summit, and then dropping over the other side, never once relenting until he reaches the finish in Buncrana. He will have spent more than 80 kilometres alone at the head of the race by the time he crosses the line. More than three minutes will pass before the second group on the road limps home. An exhibition.

The Gap of Mamore is little more than a kilometre in length, but its severity is such that when it first featured in the Tour of Ireland in 1970, eventual stage winner Paul Elliott was forced to dismount and walk near the top. Yet, of the newspapermen on the 1975 race, only Brendan Mooney, writing in the *Cork Examiner*, seemed to realise he had been present for something special, describing Kelly's showing as 'one of the finest exhibitions of solo climbing ever produced in this country'. Kelly's display would only take on the dimensions of legend once the telling of it travelled by word of mouth. 'Everybody knew that you needed a 22 sprocket on Mamore but Kelly was a horse and could do things that nobody else would even consider,' Stephen Roche put it more than a decade later.

Kelly, a hesitant Cúchulainn, insists the truth was more prosaic. He simply used the lowest gear he had, 42x24, and dragged himself up any way he could. 'It was a case of just grinding your way up with that. You just go from side to side to try to make it,' he says. 'The Gap of Mamore, I just ploughed my way up.'

Still, Mamore was special, and Kelly added another saga to his Ulster Cycle the next day by outsprinting Australian John Sanders to win in Bundoran, before proceeding to quell the internecine squabbling within the Irish national team on the penultimate stage. Alan McCormack had spent much of the week attacking Pat McQuaid's yellow jersey, and his most ambitious offensive came when he gained six minutes on the road to Mullingar, but Kelly made the decisive contribution in pegging back the move, and then helped himself to the stage win.

Kelly reached Dublin in 6th place overall, and after the final stage he availed of the hospitality of Christy Kimmage, who had served as the Irish team masseur, before travelling home to Carrick-on-Suir. That evening in Coolock, Christy's 13-year-old son Paul was transfixed by the quiet but courteous visitor. With the physique and weathered face of an older man, Kelly had the bearing of the silent hero of a Western, but was blessed with the attendant promise of youth. Nobody quite knew where he had come from, but people were daring to dream of where he might go from here. 'You'd have to think Kelly was a once-off. After the Tour of Ireland when he won that stage over Mamore, he came back and had a bath in the house that night,' Kimmage says. 'Dad would have thought this guy was fucking tough, and different to what we'd got.'

►⊙◄

In the years leading up to the Munich Olympics, while the NCA–ICF split was still slowly bubbling towards its apotheosis, the underlying tensions were apparent all over Ireland. One such fault line, albeit an inadvertently formed one, was to be found in Carrick-on-Suir, a sleepy town of 4,000 inhabitants on the Tipperary-Waterford border. Inspired by the first Rás, Carrick Wheelers Cycling Club, an NCA outfit, had been established in 1954, and its St Patrick's Day race was one of the most important early-season events on the NCA calendar. In 1969, a group of members led by Tony Ryan and Dan Grant decided to break away to form a new club, which they promptly affiliated to the ICF, though appearances can be deceptive. The split in Carrick-on-Suir had nothing to do with the wider NCA–ICF dispute, but rather was based upon a local row, the genesis of which has since been obscured, by time and diplomacy.

'It was just a burst-up within the club,' Kelly explains. 'They had a bit of a row with the committee over I don't know exactly what, but it had nothing to do with the different federations or anything like that. But of course, there was the other federation at that time, so when they started the new club, of course they went to the other side, to the ICF.'

To compound matters, Ryan and his associates dubbed their new outfit Carrick Wheelers Road Club. Operating in the same small town as Carrick Wheelers Cycling Club, and sifting through the same shallow pool in search of potential riders, the new club quickly rolled out a proactive recruitment policy. In a microcosm of the wider NCA–ICF divide, the two clubs coexisted in parallel worlds on the banks of the Suir, with the Waterford-based *Munster Express* carefully devoting equal amounts of column inches to each Carrick-on-Suir club.

Carrick Wheelers Cycling Club president Tommy Sheehan had already established a schoolboy cycling league in 1967, and the fledgling ICF club naturally followed suit. In the autumn of 1969, a delegation from Carrick Wheelers Road Club paid a visit to the Christian Brothers Secondary School in Carrick-on-Suir to promote its series of underage races. A 15-year-old called Joe Kelly, who cycled a round trip of six miles every day from nearby Curraghduff, signed up and became a fully fledged member of the club shortly afterwards. A few months later, his younger brother would join him.

John James Kelly was born in Belleville maternity home in Waterford city on 24 May 1956, the second son of Jack and Nellie Kelly. To avoid confusion with his father, also christened John James Kelly, the newborn was known immediately as Sean. There were already two boys on the farm in Curraghduff: Joe was two years Sean's senior, while Martin Power was the child of Nellie's first husband, also named Martin, who had died from a stroke as a young man. The family would be completed by the arrival of the youngest son, Vincent, in 1962.

Home life was quiet. Jack was a man of few words and Nellie was scarcely more talkative. That country reserve was bequeathed to their son, who as a bike rider and, later, as a television commentator, would make a virtue out of saying as little as was necessary to make his point. As soon as he was old enough, Kelly was expected to help on the farm, while his formal education took place entirely within the walls of

Crehana National School, in the countryside on the Waterford side of Carrick-on-Suir. Like most children in rural Ireland, his first experiences of organised sport came on the GAA field, though, strangely, he played solely at school and only fleetingly. 'In school, we played hurling and football matches with other schools, but it would only have been maybe two or three games a year,' Kelly says. 'I was OK, no better than any other guys. I probably didn't play it for long enough to find out if I was any good.'

In the classroom, the young Kelly struggled, perhaps due more to his intense shyness than to any lack of academic prowess. He was not wholly enamoured by the prospect of continuing his education beyond the end of primary school, but despite his misgivings, he enrolled in the town's vocational school with the vague aim of learning a trade. Just before classes started in September, however, a stomach ulcer necessitated Jack spending a stint in hospital and Sean, perhaps sensing an out, volunteered to fill in on the farm. More than a month passed before his father was well enough to resume work, by which point Kelly successfully argued that it was not worth his while trying to catch up. School was out.

At 14 years of age, whether he realised it or not, the rest of Kelly's life seemed to be already mapped out. He would now help his father on the farm until such time as he inherited the land for himself. He would live and die within his own little postage stamp of soil in the shadow of the Comeragh Mountains. It could easily have been a lonesome existence had Kelly not tagged along with Joe to an internal league race in Carrick-on-Suir in the summer of 1970. Fifteen or so teenage boys were already sitting astride their bikes at the entrance to Kennedy Terrace as the Kelly brothers arrived. When Tony Ryan asked the newcomer his name, so the legend goes, Kelly nodded hesitantly towards Joe: 'I'm his brother.'

The riders were split into small groups along loose lines of age and experience, and Kelly was placed in the first wave to set out, with a three-minute head start over the oldest riders. The race was six miles long, out to the Millvale Creamery and back. What Kelly lacked in nous, he made up for in strength. He set out as quickly as he possibly could and shed himself of his fellow neophytes, but rather than tire on the return leg, he extended his advantage over the scratch group to claim the spoils.

With the ice duly broken, Kelly settled into life as a member of Carrick Wheelers, and graduated to compete in formal ICF-organised races in places like Fermoy and Mallow in 1971, progressing steadily under the tutelage of Ryan and Grant. In 1972, still only 16 years of age, he won the junior national championships road race in Banbridge, beating the highly touted Alan McCormack into third place, though the Dubliner – also destined for a professional career – would prove a worthy rival on the domestic scene. 'He always had the upper hand in the sprints but there was a time when we were teenagers when I was equal with him and sometimes better in races,' McCormack says. 'But there was never any animosity. He'd stay in our house in Dublin when we were on national teams.'

McCormack and Kelly's talents were such that they were fast-tracked through the system, stepping up to the senior ranks in 1974 even though they were still eligible to race as juniors. Kelly won the Shay Elliott Memorial, Ireland's toughest one-day race, at only 17 years of age, and that summer, he and

McCormack were selected for the Irish team for the Tour of Scotland. Nobody batted an eyelid. The experience seemed to stand to Kelly. 'We were only children,' McCormack says. 'That would never happen nowadays, 17-year-old kids riding international stage races against all the hardcore Russian and Polish riders.'

Off the bike, too, Kelly was reaping the benefits of membership of Carrick Wheelers. Through a clubmate named Martin Wall, he procured a job as a bricklayer that put money in his pocket and provided a more sociable working environment than the relative isolation of the farm. Although Kelly's words were spent as reluctantly as ever – 'I'm not exaggerating when I say no more than 20 words would pass his lips on the journey from Carrick to Dublin and home,' said his regular chauffeur Grant – he enjoyed the camaraderie of the club. If cycling itself proved a more satisfactory form of expression for Kelly than his timid words ever could, simply being part of a club at all meant that the profoundly shy teenager could interact with his peers without having to surrender his natural reserve.

'I don't think you could say it gave me a social life beyond what I had before I started the cycling,' Kelly says. 'The thing it did give me was the chance to travel to races around the country at weekends, and get away from home and the work on the farm. I think that was one of the things that attracted me the most.'

Carrick Wheelers would also introduce Kelly to his wife, Linda Grant, the daughter of Dan. Linda, a year Kelly's junior, would later joke that she was the 'last piece of equipment' to be packed into her father's car ahead of each race, and it was she who stitched the words 'Carrick Wheelers Road Club ICF' onto Kelly's first-ever racing jersey. Their relationship began discreetly when Kelly was 17 and continued when his talent sent him far from Carrick-on-Suir.

Towards the end of 1971, Dan Grant had visited the Kelly house to persuade Jack to part with £150 so his son might upgrade from his Raleigh All-Steel bike to a bona fide racing machine. He based his pitch around the sacrifice and commitment required by the sport, correctly guessing that such characteristics would resonate with an essentially austere man. 'I pointed out that drink, discos and the rest would cost considerably more in the course of a year and eventually he agreed,' Grant told the *Irish Times* in 1985. It would prove to be a sound investment.

As far back as they could remember, the McQuaid boys always wanted to be cyclists. At home in the flat above the family grocery store in Glasnevin, there was talk of precious little else. Their father, Jim, was Irish champion in 1950 and again in 1951, and competed at the World Championships on four occasions. He was selected for the 1948 Olympics in London, too, but was unable to compete due to the NCA's expulsion from international competition. Together with his brother Paddy, Jim was among the founder members of the breakaway CRE the following year, and he would serve as an administrator in the newly founded body even before his own racing career came to an end. The McQuaids were bluebloods.

Pat McQuaid, the eldest of Jim's 10 children, was born in 1949, with Kieron following a year later, and they grew up surrounded by cycling. One of the young Pat's earliest memories was of his father crashing during a Grand Prix of Ireland in the Phoenix Park, and tagging along as he was patched up in St Stephen's Hospital, waiting for stitches and liniment to be applied to open wounds. At the dinner table, cycling talk abounded. Jim McQuaid liked to recall the tale of how he had given Shay Elliott a small but significant leg-up towards his professional career at the 1954 Tour of Ireland, by helping him win the King of the Mountains prize that secured his ticket to the Simplex training camp the following spring.

Their father's standing allowed the young McQuaids fleeting glimpses of cycling royalty. Pat was nine years old when his uncle, then CRE president, and father were the men charged with collecting Fausto Coppi from Dublin airport when he came to ride with Elliott in the exhibition at Morton Stadium. A 14-year-old Kieron, meanwhile, travelled all the way to San Sebastian with his father in 1965 to watch Tommy Simpson win the World Championships road race.

The split in Irish cycling was a regular topic of discussion at home. Paddy ran a vegetable shop opposite Jim's grocery store on Ballygall Road, and at 11 o'clock each morning he would cross the street to join his brother for coffee in the back room. The children would hush and eavesdrop. 'He'd sit down and they'd be talking about the politics of cycling – who was on the board, who was with who, who was against, and so on,' Pat McQuaid recalls. 'I got used to listening to it.'

The McQuaids were originally from Dungannon in County Tyrone, where they had raced with some success. Paddy was the first to move south of the border, arriving in Dublin in 1947, with his younger brother following a year later, and when Jim met and married a fellow Tyrone woman, Madge, it strengthened his resolve to build a life in Dublin. The McQuaid brothers' 1949 establishment of a new Dublin-based cycling club called Emerald marked the definitive laying down of roots. 'They came down south because of business opportunities, but also because Northern Ireland wasn't really a place my parents could live in, with a mixed marriage,' Pat McQuaid says. 'My father joined the CRE because even though he was a northern Catholic, he wouldn't have had strong nationalist views like the NCA, which was closely connected with the Old IRA and maybe ultimately the Provisional IRA.'

Not that their federation was bereft of its own internal politics. Kieron and Pat McQuaid were both in the longlist for the Munich Olympics, but only the younger brother made the trip to Germany, much to Pat's chagrin. The selectors were of the opinion that Pat's stint studying in London had left him under-raced, and even at a remove of over four decades it remains a sore point. 'Part of that was politics within the federation. They wouldn't select two McQuaids for the Olympic games,' he insists. Three years later, however, Jim McQuaid was national team coach, and his three eldest sons – Pat, Kieron and 21-year-old Oliver – were all picked for the six-man squad for the 1975 Tour of Britain, the first family to achieve such a feat. 'People would have been asking, "Are they running the show or what's the story?"' Pat McQuaid says.

Like their father, the young McQuaids were fast finishers with a knack for hanging tough on climbs, winning races by dint of their wits as much as their ability. Off the bike, the

McQuaids were preternaturally confident young men. 'Ah yeah, they weren't shy about it. Jim came from a cycling background. He was a very good rider himself, and the sons were as well,' Kelly says. When an ICF selection was invited to compete in the 1974 Rás, which was won by Peter Doyle, the most notable frisson between the two federations came when Pat McQuaid clashed with Meathman Colm Nulty in Killarney. 'We were knocking hell out of each other. It might have been the only time I did it in my life,' McQuaid recalls. Pat, with his sideburns and ready smile, exuded a particularly worldly air for a man still in his mid-20s, and such self-assurance seemed to have the added benefit of inuring him to external criticism. 'We were a successful family,' McQuaid says. 'We were brought up to be winners.'

Yet while the McQuaids would dominate the headlines at home ahead of the Tour of Britain, they would be wholly overshadowed by Kelly – who was, along with McCormack, one of two teenagers in the Irish line-up – on their return. Held in May and June each year and by then better known as the Milk Race, the Tour of Britain was, by the mid-1970s, viewed as the sternest test of an ICF rider's mettle, perhaps even the limit of his ambition. Emulating Elliott's career on the Continent seemed far-fetched; the Tour of Britain, on the other hand, was a goal of more digestible proportions. Two weeks long and attracting some of the best amateur riders in the world, it was a more arduous race than any on offer in Ireland, yet it had a comforting familiarity, too, as the best ICF riders regularly travelled to Britain for weekend racing.

Even so, the Milk Race was a daunting proposition. Peter Doyle had won stages and even placed 3rd overall, in 1968, but as a rule, the men in green jerseys had tended to turn up clasping to hope but largely unfettered by expectation. Though Kelly was highly rated at home, he was still a first-year senior competing in the toughest race on the calendar, and a promising 12th place on the first road stage to Bournemouth was soon forgotten when four of the Irish team fell victim to food poisoning on the road to Bath the following day. A tin of salmon was identified as the culprit, though be it due to an iron constitution or a simple dislike of canned fish, Kelly was not among those affected.

As the race swept northwards, the 19-year-old Kelly continued to be mentioned in dispatches as the standout performer on the Irish team. 'There was no such thing as one riding for the other because we were a long way off the level coming into the Tour of Britain against the Eastern Europeans, so you just did your own thing in the race and if you were good enough, you'd get up there,' Kelly says. He did just that on stage 7, a tough, 98-mile leg from Southport across the Pennines to Sheffield. Though it was the first of June, it was during a spell of unseasonable cold across Britain, with flurries of sleet recorded as far south as London. On the climb of Saddleworth Moor, a group of seven hardy souls forged clear, with Kelly among them. The stiff ascent of Holme Moss followed as the race skirted the Peak District, and only three men remained in front by the summit – Kelly, Poland's Jan Trybala and the Swede, Bernt Johansson.

Jim McQuaid was following the race on the back of a motorbike, and he rode up alongside Kelly on the long drop towards Sheffield, advising him to sit on the back of the group and wait for the sprint. Johansson didn't need to eavesdrop to realise what was happening, but it didn't deter him from burying himself on the front to ensure the break stayed clear and the trio reached the finish together. It seems clear that neither Johansson nor Trybala understood what they were facing. Perhaps Kelly's unrefined riding style masked his cunning, like Odysseus in beggar's rags. Maybe they simply assumed that Kelly, having hitched a ride from Holme Moss to the finish line, would now have the decorum not to contest the sprint for the win.

On the slightly uphill finishing straight in Norfolk Park, Kelly nudged his wheel between Trybala and Johansson, before climbing from the saddle to wind up his sprint with 200 metres to go. Johansson reached out to grab at him and tore off his race number in the process, but Kelly shrugged him off. Stage victory was his, while the yellow jersey went to Johansson, though it was no consolation to the Swede, who immediately sought a confrontation. Even in his hour of triumph, Kelly remained a man of few, carefully chosen words. 'Fuck off,' he growled as he made for the podium.

After the prizegiving ceremony, Kelly was slightly more forthcoming, and, now 3rd overall, surprisingly unguarded about his ambitions for the remainder of the Tour of Britain. 'He tried to send me into the fence so I elbowed him off. I don't only want to win stages, I want to win the whole tour,' he told reporters, even if he confessed to discomfort at the attention his win had garnered. 'I'd rather not win the tour than have to face all these interviews again.'

A greater ordeal awaited. Back at the Irish team's hotel, Kelly sat contentedly listening as his teammates swapped war stories from their crossing of the Pennines when Jim McQuaid entered with a curt announcement: Kelly's attendance was required at the Lord Mayor's banquet that night. 'Any of the rest of us would have been delighted to have been there, sat beside the podium hostesses, the Pinta Girls, in their hot-pants suits,' Kieron McQuaid laughs. 'But all we heard from Kelly was, "Fuck no, fuck no, fuck no. I'm not going, I'm not going."'

For a moment, Kelly thought his lack of a suit might buy him a reprieve, but the McQuaids, typically, had all but packed a wardrobe apiece. Between them, they provided Kelly with the requisite attire, though there was one further issue. He had never worn a tie before. 'I was knotting a tie every day for work as an accountant and now I'm standing there knotting his tie,' Kieron McQuaid recalls. 'And I'm thinking to myself, "I'd prefer to have your legs and not know how to knot a tie than have my legs and be knotting a tie every day of my life."'

Kelly was more at ease in cycling garb, even if the kit provided by the ICF was notoriously ill-fitting. The slighter McCormack would have to defend his right to wear the smallest available jersey. 'They'd be laid out on a bed, and Sean would grab my jersey, saying he liked a nice tight fit,' McCormack says. 'Jesus, the medium would be like a dress on me, so I used to have to fight him to keep my small jersey. They were pure cotton and they'd sag in the rain.'

Despite his flapping jersey and a strained Achilles tendon, Kelly reached the last day of the race still lying in 3rd place overall, and a mere 90 miles away from equalling the best-ever Irish performance. The final leg to Blackpool, however, was calamitous. After puncturing on the start line, Kelly suffered another flat tyre after 30 miles, and then needed two further wheel changes due to broken spokes and rubbing brakes. He rolled home more than 10 minutes down on the day, and tumbled to 25th place overall.

In cycling, Kelly was learning, there are no guarantees beyond the here and now, though he was given cause to think seriously about his long-term future in the sport after the race when the manager of the Dutch national team, Jan Kuiper, extended an invitation for him to come and compete in the Netherlands for the remainder of the summer. 'It was the actions of the man when he was in trouble that I liked,' Kuiper told the *Irish Times*, but the offer was never taken up. In ICF circles, meanwhile, there was a growing sense that Kelly, still only 19, was already among the favourites to claim gold in the following year's Montreal Olympics, even if formulating a development plan for such a force of nature must have felt as redundant as erecting signposts to divert the path of a meteor.

3

BIG GAME

Pat McQuaid was 26 and the father of a young family. He had spent three years working as a PE teacher at Greenhills College in Walkinstown and was seemingly settled in his chosen career, yet he still evinced a certain restlessness, his eye drawn to the comparative glamour of his alternative existence on two wheels. In August 1975, having applied for a permanent post at the school, McQuaid was invited for an interview, and though the date of the appointment fell during the Tour of Ireland, the clash does not seem to have caused him much concern. Rather than fretting over a dilemma, McQuaid sensed something of an opportunity. A year away from the classroom would, after all, allow him to devote himself full-time to the business of securing selection for the Montreal Olympics. He skipped the interview and rode the race.

'I was temporary whole-time in Walkinstown and my wife was teaching as well. Cycling was my major interest at the time, and I was prepared to make major sacrifices for it,' McQuaid says, though he had already made a considerable investment in pursuing his teaching career, having trained at Strawberry

Hill in London, where his contemporaries included Gaelic footballers Billy Morgan, Jimmy Deenihan and Liam Sammon. His sojourn in London proved fruitful, but if forgoing the opportunity to try his luck as an amateur in France was no great disappointment – 'I knew I didn't have the level to be a Tour de France rider,' he says – missing out on selection for the 1972 Olympics was a rather sorer point.

Montreal would be different, McQuaid insisted, and, with the 1975–76 academic year suddenly bereft of teaching commitments, he was free to fill it with racing and training. During the Tour of Ireland, the Scottish rider John Curran approached McQuaid with an offer to compete in South Africa in October, at a two-week stage race called the Rapport Toer, which ran over 1,600 kilometres between Cape Town and Johannesburg. Curran, who had raced there the previous year, outlined the benefits of competing in South Africa's leading race, including expenses and a week's holiday paid for by the sponsors. There was, of course, one hefty snag: the sporting boycott of apartheid South Africa, which had gathered momentum following the country's exclusion from the Olympic movement in 1970.

The UCI had been among the federations to bar South Africa from international competition and forbid athletes from travelling to compete in a state where racial discrimination was enshrined in policy, but still the South African cycling federation continued to organise domestic events. When the Rapport Toer was established in 1973, the brainchild of Bloemfontein carpet merchant Raoul de Villiers, overtures were made to foreign riders to compete. Cycling was, after all, a niche sport in the country, and while the arrival of rebel cricketers and rugby players during the apartheid era would be widely reported, cyclists were, for the most part, able to compete quietly under assumed names and, if caught, the condemnation back home was rarely sufficient to earn them much more than a slap on the wrist. Indeed, Curran had received a six-month ban on his return from South Africa in 1974, but the sanction wasn't heavy enough to deter him from returning, nor to dissuade McQuaid from joining him and convincing his brother Kieron and Kelly to come along. They would ride under false identities for a 'British' selection bearing the name of the fragrant sponsor Mum for Men.

Afterwards, the perception was that the callow Kelly had been coaxed into travelling to South Africa thanks only to the powers of persuasion of the more streetwise McQuaid, but the reality was more nuanced. McQuaid was the intermediary, true, but Kelly, now alive to the earning potential of the bike, needed little by way of encouragement. Three weeks in South Africa meant time away from the farm and laying bricks, while the prize money on offer, however meagre, was as good an incentive as any. 'Later it was made to look like I was the one who had taken Kelly there by the hand, but Kelly made up his own mind. He didn't need much convincing. He thought the same as me. It was 14 days of racing, with 12 double stages. It was a fucking hard race with good competitors,' McQuaid says. 'We knew the decision we were taking. We thought we'd get away with it and we thought it would help us towards the Olympics.'

The Irish team at the Tour of Ireland had split into two loose camps, with the McQuaids and Kelly on one side, and Tony Lally and Alan McCormack on the other. The South Africa plan was discussed in private, lest the others muscle in on it or, worse still, tip off the authorities. 'It wouldn't have been during dinnertime but when we were on our own somewhere, because they definitely didn't want Lally to know,' Kelly says. 'Pat explained it and said, "We can go there all-expenses paid, race in good weather and stay on for a week afterwards with the sponsors paying for it all. We'll go there as a British team, under false names and nobody can know anything about it." So of course when I heard that, at 18 years old, it was a dream really. I said, "Yeah, I'm interested," and the planning started.'

Neither the McQuaids nor Kelly, it seems, had any misgivings about breaking an international boycott to compete in an explicitly racist country, where the non-white majority – some 80 per cent of the population in 1975 – was denied a vote. Kelly, for one, dealt with the moral question by shrugging his shoulders rather than wringing his hands. 'We lived our way in Ireland, they lived another way here. What was I going to do to change it?' he would recall in his 2013 autobiography, *Hunger*.

'The main reason I accepted to go was to ride the race, but in the back of my head, I wanted to see apartheid for myself and how it affected the people,' Pat McQuaid says. 'The race itself had both white and black teams from South Africa, so there was no apartheid within the race itself, but I did see it in the country.'

Even now, McQuaid defends his decision to break the boycott and compete in a racially segregated South Africa, arguing that it was unfair for sport to be held to a standard of behaviour not demanded of business or politics. Ireland and Europe's trade and diplomatic links with South Africa continued even as the sporting boycott grew. 'British rugby and cricket teams were pilloried for going over there, yet British businesses were doing business with South Africa all the time,' McQuaid says. 'Why were they selecting sport? If it was balanced and governments were stopping their businesses trading with South Africa, then I wouldn't have gone. But that wasn't happening and I thought it was hypocritical just to hit the sports people.'

After completing his final race of the domestic season in Enniscorthy on 28 September, Kelly spent the night at the McQuaid house in Dublin before they flew to Johannesburg by way of London and Paris the following day. The presence of Scottish cycling official Gerry McDaid on the London–Paris flight provided a brief scare, but having avoided drawing his attention, the trio must have felt they were in the clear. Back home, meanwhile, anybody inquiring as to their whereabouts was to be told they were engaged in some warm-weather training in Mallorca.

On reaching South Africa, Kelly and the McQuaids linked up with their teammates, Curran and his fellow Scot Henry Wilbraham, as well as Tommy Shardelow, the South Africa-based Briton who would serve as their team manager. As well as being measured for Mum for Men kit and team blazers, the five were invited to try out their new identities for size. Pat McQuaid would compete as 'Jim Burns,' while Kelly would ride under the moniker of 'Alan Owen'. There were some familiar figures from the European scene in the Rapport Toer peloton, too. Jean-François Pescheux, later race director of the Tour de France, was among the French riders on show, while the American Jock Boyer, a future teammate of Kelly, also featured. According to Boyer, even the reigning Tour de France champion Bernard Thévenet was in attendance at the behest of Peugeot, though not as a competitor. 'There were loads of European teams riding there, and they would go back home and their federations would do nothing,' McQuaid says. Safety in numbers, in other words.

From a sporting point of view, the Rapport Toer was a resounding success for the Irish Olympic hopefuls, as Jim Burns, aka Pat McQuaid, won two stages, while Alan Owen, aka Sean Kelly, rode well enough to move up to 8th place in the overall standings. As the race drew on, it seemed a most auspicious expedition, and having escaped the notice of a cycling commissaire in transit, they certainly couldn't have imagined that something so distant from cycling's small world as the arrival of a Hollywood glamour couple in South Africa would – very indirectly – trigger their unmasking.

That, at least, was the story that eventually travelled back home, though it has been told and retold with such relish ever since that it is increasingly difficult to separate fact from fiction. On 10 October 1975, little more than a year on from their first divorce, Liz Taylor and Richard Burton married for the second time in Kasane, Botswana, and decided to honeymoon in South Africa, with a retinue of gossip columnists and photographers recording their every move. When Taylor and Burton stopped in the town of Oudtshoorn to see the ostrich farm, their visit coincided with the arrival of the Rapport Toer's fourth stage, and one enterprising reporter, John Hartdegen, a South African freelancing for the *Daily Mail*, apparently saw a potential story in having 'Liz and Dick' greet the 'British' cycling team Mum for Men before the next day's stage.

Shardelow's reluctance to accede to Hartdegen's request triggered his curiosity. After being challenged, Shardelow eventually confessed that Kelly, the McQuaids et al. were competing in South Africa surreptitiously, but his plea for Hartdegen's discretion fell on deaf ears. The journalist apparently realised that this story of illegal bike riders had even greater value than a simple photo opportunity with Burton and Taylor.

That was the gist of the tale relayed by Kelly and McQuaid, and faithfully recorded in David Walsh's 1986 biography of Kelly, though Shardelow himself disputed that account in an interview with South Africa's *Mail and Guardian* in 2013. The Burton and Taylor angle, he insisted, was a mere embellishment. Mum for Men's cover was, in fact, blown due to internal squabbling between the English and Afrikaner factions within South African cycling. 'The journalist who reported them was a guy who was tied up with South Africa cycling,' Shardelow said. 'He made his money out of it.'

Regardless of Hartdegen's motives, the outcome was the same. At the following day's start in Plettenburg Bay, he had a photographer capture close-up shots of the riders in Mum for Men jerseys who were listed as J. Burns, G. Main, D. Nixon, P. Nugent and A. Owen in the race programme. The pictures were wired to the *Daily Mail* in London and forwarded to the British Cycling Federation. 'They said, "Well those three guys, they're not British, they're from Ireland – that's Sean Kelly, Pat McQuaid and Kieron McQuaid," Kelly says and grins: 'That's when the shit hit the fan.'

The story appeared in the *Daily Mail* the following morning, under the banner headline 'The Secret Team Who Masquerade as Britain', and by that evening, it had reached newsstands in Ireland. 'The news travelled fast and once we were found out, there was nothing we could do,' Pat McQuaid says. 'During those couple of hours, the *Irish Press* managed to phone my mother-in-law in Bristol but she didn't know where I was. When they phoned my father, he said I was on holidays. They got no joy there, but they still went with the story that evening.'

Within 24 hours, and with the Rapport Toer still ongoing, McQuaid found himself, by dint of his loquaciousness, acting as the de facto spokesman for the trio of Irishmen in South Africa. While Carrick Wheelers would neither confirm nor deny Kelly's presence in South Africa, McQuaid spoke on the telephone with Jim McArdle of the *Irish Times*, and seemed already resigned to the worst-case scenario. 'That's it, I won't see the Olympics now,' he said.

By the time the South Africa Three returned to Ireland after a week's holiday that included a trip to Kruger Game Reserve, the lie of the land had begun to shift, even if McQuaid's official version of events at an ICF meeting shortly afterwards – that they had raced under false names only because they had arrived at the last minute and the sponsors had already filled in those names on the start list – did not in any way tally with reality. In November, the ICF decided to hand the trio a seven-month ban, which would have allowed them to return to action in ample time for Montreal. That sanction was later reduced by two months on appeal, meaning that they could even line out at the Tour of Britain, and when they resumed racing in April, Pat McQuaid and Kelly assumed they were beginning their preparations for the Olympic Games in earnest.

It wasn't until May 1976 that the International Olympic Committee took a formal interest in the matter, and at a meeting in Lausanne that month, it was decreed that all riders who had taken part in the Rapport Toer would be barred from that year's Olympic Games. The Olympic Council of Ireland relayed the decision to Kelly and the McQuaids the following day, shortly before their departure for the Tour of Britain. An appeal on their behalf from the ICF came to nothing. Kelly would not be travelling to Canada. To add to Kelly's chagrin, the gold medal in the road race in Montreal would be won by the man he had defeated at the Tour of Britain the previous year, Bernt Johansson.

Forty years on, McQuaid blames John Mangan's nemesis, Lord Killanin, for the belated decision to come down heavily on the cyclists. 'As an Irishman, he would have been embarrassed by it to some extent,' McQuaid says. In the decades that followed, it erroneously passed into lore that McQuaid and Kelly had received a permanent ban from the Olympic movement. That was untrue, though the mix-up is perhaps understandable, given that Kelly never went on to become an Olympian afterwards. So it goes. Rather than a detour, the roadblock would bring him on a shortcut towards his real destination.

It is a common misconception that Kelly was an accidental star, a young man who raced as something of a hunter-gatherer, picking up bouquets and plaudits without any thought of his long-term future, only to land almost unwittingly in the professional ranks. Yet even as a 19-year-old in Ireland, a country that had produced just one Tour de France rider and provided no obvious pathway to the professional ranks, Kelly was nurturing rather loftier and longer-term aspirations than a base desire for the next race and the next paycheque. 'This is the race you have to be in if you are going to be a top-class rider,' he had told reporters at his debut Tour of Britain. In the summer of 1976, with the Olympics off the agenda, his appetite was clearly not going to be sated by the same old diet of domestic racing and the occasional foray abroad with the national team. The time had come for him to set out on his journey southward.

The Olympic ban meant that Kelly's move to the French amateur scene, always likely to happen in 1977, could be brought forward to the summer of 1976. 'I've no doubt he was going to go down that route at some time,' Pat McQuaid says, waving away the notion that Kelly had no grand designs on a professional career. 'He had the ability and he was ambitious.' Kelly, as ever, is more circumspect on his rationale for accepting an offer to join amateur outfit Vélo Club Metz-Woippy midway through the season. 'I said I wasn't going to hang around and just race all year in Ireland if I wasn't going to the Olympics, so I decided at a certain point that I'd go to Metz,' he says. 'They said "Yeah, no problem," so I went over after the Tour of Britain.'

The decision to go to Metz did not simply drop out of the ether, as the club had already made a concerted attempt to secure the Irishman's services the previous summer. John Morris, a Briton who acted as a talent scout for French clubs, had first made contact on Metz's behalf following Kelly's Tour of Britain stage win in 1975, and club member Alain Steinhoff approached him in person after the amateur road race at the World Championships in Mettet, Belgium. Kelly demurred, citing his preference to prepare for Montreal in Ireland, but penned a short letter to Steinhoff almost immediately after learning of his Olympic ban in May 1976. The response from Metz was prompt, and offered free lodging and a bonus of four francs per kilometre of each race Kelly won. That last detail sufficed to strike a deal. Kelly would join the club after competing at the Tour of Britain, where he claimed another stage victory, this time beating the Pole Ryszard Szurkowski in a white-knuckle sprint on a downhill finish in Stoke.

Kelly flew directly from the Tour of Britain to Luxembourg in mid-June, where he was collected and driven to Metz to meet with the club president Aldo Bevigniani, a garrulous man of Italian origin whose transport company sponsored the club. Bevigniani considered the acquisition of Kelly a considerable coup for a relatively modest outfit, but the warmth of his welcome was offset by the spartan nature of the accommodation he provided. During his time in Metz, Kelly lived in a disused office with two teammates from New Zealand, where chipboard was used to divide the space into 'rooms' and old bedsheets covered the windows in place of curtains or blinds.

Unlike most members of the so-called 'Foreign Legion', the generation of English-speaking riders who came to seek their fortune on the French amateur scene in the late 1970s and early 1980s, usually enduring the harshest of educations, Kelly took quite readily to his new environment. In a strange way, his introverted character and upbringing seemed to have prepared him better than most. Never one to spend too many words in his native tongue, Kelly's lack of French was hardly a source of frustration. 'I spoke so little it didn't really matter whether I knew the language or not,' he wrote later. Similarly, the early nights and curtailed social life demanded of an aspiring bike rider were no real hardship to a farmer's son who had spent his teenage years in relative seclusion three miles outside Carrick-on-Suir. Occasional phone calls from Bevigniani's office to Linda Grant and his family sufficed for Kelly to stave off the worst of his homesickness. Psychologically, it helped that he was arriving with only little more than four months of the season remaining, rather than facing into an entire year abroad, and the stint would be broken up further by a trip home for the Tour of Ireland in August. And, of course, the prospect of earning hard cash put the privations of foreign living in perspective.

On the bike, the transition was also a comparatively painless one. Kelly's post-South Africa ban had delayed the start of his season, and the truncated spring meant that he reached the summer fresh and on form. He benefited, too, from the fact that Metz was a provincial club, as he competed predominantly against fields of middling quality that made for an ideal induction to Continental racing. 'At that time, I think the level in races around Paris would have been higher than Metz, because that's where the real good riders were,' Kelly says. 'At Metz, a lot of the races were a level down from that, so that helped. And I was also in super shape going over there after the Tour of Britain.'

Within a couple of weeks, Kelly was already winning races, including a solo triumph on a hilly course at Cousances that bore echoes of his Gap of Mamore exploits, and his morale was boosted further by the money he was accumulating as a result. Although the French cycling federation withheld payment of prize money for up to two months, Kelly could yield an immediate dividend by winning intermediate sprints, which were paid out at the finish of each race. The joke goes that the first French expression he learned was 'Sprint Prime', and while money was undoubtedly Kelly's main motivation, his string of victories – some 18 in total – was not going unnoticed.

Kelly's win at the Tour de Haute-Marne was particularly notable. Caught on the wrong side when a level crossing lowered just as the leading group was coming through, he was one of only two riders who opted to wait rather than scurry underneath the barrier. Working together, the chasing duo strained to make up their deficit, before Kelly resolved the situation by taking off alone and closing the gap by himself. He caught the leaders in the finale, then won the sprint by a handsome margin. Jean-Pierre Douçot, a mechanic and former amateur rider who served as an informal talent scout in eastern France, was present, and he became an early advocate of Kelly's talent. He alerted Jean de Gribaldy, a directeur sportif from Besançon tasked with putting together a new French arm of the crack Belgian professional outfit Flandria. 'Everybody claims to have discovered him, but I remember well that I was the first person to talk to de Gribaldy about him,' Douçot said in 2006. At a race later in the summer, a local amateur tipped Kelly off about de Gribaldy's interest, but the finer details were lost in translation. 'At that time my French wouldn't have been great. I understood what he was saying, but exactly who this guy was, I didn't understand at all,' Kelly says.

Although Kelly raced less than half a season for Metz, and mostly in provincial events, he would win enough to place 90th in the French federation's end-of-year ranking of amateur riders, seven spots ahead of John Mangan, who was racing on the other side of France with VC St-Malo. News of

Kelly's exploits was also beginning to filter through to French cycling's nerve centre around the capital. Philippe Bouvet was an amateur rider in Paris and among those who had noticed this Irishman's remarkable dominance in north-eastern France that summer. When they lined up alongside one another at a Trophée Peugeot race in Troyes, Bouvet, who was already leaning towards a career in journalism – he would spend 32 years as a cycling reporter at *L'Équipe* – made it his business to get a closer look at this would-be phenomenon. 'I'd heard talk of this big, strong Irish rider from Metz-Woippy, and that's the first time I saw Kelly,' Bouvet says. 'It was Pascal Simon who won the race ahead of Jonathan Boyer, and we were a long way back in the peloton, but I can remember Kelly at one point riding on the front and stringing it out.'

The approving nods of connoisseurs like Bouvet were one thing, but the amateur who makes the step up to the professional peloton usually needs to produce at least one landmark victory in a major race, a sort of masterpiece to complete the apprenticeship. Kelly's would not arrive until his final outing of the season, when Bevigniani brought his charges for a rare test abroad at the amateur Tour of Lombardy on the first weekend in October. At Il Piccolo Lombardia, among the most prestigious races on the amateur calendar, Kelly took advantage of his relative anonymity on a day of driving rain north of Milan.

When the highly rated Dutch amateur Henk Lubberding attacked on the final climb, only Kelly and two Italians, Vittorio Algeri and Filippo Marchirato, could follow. On the run-in to the finish, all eyes were on Algeri. A rapid finisher, he had placed 8th in the Montreal Olympics and as a native of Torre de' Roveri near Bergamo, he was desperate to sign off on his amateur career with a win in his home classic. Not for the last time in his career, Kelly benefited from a local rider's eagerness in a big Italian race. Algeri opened the sprint from distance but was beaten soundly by Kelly, who now had a victory of rare quality to add to the quantity he had amassed in France.

The Lombardy triumph was enough to convince de Gribaldy to act more purposefully on Douçot's earlier recommendation, but Bevigniani had already figured out that the swiftest way to win Kelly's favour was with the chequebook, and he offered to double his protégé's allowance and improve his win bonuses if he returned in 1977. 'I thought that another year would do me very well because I was still very young,' Kelly says. Having collected the bones of £800 from barely four months of racing, his interest was stoked, especially when he succeeded in persuading Metz to sign Pat McQuaid for the following year. 'When Kelly came back from those few months, he said he couldn't go back alone for a full year. He couldn't last that long out there by himself,' says McQuaid, who had since taken up another teaching post in Ballinteer but still nursed hopes of devoting himself full-time to cycling. Some dreams die hard.

The swift December dusk had already come tumbling by the time the taxi crossed the bridge in Carrick-on-Suir and headed out the Curraghduff road. A middle-aged man in a pilot's uniform, the only English speaker in the group of visitors, sat in the passenger seat, translating the curt instructions that the older man with slicked back hair and a pin-striped suit was issuing in French from the back seat. Their party was completed by a courteous, shy young man who spoke only when spoken to. When the driver had collected his motley crew outside the arrivals hall of Dublin airport that morning, he could hardly have expected the orienteering course that lay in store, though the protracted haggling over the asking price probably ought to have tipped him off.

On reaching a lonely farmhouse, the man in the pilot's uniform knocked on the front door and requested to speak with Sean Kelly. Sean, he was told, was not home, as he was out collecting a fertiliser tank on behalf of his brother Martin. The three visitors were invited to await his arrival, but after a hasty consultation in French, they elected to drive out the Dungarvan road and intercept him on his way back. Shortly afterwards, they happened upon a tractor in the late afternoon gloom, and the old man leant forward in the back seat. 'Is that Kelly?' he asked the young man alongside him. The young man squinted and hesitated. The old man ordered the taxi to a halt, and the man in the pilot's uniform sprung from the passenger seat and hailed the tractor.

'Are you Sean Kelly?' he called up to the youth aboard the tractor.

There was a pause, as though the words had lost their way in the dark.

'Yes, I am Sean Kelly,' came the cautious response.

The pilot turned to the taxi and nodded, and Jean de Gribaldy emerged to introduce himself. He had travelled that morning from Dole airport on his private jet, flown by his friend Bernard Dagot, while Kelly's Metz teammate Noel

Converset was brought along with the dual role of recognising the Irishman and then convincing him of the merits of signing for the Flandria professional cycling team. Converset's carrot was a considerable one. If he succeeded, then he too would get to turn professional, at the belated age of 27.

'Of course, I recognised Converset because I raced most of the year in Metz with him. He hopped out of the taxi and he was saying "Jean de Gribaldy" and "professional" and he was going on in French there, full bore,' Kelly says.

They agreed to return to the farmhouse to open negotiations in earnest, with Dagot acting as interpreter, and de Gribaldy insisting over and again that he wouldn't leave Ireland without Kelly's signature. Converset nervously continued his sales patter, looking to sell Kelly on the idea of racing for Flandria alongside the newly crowned world champion Freddy Maertens. 'I was there to push him to sign,' Converset says.

Kelly took some persuading. He was already set on the idea of returning to Metz with Pat McQuaid, and reckoned that de Gribaldy's opening offer of £4,000 wasn't far north of what he could expect to earn as an amateur in 1977 between living expenses, sprint primes and win bonuses. He politely declined to sign there and then, preferring instead to consult with McQuaid, who in turn sought the advice of the British cycling photographer John Pierce, a regular competitor, team manager and journalist at the Tour of Ireland.

'Pat rang me because I'd done a contract with Phil Edwards from Bristol when he signed for Sanson, the Italian team, so I'd been involved a little bit with contracts and had some idea of how much they should be,' Pierce says. 'Pat said to me that Kelly had been offered £400 and I said, "That's nonsense, it's

£4,000. You tell him to ask for 6 and if he gets offered 5 then he's doing alright.'"

When de Gribaldy phoned Carrick-on-Suir the following week, Kelly duly negotiated his asking price upwards to £6,000 and a contract with Flandria was agreed. He seemed uncannily well-versed in the art of the deal.

AMONG ROYALTY

Jean de Gribaldy was a man of contradictions. He claimed his family was descended from Piedmontese nobility, and he encouraged and revelled in the nickname of *Le Vicomte* ('The Viscount'), yet in the cycling world, he enjoyed painting himself as an outsider and a champion of the downtrodden. He ran cycling teams on precarious funding, yet his preferred modes of transport were private plane or very fast car. As a manager, he expected dedication, sobriety and, in some instances, chastity of his riders, yet he was a frequent habitué of Paris nightspots like the Alcazar and Chez Castel, where he counted French pop stars like Johnny Hallyday and Sylvie Vartan among his friends

De Gribaldy was born in 1922 in Besançon. The Franche-Comté region was a watchmaking hub, and his parents wanted him to take up the trade, but the young de Gribaldy preferred bikes. He turned professional after World War II, riding the Tour de France three times, though if he was calling himself the Viscount back in that golden era of cycling nicknames, the press was paying little heed. On retirement, he opened a bike shop in Besançon and, though his business interests in the early 1960s extended to establishing his own small airline, Air Franche-Comté, he never strayed far from cycling. After being invited to put together a semi-professional team to compete in the Route de France in 1964 – legend has it he brought Jacques Brel along to watch – de Gribaldy began a 23-year run as a directeur sportif. *Le Vicomte* had arrived.

De Gribaldy's teams generally operated on a minuscule budget, evidenced by the number of small sub-sponsors occupying real estate on the jerseys. To compensate, he scoured unexpected places for talents like Joaquim Agostinho, the Portuguese rider encountered at the 1968 Tour of São Paulo, who would go on to place on the podium of the Tour de France twice in his late 30s. Agostinho was a quiet, uncomplaining man of rural stock from a relative cycling backwater. In Kelly, de Gribaldy hoped he had unearthed a similar diamond.

Not that the Flandria-Velda team was in much need of further adornment, given that it was built around the glittering talent of rainbow jersey Freddy Maertens, winner of 54 races the previous season. The team, sponsored by a Flemish bicycle and moped manufacturer, had existed since 1957. The imposing Lomme Driessens was team manager, with 'Iron' Briek Schotte, a double world champion and Tour of Flanders winner in the 1940s, his number two. It was a team with a history. Flandria's red-and-white jerseys, already among the most distinctive in the peloton, had been bedecked with a rainbow trim since tragedy befell the team in 1971, when then world champion Jean-Pierre Monseré died following a crash in a *kermesse* race in Retie.

Though an avowedly Belgian institution, the sponsor was keen to expand its market, and de Gribaldy was asked to put together a French arm to the team for the 1977 season. Marcel Tinazzi, René Bittinger, Converset and Metz recruit Kelly were among those he signed for what was notionally designated as the French squad, but was, to all intents and purposes, the B team. At the press presentation in Brussels in January, Kelly and the French stood shivering in the background as Maertens fielded questions from Belgian reporters. Although the entire Flandria squad subsequently trained together at a preseason camp in the Ardèche, once the season began, Maertens and the Flemish stars went one way, and de Gribaldy's fledglings another.

In the early-season races in the south of France, it was soon apparent that Kelly was the pick of Flandria's new intake. De Gribaldy, never much given to issuing pre-race instructions, left his Irish recruit largely to his own devices in his first outing, the five-day Étoile de Bessèges stage race, and Kelly's strength and instincts served him well, as he placed third overall. He elicited further notice at the Tour of the Mediterranean that followed, even if he took home no bouquets. In a tight sprint finish in Marseille, he looked to have edged out Jan Raas, but the race jury decided otherwise and awarded the win to the Dutchman, amid furious protestations from de Gribaldy, who later procured a photograph demonstrating that Kelly had, in fact, been first across the line. It was all to no avail, though the 20-year-old didn't have to wait much longer for his first win in Flandria red. Little over a month into the season, on 6 March, Kelly travelled to Switzerland and won a six-man sprint to claim victory at the pro-am GP Lugano.

Kelly's living quarters for the 1977 season seemed apt for a man on the threshold between the amateur and professional ranks, as they were scarcely an upgrade on the converted office he had inhabited in Metz. De Gribaldy liked to keep tactical discussions to a minimum, but he was fanatical in controlling every facet of his riders' training, and insisted that his young charges spend the bulk of their time between races living in Besançon in a cramped upstairs apartment at 18, Place du Marché. The business beneath the apartment was de Gribaldy's own bike shop, and even when his cycling duties and extracurricular activities took him away from Besançon, he demanded information on how his boys had trained and precisely how much they had eaten. Weight, and the lack of it, was a fixation.

'There was a kitchen in the shop, so I'd go there for a bit of lunch. In the evening time, sometimes I'd cook something in the apartment myself but most of the time de Gribaldy wanted me to come to his house, so he could see what I was eating and how much I was eating,' Kelly says. 'He was always there after we'd come back from training as well and he'd ask how far did we train, and he'd tell us if we needed to do more in the afternoon.' As an immigrant, Kelly was a permanent resident in the apartment, but his fellow French neo-professionals, including Converset, though he hailed from nearby Héricourt, were regularly summoned to barracks in Besançon.

'Sean obviously had a room in the apartment because he stayed there more often than us French riders, but we all would have slept at that apartment at least some of the time,' says Marcel Tinazzi, who would win the French national title in his debut season at Flandria. 'That was de Gribaldy's philosophy. De Gribaldy wanted to keep us away from food and women. He used to say that if we went home, we'd only eat too much and spend too much time with our wives. He kept us in that apartment deliberately, and he was right to do it! It was de Gribaldy who used to bring us our food every day, too. Nobody else at the time was as obsessed with keeping weight off.'

Tinazzi, like Kelly, would come to adore de Gribaldy as much as he respected him. Despite his aristocratic affectations, he was not an authoritarian figure, and despite his demanding regimen of training and diet, de Gribaldy also knew when to dangle the occasional treat. Tinazzi was among the riders summoned to Paris for a night out with the boss. 'It was only ever at the end of the season, mind,' he says. 'We'd go see the shows, and visit Sylvie Vartan in her dressing room. Halfway through, de Gribaldy might disappear backstage for quarter of an hour for a chat with her. He was very well known in Paris. He knew everybody. *Everybody.*'

Kelly, even later in his career, was not a regular on those Parisian excursions. 'Sean didn't come very often, maybe just once or twice. I went more than him,' Tinazzi says, and laughs: 'That's probably why he won a lot of races and I didn't.' He defends de Gribaldy, too, against the charge that he was an especially parsimonious paymaster. 'If he paid the minimum, it was because he simply couldn't afford to pay his riders more than that,' he insists. 'And don't kid yourself. It's not like Guimard or Peugeot paid that much more. Money was limited everywhere at that time.'

Not everyone from Flandria's French class of 1977 holds benign memories of de Gribaldy's style. His modus operandi was to take a punt on five or six minimum-wage neo-professionals every year in the hope that one or two might make the grade, dumping the rest unceremoniously at season's end. While de Gribaldy honoured his promise to make Noel Converset a professional, he quickly decided the Frenchman had no future at that level. Converset's dream of riding the Tour de France would remain just that. 'There were too many riders on the team, with the Belgians and the French,' he says. Instead, in 1977, his primary task was to stay close to Kelly early on in races, lest the Irishman suffer a mechanical problem. 'I'd have to give him my bike, because it was the same size. I helped him to win a lot of races and never got much thanks for it,' Converset says.

More pressingly, Converset claims he never got any money, either. 'He didn't pay me, de Gribaldy,' Converset says forlornly. 'I had to hire a lawyer and open a case against him because I wasn't paid. He was a bandit, de Gribaldy. He didn't pay me at all. He was a bandit.'

By 1978, Converset was back in the amateur ranks, and working in his family's clockmaking company. He says he never heard from his Flandria teammates again.

Flandria's French team was but a provincial outpost in an empire that revolved around the Belgian triumvirate of Maertens, Michel Pollentier and Marc Demeyer, and, as though rendering a tribute unto Caesar, de Gribaldy was asked to dispatch his strongest man to ride in their service at Paris-Nice in March 1977. 'De Gribaldy says to me, I don't know, maybe three or four days beforehand, "You could make Paris-Nice with the Belgian guys,"' Kelly says. De Gribaldy duly ferried him to Aulnay-sous-Bois, on the north side of Paris, and into the court of the man who would be king.

Freddy Maertens was only 25 years of age in the spring of 1977, but he was already at his zenith. As well as being the fastest sprinter in the world, his sheer power made him formidable across just about every terrain bar the highest mountains. Resplendent in the rainbow jersey, he had just won Belgium's season-opening classic, the Omloop Het Volk, and later that spring he would go on to annex the Vuelta a España, matter-of-factly winning 13 of its 21 stages along the way. With Eddy Merckx entering the twilight of his career, the expectation in Belgium was that Maertens would assume his mantle. There had never, it seemed, been a winning machine quite like this squat, muscular man from the *plat pays* along Belgium's North Sea coast.

Pollentier knew Maertens from childhood, and, for the most part, his talents dovetailed with those of his friend. Lacking Maertens's style and finishing speed, the wiry, balding Pollentier was a fine climber, good enough to win the Giro d'Italia later in 1977. The trio was completed by the 1976 Paris-Roubaix winner Demeyer, and though he was not of the same calibre as Pollentier and Maertens, he compensated with raw strength and the force of his character. He was a natural road captain, at home negotiating deals with other teams and bellowing orders at his own. The hierarchy was an intuitive one. In his 2008 book *Forcenés*, a stylised account of cycling history, the French author Philippe Bordas described them as Byronic figures, 'searching for whom to die. Freddy is the chosen one. Marc the Giant and Michel the Little Thumb know it instinctively.'

Maertens mashed his monstrous gear to win the prologue of Paris-Nice and then rattled off sprint victories on each of the first three road stages, with his red Flandria guard dictating terms on the front of the peloton. The war long won, he added the concluding time trial on the Promenade des Anglais to cap his final overall victory. Kelly contributed as best he could throughout the week, largely by helping to wind up the pace in the closing kilometres on flat stages, before Demeyer would lead Maertens out for the final sprint.

A hectoring presence even in victory, Demeyer was furibund when Maertens was beaten into third place on stage 4 in Digne-les-Bains. He identified Kelly as the culprit, reasoning that the Irishman had fatally allowed the pace to slacken with two kilometres to go. Past the finish line, Demeyer delivered a string of invective in Flemish, which the Irishman didn't understand, and then in French, which he barely spoke. Maertens, by contrast, made it his business to offer words of encouragement in English each evening.

'I got on well with Maertens. I was able to work pretty well for him, and he could see I was a Paddy shy guy so he was helpful,' Kelly says. 'Sometimes at night-time, he'd talk to me and explain things that we did, and say if maybe it was the wrong way to do it. He'd just give me guidance.' For all that he subsequently developed a reputation as a hell-raiser – problems with the taxman and rumours of doping and alcoholism would plague the latter part of his career – Maertens was at heart a sensitive individual. He had given the late Jean-Pierre Monseré's son Giovanni a bicycle as a communion present, for instance, and when the seven-year-old was killed after colliding with a car while Maertens was at the 1976 Tour de France, the Flandria team, his family and even the Belgian press all agreed not to reveal the news to him until he had reached Paris, mindful of how profoundly it would affect him.

Apart from Maertens's kindness, few concessions were made for the newcomer from Ireland at Paris-Nice and on his other, occasional appearances with the A team in his debut season, including the classics Flèche Wallonne and Amstel Gold Race. He had to learn by observation. Flemish was the main language at the dinner table, but from watching his more experienced teammates, Kelly would in time receive a crash course in the wink and elbow language of professional cycling. Though the rivalries between the stars and their teams, especially in Belgium, were often venomous, there were occasional cessations of hostilities when common interests prevailed or when victories were exchanged for favours.

Ahead of that year's spring classics, Driessens even had Maertens sign what amounted to a non-belligerence pact with Roger De Vlaeminck of the rival Brooklyn team for Paris-Roubaix and Liège-Bastogne-Liège. Maertens reproduced the contract in his 1988 autobiography, *Fall From Grace*, and gave short shrift to the idea that the public might have felt short-changed. 'I don't have to account to the average cycling fan for the fact that I wanted to earn as much as I could,' Maertens wrote. 'Later on, when I was in financial trouble, I never saw this average cycling fan standing at my door with a bag of money.'

The spring of 1977 would also serve to draw the average cycling fan's attention to the prevalence of doping in the peloton, although in that prelapsarian time, long before the Festina Affair or Operación Puerto, neither the public nor the authorities reacted with any real outrage. Bernard Thévenet was docked 10 minutes when he tested positive at Paris-Nice, but it was deemed a mere embarrassment rather than a scandal, and he would win the Tour de France in July. Maertens was stripped of his Flèche Wallonne victory when he tested positive for the stimulant pemoline, better known by its brand name of Stimul. He was just one of several Belgian riders to do so that spring. Eddy Merckx also tested positive for Stimul at Flèche Wallonne, while Pollentier had been caught using the substance at the Tour of Belgium. 'You can't make a racehorse out of a donkey,' Merckx said by way of response. The cycling world shrugged. No bans were doled out and life went on as before.

Kelly, still only 20 years of age, was deemed too raw to participate in any of the three-week tours in his debut season, and while Maertens and Pollentier set about winning the Vuelta and the Giro, he fell in again with the French team and claimed a brace of lofty scalps. At the Tour de Romandie, he out-kicked Patrick Sercu, the so-called Walloon Arrow, to win the opening stage, after Tinazzi and Muselet led him out. Two weeks later, Kelly beat Merckx himself in a sprint at the end of the minor Circuit de l'Indre in Chateauroux. That Merckx was long past his prime and scarcely a month on from testing positive for a stimulant did little to temper Kelly's sense of achievement.

For the most part, Kelly performed off Broadway that season, adding a fourth win at the Étoile des Espoirs race, though he would ride more regularly with Freddy and company than his French teammates, partly due to his ability and partly due to demographics. 'With the language and everything else, you had kind of a clique between the two sides [Belgian and French], but I was kind of in the middle,' Kelly says. 'And the Belgians speak good English, so they talked to me a lot.'

At season's end, Kelly received the ultimate seal of approval from the Flemish cohort. The ICF's budget did not extend to sending Kelly to Venezuela for the World Championships, so Flandria stepped in and paid for him to travel to San Cristobal – not because the youngster was a medal hope, but because he could be relied upon to ride in support of Maertens, his trade teammate. Indeed, precisely for that reason, the French selectors opted not to pick Tinazzi, even though he had won the national title as a neo-professional: they feared his loyalty would be to his Flandria teammate Maertens rather than to France. It wasn't straightforward to be an Irishman in a professional peloton dominated by cycling's old world powers of France, Italy, Belgium and Spain, but it was not without the occasional residual benefit.

The apprenticeship continued in much the same vein in 1978, when Kelly returned to Flandria on close to double his previous salary. Once again, he flitted between leading the line for de Gribaldy's team and riding as a domestique for the Belgian squad, which was now managed by Fred De Bruyne after Demeyer, backed by Maertens and Pollentier, had instigated a heave against Driessens during the winter. The power of Flandria's star men seemed absolute. They must have felt themselves untouchable.

That spring was notable for Kelly's first appearance in Paris-Roubaix, but racing on rough roads as an amateur in Ireland proved no real preparation for traversing the tracks of jagged cobblestones that punctuate the pocket of northern France that was so devastated in the First World War. The race's nickname, the Hell of the North, which stems from that very desolation, is apt. From the first cobblestones after 100 kilometres or so, there is only chaos, as early fallers and muddied backmarkers are cast adrift like lost souls. For neophytes, there is something of Stendhal's description of the Battle of Waterloo about the experience: they are not so much participating in the race as chasing it. Most leave the fray scarred, yet unsure if they had truly been in Paris-Roubaix at all. Kelly abandoned all hope shortly after the midway point, and he reached the Roubaix velodrome in the broom wagon. 'When you start doing the classics, you get an eye-opener, of course, and that's what I got,' Kelly says. 'I went to my first classics – Gent-Wevelgem, Paris-Roubaix and some of those races – and I thought, "Oh my God, this is something totally different." It's a shock, really.'

At June's Critérium du Dauphiné Libéré, on the other hand, Kelly was part of a team that was doling out its own version of shock and awe. Though Flandria claimed 'only' three stages, their dominance that week in the Alps felt total, and Pollentier scored a commanding overall victory. 'We set off and we just knew we'd win the Dauphiné Libéré, because Freddy and Michel were going like motors,' Tinazzi recalls. 'It was around the time the 12-tooth cog came out, and Freddy and Michel knew how to push that big gear like no one else.' The headlines were all for Pollentier and Maertens, but Kelly had done enough to earn a berth in the team for the Big Show the following month. Fourteen years after Shay Elliott's final appearance, an Irishman was going to the Tour de France.

►⊙◄

In 1978, the Tour was decidedly old world in feel, nothing like the globalised, made-for-television spectacle it would steadily become over the next quarter of a century. Of the mere 110 riders who lined up for the Grand Départ of that year's race in the Dutch town of Leiden, just shy of half were from France, and only three – Kelly and the Britons Barry Hoban and Paul Sherwen – hailed from outside mainland western Europe. Not a single Italian team or rider had seen fit to travel north of the Alps, and the press room was composed predominantly of home-based and Belgian journalists. Live television coverage was limited almost exclusively to France.

In such a context, then, it was perhaps only to be expected that news of Kelly's victory on stage 6 to Poitiers would struggle to make an impact in Ireland. Of the main daily newspapers, it was the *Irish Times* that dedicated the most space to the triumph, including a photograph on page 3 to accompany the short, unsigned newswire report that gave the result, outlined the barest of details of how it had happened and mentioned that it was Ireland's second stage win after Elliott's 15 years previously. When Kelly finished safely in the main peloton after helping Maertens to stage victory the following day, however, the *Irish Times* subeditors showed their lack of understanding of the rudiments of the sport by running a paragraph of newswire copy under the heading, 'Kelly slumps in Tour de France.'

A Tour stage victory held rather more value in the professional peloton than in Ireland. In Kelly's case, the win was by no means a confirmation of greatness, but it was a firm indication of future potential, and that would be a precious commodity when it came to negotiating a new contract at the end of the season. It was also an unexpected windfall for

Kelly, given that his primary task at this Tour was to lead out Maertens in the sprints, but a rare opportunity presented itself on the road to Poitiers.

Beneath leaden skies, Kelly, wearing arm-warmers to guard against the chill, was alert to the danger when Gerrie Knetemann and Joseph Bruyère, then 2nd and 3rd overall, shot off the front of the peloton with 30 kilometres to go. Maertens gave Kelly the nod to follow, and when two more riders, the Swede Sven-Åke Nilsson and Flandria teammate René Bittinger, joined them, it was clear that this break had legs. It soon became a battle of nerves, with Kelly and Bittinger both refusing to contribute to the pace-making, mindful that Knetemann and Bruyère had designs on the yellow jersey and were desperate to keep the move alive. Only on the final approach to Poitiers did Kelly take some cursory turns on the front, doing just enough to ensure the quintet stayed away. His reputation as a fast man made Kelly the likely winner, and so it proved. He opened his sprint on the cusp of the gently unfolding final bend, and powered clear, gear cables flapping in the breeze. Although he overestimated his strength by sprinting too soon and was almost caught by Knetemann, Kelly raised a fist to the air as he crossed the line. On the podium, Kelly cut an awkward figure, smiling bashfully as he accepted the bouquet, with a Flandria cap balanced precariously atop his unruly mound of hair. 'I nearly misjudged the final part because it was uphill,' he admitted.

The victory was a welcome infusion of morale in a most arduous debut Tour, which included a mammoth 153-kilometre team time trial in the opening week, two split stages and a preponderance of long-distance transfers before and after each day's racing. Indeed, such were the hardships endured by the peloton that they went on strike on the morning stage to Valence-d'Agen, walking across the finish line en masse in protest at their working conditions. Bernard Hinault, the young French champion riding in his first Tour, led the way, his chest jutting out defiantly amid the jeers and boos of the crowds at the roadside. The other big leaders – Maertens, Joop Zoetemelk et al. – stood alongside him, while Kelly and his fellow neophyte Paul Sherwen took up position in the second row. For years afterwards, Sherwen would enjoy dusting off the old tale of how Kelly had turned to him and said, only half in jest, 'If anyone moves, we're going for it.'

The polemics subsided and racing resumed, but the preordained script for this Tour remained askew. The consensus beforehand had been that Hinault, though still only 23, would cruise to victory on his debut, but his Tour threatened to run aground when he performed poorly on the mountain time trial at Puy de Dôme, and he was cast adrift by Pollentier on the climb of l'Alpe d'Huez. Hunched over his bike, his head drooping almost to his handlebars, the Belgian hardly cut the most graceful of figures on the climb's 21 hairpin bends, but his ungainly style proved effective. He soloed to stage victory, more than half a minute clear of Hennie Kuiper and Hinault to move into first place overall. A week from Paris, Pollentier was in the yellow jersey of race leader and the polka dot jersey of King of the Mountains, while Maertens was in the green jersey of points leader. Flandria's supremacy was absolute.

And then it was gone.

Kelly might have expected an air of bonhomie as the Flandria team dined at the Hôtel Le Castillan that evening, but the mood was downbeat. Instead of toasting his success with champagne, Pollentier's teammates were digesting the news that he had been expelled from the Tour for attempting to pass off someone else's urine sample as his own at anti-doping control. He had been caught with a rubber bulb full of urine under his armpit, which was attached to a plastic tube that ran into his shorts. French rider Antoine Gutierrez was also discovered using the same kind of apparatus.

Maertens's first reaction was to telephone the Tour organiser Jacques Goddet to inquire 'if some sort of arrangement couldn't be reached'. Nothing to be done. His second impulse was to suggest the Flandria team leave the race in protest. Kelly and his fellow Tour virgins from the French squad – Tinazzi, Bittinger and Muselet – kept their counsel throughout the internal debate that followed, though, to a man, they were quietly relieved when the order came from Flandria's head office that they were to stay put.

A forlorn Pollentier set about packing his suitcase, but he remained in the hotel the following day, a rest day, and an orderly troupe of journalists arrived to document his final moments on the race. 'They made a big story of it, like he'd gone and killed 30 people,' Tinazzi complains now. With his receding hairline and haunted expression, Pollentier looked at least two decades older than his 27 years as he sat on the end of his bed, dressed in his bright red Flandria tracksuit. In an interview with French television, he complained that there had been no doctor present when Kelly was tested in Saint-Étienne two days earlier, and offered a summary of his own case that served neither as an admission nor an outright denial. 'I didn't cheat. I was caught with things but I didn't use them,' he said gnomically, before lobbing in a thinly veiled accusation that he had been the victim of foul play: 'We were winning too much.'

Six years later, in an interview with David Walsh, Kelly would echo Pollentier's suspicions. 'In the back of my mind I imagined that Michel wasn't the type of rider that Félix Lévitan, the Tour director, wanted to win the race,' Kelly said. 'What Michel did was wrong, the organisers were entitled to put him out, but if that had happened with another rider, the reaction might have been different.'

In Pollentier's absence, Bernard Hinault rolled onto the Champs-Élysées in yellow to win the first of his five Tours de France, while Maertens joylessly toasted victory in the points classification. Despite struggling in the heat of the Alps, Kelly came home in 34th place overall, and went on to finish his second season in the professional ranks with his market value considerably boosted by his Tour stage win. He rejected Flandria's offer of an improved contract in favour of a higher offer from rival Belgian outfit Splendor in 1979. They would pay out £12,000 in compensation to Flandria and, according to contemporary reports, Splendor's bonus system could see Kelly earn up to £50,000 in a season. Though de Gribaldy counselled strongly against the move, it was difficult to pass up.

'The money was better and I could see the opportunity to get away from Maertens,' Kelly says. 'If I stayed put, I was going to be working for Maertens again at the bigger races. If I went to the Tour de France again, it would have been Maertens for the sprints, and it would have been the same at some of the other stage races like Paris-Nice. But with Splendor, I was told that I would be the guy for the sprints.'

Splendor manager Robert Lauwers travelled to Ireland in November to finalise the contract, and stayed at Alan McCormack's home in Dublin during the trip. McCormack had raced for Lauwers's team, then called Lord's-Splendor, during the 1978 season, and even completed the Vuelta a España, but had then returned home abruptly during the summer, in somewhat mysterious circumstances. He told Jim McArdle of the *Irish Times* that he was 'completely drained with no energy', and he would rather drop back to the amateur ranks than return to the Continent, yet Kelly did not see fit to consult with him about the precise details of life at Splendor.

'No, but when Alan was there it was a very small team and then they decided they were going to have a bigger team,' Kelly says. 'I think it had changed.' In any case, Kelly was already familiar with many of his new comrades at Splendor – the team leader, after all, would be Michel Pollentier.

5

WONDER BOY

In the late 1970s, as a band called The Hype, yet to morph into the behemoth known as U2, bounced from one half-empty Dublin nightspot to another, its frontman behaved as though he were performing somewhere else entirely. Each night, Paul Hewson, already demanding to be known as Bono, would prance about the stage and climb amps with a confidence that belied the unsteady quality of the group backing him. He would sing for the rafters on nights when the audience scarcely filled the front third of the room. At the time, it must have seemed an affectation, or perhaps even a delusion. Yet within a few years, the same punters who rolled their eyeballs and muttered, 'State of your man' then were now lining up to boast, 'I was there.' The line between misplaced arrogance and justifiable confidence is sometimes a hazy one.

The 19-year-old Stephen Roche was, at least in one respect, cut from similar cloth. Popular as the Rás Tailteann was in North Kerry, there was hardly a spectator to be found on the roadside 30 miles into the fourth stage of the 1979 edition of the race, but Roche appeared to ride as though his every pedal stroke was being watched intently by an audience of thousands. Part of the day's early break, his progress was halted by a rear wheel puncture ahead of the climb of Knockawaddra. He stood calmly as a mechanic changed his wheel and struggled to reship the chain, before setting off again. Rather than begin his pursuit immediately, however, Roche raised his hand and called up the service car once more. Though the young mechanic had managed to avoid tangling his bell-bottomed jeans in the chain, he had left an oily handprint on the frame of Roche's bike, a bright red Raleigh. Always fastidious about his kit and equipment, Roche requested a rag from the car and wiped the offending handprint away before eventually seeing fit to increase his pace and commit to the chase.

'The rest of us would be going ballistic trying to get on, but he's there saying, "Ah Jesus, look at the state of me bike,"' says Damien Long, a childhood friend of Roche who also competed in that Rás for a Dublin selection.

Such sangfroid was impressive considering that Alan McCormack, a teammate in the ICF national team but Roche's chief rival for overall honours, was driving the break up ahead. Roche caught the leaders over the other side of the climb and then helped to propel the move to the finish in Caherciveen. McCormack claimed stage victory in a three-man sprint but Roche moved into the overall lead, and he would hold the yellow jersey all the way to the finish in Dublin to become the youngest-ever Rás winner.

It was a special edition of the race, as 1979 was the first season of Irish cycling under the so-called Tripartite Committee, with NCA, ICF and NICF riders now competing freely in each other's events. For riders of Roche's generation, who had grown up only tangentially concerned by the civil war in Irish cycling, an arguably more exciting development was that RTÉ had seen fit to film the Rás and broadcast the highlights at the end of the week. In Roche, a youthful yellow jersey who still carried some puppy fat but few inhibitions, Michael O'Carroll and his camera crew found themselves blessed with a natural star, always game for a running commentary or a quip whenever they drew up alongside him for a close-up. Small wonder he didn't want oil stains on his bike.

'Who would you worry about in this group?' they asked Roche on stage 2. 'No one!' came the playful response, and, as if to prove the point, he went on to claim a rare sprint victory at the finish in Westport. Roche's second stage win of the week came on the morning of the final day, when he scorched to victory in the Navan time trial despite breaking a spoke early in his effort. That afternoon, he was part of the three-man break that escaped on the finishing circuit in the Phoenix Park. Minutes away from overall victory, Roche was happy to ham it up for the cameras once more.

'Are you thinking of work tomorrow?' he was asked. Roche shook his head: 'Oh no – the girls and work. I'm going to enjoy myself tonight.' Though before the post-race festivities, he would, he acknowledged, go home to Dundrum for his mother's cooking. 'Steak and ice cream,' he beamed.

For all the levity, it had been at times a tense week for Roche. McCormack, a forceful presence on the Irish scene following his curiously sudden return from the professional ranks in Belgium, had not taken kindly to being usurped by a man almost four years his junior. Roche's overt displays of confidence may have appealed to the cameras but they grated with some of his teammates. 'I always called him Wonder Boy – he and I never really got along,' says McCormack. 'He was always a little cocky and full of himself, too much to say. I didn't dislike him, but I wouldn't say he was my Guinness drinking partner. I'm not bitter, but he definitely had a bit of an attitude. I'd rather have hung out with Sean [Kelly]. But then he was a little later and younger than us as well.'

As at the 1975 Tour of Ireland, McCormack thought nothing of attacking a teammate in the yellow jersey. It was an unwanted but no less useful education for Roche. 'I had to learn and learn quickly because Alan McCormack was very quick at jumping in the front break, whereas I was only a novice to the game. He got away on the road to Carrick-on-Suir, and I had to react and chase him down,' Roche recalls. 'But looking back on it, I can see that I was a little bit classier than my teammates.'

At the time, too, Roche already seemed to have a fair idea of that fact. At an age when Kelly had, at least according to the popular myth, nodded shyly in response to Brendan O'Reilly during a *radio* interview, Roche was already blithely issuing statements of intent. When the RTÉ crew visited him in his room late in the week, he spoke with startling confidence. 'People are saying I've got a lot of class alright, but I want to leave my mark on cycling,' Roche told them.

'Wasn't it a good job I had a good career?' Roche says now. 'Otherwise I wouldn't be able to look back on that.'

►⊙◄

It hadn't always been thus. Before Roche became a cycling star, he was a boy who struggled to get picked for soccer and hurling teams. And before Roche flaunted his credentials as a ladies' man to the nation, he was, according to Damien Long, 'useless with women, just like the rest of us'. Long chuckles at the memory. 'We'd be chasing girls and getting nowhere. We were just awkward young fellas.'

Once aboard a bike, however, Roche was a man transfigured, pedalling with a grace and facility that set him apart from his peers almost from the night he first showed up for an Orwell Wheelers club run as a 13-year-old in the summer of 1973, aboard a Jack of Clubs bike fitted with flat handlebars. 'He would have had this great label: class,' says Paul Kimmage, who, though three years younger than Roche, was a friend and even more fervent admirer throughout their teenage years. The tag was a double-edged one. In a cycling culture where the 'savage road men' of the Rás were the preferred archetype, as Roche progressed through the ranks, such style would often come to be confused with a lack of effort. In turn, he would be compared negatively with the more obviously industrious Kelly. Long before he joined the Waterford man as a professional, the dichotomy between the hard man from the country and the soft boy from the city gained currency.

Yet Roche was hardly born into privilege when he arrived into the world on 28 November 1959. He was the second of six children, and until he was six years old, home was a one-bedroom basement flat in Ranelagh, before the family moved to a corporation house in Dundrum. His parents, Larry and Bunny, had met as members of a cycle touring club in Dublin, but emigrated to London in 1958, not long after their wedding. Larry procured a job with London Transport, but a two-month strike not long after he started persuaded the couple to return to Dublin. Through the 1960s and 1970s, he worked as a milkman. Stephen, his eldest son, regularly joined him on his rounds when he was still in primary school, and would later attribute his outgoing personality to the work.

Much like Kelly, Roche fell into competitive cycling thanks to the proactive youth policy of his local club. Noel O'Neill and Paddy Doran were responsible for Orwell Wheelers' recruitment drive on the southside of Dublin, though it was Pat Flynn, the wife of local amateur rider Steve, who first ran the idea past Roche as he took a break from playing soccer on the green in Rosemount housing estate. The following Wednesday night, he reported for duty outside the H. Williams Supermarket in Dundrum and began life under O'Neill's tutelage. 'Noel had an open-door policy. Once you had a bike and wanted to ride, you were very welcome,' says Long, who would join the club a year later. Roche, incidentally, was dispatched to bring Long to his first training session. 'I was very shy, and he brought me around and introduced me into it.'

Orwell's efforts were replicated by other ICF clubs in Dublin, and soon a miniature peloton of teenage riders was meeting every second weekend on O'Connell Street. 'There was a bit of a drive from the federation, that was how I got into it. They actually used to have a meeting from the GPO every second week, so we met from all over Dublin and went on bike rides,' Roche says. Thanks to being one of the few riders competing on high-pressure tyres, Roche was among the prizes from the outset, but in time he progressed to winning races outright. Though he had shown no particular aptitude for sport beyond a fondness for swimming – a trait inherited from his father and grandfather – bike racing seemed to come easily to him.

Even so, in those early years, a great deal of cycling's appeal lay elsewhere. Already a spectator and participant as his father worked on old car engines in his free time, Roche took pride in stripping down and rebuilding his bike, while hostelling trips, either to the Wicklow Mountains or into County Meath, were another draw.

Paul Kimmage first met Roche on one such weekend in Wicklow, in the company of a mutual friend, Paul Smith, and was instantly impressed. Not only was this Roche a gifted bike rider, he was also, at least to Kimmage's impressionable eyes, the epitome of cool, from the little flask of coffee he carried on his bike to his unfussy mastery of bike repair. 'He was like a big brother,' Kimmage says. 'I remember another weekend when we were going down to Clogher Head and my brother Raphael's chain fucking snapped on the big climb coming out of Naul. There's no mobile phones in those days or calling Dad to come and pick us up, so we thought, "What the fuck are we going to do?" Roche just opens his bag up, pulls out a chain extractor and cuts the links off. And I just thought, "Fucking hell, that's amazing. You are amazing."'

Not that Kimmage's relationship with Roche was based purely on fawning admiration. 'There was great camaraderie on those weekends, a great buzz. Six or seven of us just yapping and laughing,' Kimmage says. 'I loved Stephen. He was a class bike rider, but just a good fella too. I remember he loved Abba, loved that bird out of Abba, the blondie one. And Bulmer's fucking Cidona, he loved that. He was good fun, a good lad.'

By his late teens, Roche's talent on the bike was beginning to manifest itself more obviously in races. When he was 16, he was selected to compete for Ireland in the English Schoolboys'

Cycling Association trials in Yorkshire, a multi-discipline event that he might well have won but for a mechanical problem in the final event. He had the consolation of striking up a friendship with the English rider who beat him, Neil Martin from Birmingham. The two became pen pals, and would later visit each other's homes, with Martin going on to marry Roche's elder sister Maria in 1982. Back home, Roche won the Dublin-to-Drogheda handicap race in 1976, the schoolboy springing a surprise by holding off the best senior riders in the country. His progress would be stalled shortly afterwards by two ingrown toenails that prevented him from wearing cycling shoes, but Roche returned to form in 1978, beating the highly rated Lenny Kirk to win the Irish Junior Championship.

At that stage, Roche was already in full-time employment, having left school following his Inter Cert, and was serving an apprenticeship as a maintenance fitter at Premier Dairies. Although he enjoyed the work, which chimed with his interest in all things mechanical, and the pay packet, which allowed him to buy his own car at the age of 18, the schedule meant that his training suffered, particularly before the longer evenings of summer came around. 'I was doing my apprenticeship as a maintenance fitter and I was sitting guilds at night-time so I wasn't training a lot and I wasn't getting form until later in the year,' Roche says.

Even before his stint at Premier Dairies, mind, Roche hardly had a reputation as a consummate trainer, though again, he would cite his early-morning milk round as a mitigating factor. 'I remember as schoolboys and juniors, one of our favourite spins was to cycle to the garage in Enniskerry and back, which was only about 16 miles for Stephen from his house,' Long recalls. 'People used to be giving out to him, saying, "You have to do more than that," but he never did. He didn't have to. That was the difference. We had to do the training, he just turned up.'

That strategy of just turning up would carry Roche all the way to Rás Tailteann victory in his first season out of the junior ranks in 1979, but it also made him wonder how much further he could go if he devoted himself full-time to cycling ahead of the following year's Olympic Games in Moscow. France was calling.

On the evening of 9 January 1980, recently elected Taoiseach Charles Haughey made a special televised address in which he warned of Ireland's crippling national debt and spoke of plans to introduce drastic cuts to government spending. 'I wish to talk to you this evening about the state of the nation's affairs and the picture I have to paint is not, unfortunately, a very cheerful one,' he began. 'The figures which are now just becoming available to us show one thing very clearly: as a community, we are living way beyond our means.'

Years later, once the full scale of Haughey's own lavish lifestyle had become public knowledge, those words would come to be viewed with grim irony, but at the time, they were a simple summary of Ireland's bleak economic reality. The unemployment rate, already approaching 10 per cent, would reach 14 per cent within three years. Rather than a call to arms, Ireland's youth heard the speech as an exhortation to get out of the country. Ireland's net emigration in the 1980s would reach more than 200,000.

Roche joined the exodus on 11 February of that year, when he flew to Paris to join Athletic Club de Boulogne-Billancourt, better-known as ACBB. He was by no means an economic migrant, however, and Haughey's forbidding prognosis had all but passed him by. 'I was totally naïve to that,' says Roche. He had secured a permanent position at Premier Dairies the previous November, six months before his apprenticeship was officially due to end, but rather than settling into a career as a fitter, he felt his qualification gave him the freedom to pursue his ambitions on the bike. He took a six-month leave of absence to move to Paris. 'It kept my parents happy that I had that under my wings before I left. If it didn't work out in France, I could come back and find a job.'

Neil Martin had spent the 1979 season at ACBB, when future professionals Robert Millar (now Philippa York) and Phil Anderson were also on the roster, and had recommended his future brother-in-law to the club. 'They asked me if I knew anyone else who might want to come over and I said, "Yeah, I know this Irish guy,"' Martin told the *Sunday Independent* in 2013. Yet according to Roche's version of events, he arrived at ACBB only through the intercession of the French cycling federation's technical director Lucien Bailly, who conducted a training weekend in Durrow in the spring of 1979 at the invitation of the ICF. It was here, he says, that he caught Bailly's eye, who in turned tipped off Mickey Wiegant, the manager of ACBB.

'It was lashing rain all weekend and I wore my dad's oilskins from the milk round on my bike because I had no light rain jacket,' Roche says. 'At the end of the two days, Lucien Bailly came up to me and said, "Stephen, you need to go to France to prepare for the Olympics. You're going nowhere if you stay here, travelling weekends to the UK for races and what have you." He knew Mickey Wiegant, and got me accepted on the team.'

However it really came to pass, Roche's arrival at ACBB coincided with Martin's departure. Martin had started dating Maria Roche in the autumn of 1979, following the Tour of Ireland, and expected to race alongside her brother in Paris in 1980. Instead, after a long silence from ACBB over the winter, he eventually learned that he had been deemed surplus to requirements, mere days before he was due to return to France. '"We've no place for you. We've taken the Irish guy." And that was it. I was out and Stephen was in,' Martin said in 2013. Their relationship would be a distant one thereafter, even when their sons, Dan Martin and Nicolas Roche, joined the professional peloton around the same time almost 30 years later.

The day before he left for Paris, Roche's parents held a small going away party at the family home. Among those in attendance was Peter Crinnion, who had managed Roche on Irish national teams, and had long felt that his talents were better suited to the more structured style of racing on the Continent than the helter-skelter fare on offer in Ireland. From his own experience in the 1960s, Crinnion also suspected that adapting to life in France might prove a greater obstacle than coping with the hardships meted out on the road, and he urged the youngster to stick it out for the full season, no matter what. Roche hardly needed encouraging, having developed something of a complex regarding his perceived toughness, or lack thereof, following the gentle ribbing he had received over his ingrown-toenail-induced hiatus as a junior. 'I wouldn't give the Irish cycling community the pleasure of seeing me come home with an empty bag,' he says. Having a point to prove, real or imagined, never did an emigrant or a bike rider any harm.

The first test of Roche's resolve would come early. Shay Elliott had raced – and won – for ACBB in 1955 before turning professional, but a quarter of a century on, there was no welcome mat laid out for his fellow countryman. Encouraged by the successes of British rider Paul Sherwen in 1977, and the man he recommended as his replacement, Graham Jones, ACBB saw the value in attracting foreign riders to their ranks and established itself as a talent factory for young Anglophone cyclists. Unlike their French counterparts, they tended to speak little and complain less. Unversed in the rudiments of the Continental system, they sought little or nothing by way of living expenses. The strongest among them had a burning desire to turn professional and a willingness to brook all sorts of hardships. The rest were easily expendable. It was a no-lose situation for ACBB, whose Foreign Legion from Britain, Ireland and Australia would cement its status as France's pre-eminent amateur outfit in the early 1980s.

When Roche's flight to Paris was delayed by fog, his ACBB contact simply left without him, and on arriving in Charles de Gaulle later that night, he took a taxi to the team's *service course* on Rue du Point du Jour in Boulogne-Billancourt, on the west side of the city. The building was empty and shut by 10pm, so after dining on green pasta at a nearby restaurant – 'It got cold, so I ended up giving it back and he only charged me 10 Francs' – Roche donned all of his winter clothing and settled down to sleep in the porch of ACBB's headquarters. He would be woken by the parp of a horn at four in the morning, as two young men in a car with a bike rack on top pulled in. 'Are you Roche?' they inquired. He nodded and climbed in. Once in the Peugeot 104, Roche learned that the men were his ACBB teammates, Pascal Cuvelier and Jean-Louis Barrot, but understood precious little else in the 16 hours that followed, as they drove south to Sainte-Maxime on the Côte d'Azur, where the team was based for the early-season races.

The British rider John Parker, in his second year at ACBB, was on hand to explain the lie of the land to Roche, but it would have been immediately apparent that the management team of Mickey Wiegant and Claude Escalon were not in the business of making concessions to new arrivals. Wiegant, christened Paul, had reportedly earned the moniker of 'Mickey' due to a penchant for wearing a Mickey Mouse badge on his jersey as an amateur rider in the 1940s, but he was not much given to laughter in his guise as sergeant-major at ACBB. Curfews and dress codes were rigorously imposed, and dissent of any kind was not tolerated. What was good enough for the great Jacques Anquetil, whom Wiegant had coached in the 1950s, was certainly deemed good enough for this platoon of scrawny young men, some still in their teens. In one of Roche's early attempts at speaking French, he made the beginner's error of addressing Wiegant with the informal 'tu' form, and was admonished accordingly. 'You must use "vous", Roche, because Monsieur Wiegant is not your friend, he is your boss,' Wiegant said gruffly. By that point, the old man had already versed the Irishman in the hierarchical nature of the team in orange and grey. In Roche's first race, he tried to bridge across to a break that already included ACBB's designated leader, the much-touted

Loubé Blagojevic, only for Wiegant to drive up alongside him and simply force him off the road.

An early victory at the Grand Prix des Issambres, not far from Wiegant's home, bolstered Roche's standing in the team before he travelled back to Paris, where he would be based for the bulk of the year. At first, there were seven riders housed in the two-bedroom apartment in Boulogne, and so Roche, a latecomer, slept on the couch in the living room. The rate of attrition was high, however, and within weeks, they were down to just four – though as Roche struggled to resolve a lingering knee injury, he began to wonder if he, too, might soon be headed for the exit. Eventually, he happened upon a solution. As part of the team's sponsorship deal, all ACBB riders had been given new Le Coq Sportif cycling shoes, but once Roche reverted to his old, softer-soled Colnago pair – undoubtedly to the annoyance of Wiegant, a stickler for appearances – the pain subsided. After missing some important spring races, Roche set about making up for lost time, and as had been the case back in Ireland, he found form as the evenings lengthened.

'The first time I saw Stephen was at the amateur Paris-Troyes in March, and I remember I saw him at the start alongside the Dane Hans-Henrik Ørsted, who was the amateur hour record holder at the time. Stephen had these chubby cheeks but he already had that magical pedal stroke, though I don't think he got a good result there,' recalls Phillipe Bouvet, who was by then a journalist at *Le Parisien*. 'I didn't see him again until May, when he won the Tour de l'Île de France and he was a lot thinner by then. The great Stephen Roche started there.'

Strong showings at Paris-Mantes and the Route de France suggested to Roche that he was on the path to a professional contract, though a decision was looming. Roche's leave of absence from Premier Dairies expired immediately after the Moscow Olympics, and he needed to give them notice of his intentions in May. 'I popped the question to Mickey in the car on the way back from the Route de France, and he said, "It's not with second or third places that you get a pro contract,"' Roche says. 'I thought I was actually good, but I just said "Ok, I understand."'

A week later, Roche lined up at the amateur Paris-Roubaix, where victory had to that point been the exclusive preserve of French and Belgian riders. A youngster from Dundrum with no experience on the *pavé*, the jagged cobblestone tracks of France's flat, exposed Nord, was not expected to thrive in such an environment, but come the approach to the old velodrome in Roubaix, Roche found himself at the head of the race with only the Belgian Dirk Demol for company. An agitated Wiegant sat in the team car behind the two leaders, bellowing instructions through a crack in the windscreen. Demol, having marshalled Roche to the front in the closing kilometres, now sat sheltered in his slipstream ahead of the two-up sprint on the velodrome, and Wiegant was beside himself at the Irishman's naïvety. Another near miss loomed, but a traffic island in the streets of Roubaix gave Roche the chance to redeem himself. By feinting to take the long way around, he manoeuvred Demol to the front, and then edged a tight sprint by half a wheel to claim France's biggest amateur classic. A week later, he added another classic, Paris-Rheims. He would not be returning to work as a fitter.

Even so, and despite the close links between ACBB and the professional Peugeot outfit for which it was essentially the feeder club, a contract offer had yet to materialise by the time Roche travelled to Moscow for the Olympic Games road race in July 1980. In theory, a strong showing in the Soviet Union could secure Roche a deal, though he was equally motivated by what it might do for his reputation in Ireland. News of Roche's exploits for ACBB travelled slowly, if at all. Few knew that Roche had won the amateur Paris-Roubaix, which earned just one line in the *Irish Times*, and only aficionados had any idea of what it meant. An Olympic medal, on the other hand, would bring instant fame back home. After all, what good was making a mark on the Continent without making a name for himself in Ireland?

It wasn't to be. Roche fell well short on a sweltering afternoon in Moscow, coming home in 45th place, more than 20 minutes down on winner Sergei Sukhoruchenkov, the Soviet billed as the Eddy Merckx of the Eastern Bloc. 'I felt in really good condition coming into the Olympics, but it was a total flop. It was the atmosphere, the humidity, the food, everything. The legs just weren't there that day and I finished 46th or something,' Roche says. Back at the Olympic village, he swapped tales of woe with another ambitious young athlete. Boxer Barry McGuigan had come to Moscow looking to crown his glittering amateur career, but the featherweight's elimination in the third round left him wondering if he'd even continue into the professional ranks. Roche began to entertain similar doubts. 'My options were to return to Ireland and pick up my tools and find a new job, or go back to France and ride some summer criteriums with some friends, and then try to win an end-of-season classic so I could turn pro,' Roche says.

Roche spent much of August racing in criteriums in the Basque Country at the invitation of Wiegant's second-in-command Escalon, an honour not usually bestowed upon the anglophone visitors. The previous year, for instance, Millar and Anderson complained that their French teammates were regularly colluding against them late in the season as competition for a professional contract grew ever more cutthroat. Roche, by contrast, was invited into the inner sanctum reserved for Escalon's favourites. This was partly because of his talent on a bike, but also because of the efforts he made to ingratiate himself with his hosts. Roche the *emigré*, it seems, followed the kind of advice Master Boyle had doled out to Gar in Brian Friel's *Philadelphia, Here I Come*: 'Don't keep looking back over your shoulder. Be one hundred per cent American.' Although his command of the language was still imperfect, there were various means of assimilation. In the summer of 1980, for instance, Roche began courting Lydia Arnaud, the 15-year-old sister of Thierry Arnaud, a rider on ACBB's second team.

'Initially it was very hard at ACBB, because they saw me as another English guy coming in to take their bread and butter at the end of the year. And because my name was a French name, people started talking to me, but I couldn't speak French back to them, so they assumed I was English,' says Roche, explaining that his standing improved once it was established that he was not, in fact, a *Rosbif.* 'It was only when I started winning races that people started to look at me as the Irishman Stephen Roche. And it actually helped me then that I was Irish and not English. For whatever reason, there was a certain difference in tolerance there, you know.'

Along with Cuvelier, Barrot and three others, Roche was part of a combine that dominated the criteriums along the Franco-Spanish border – 'We made our own mafia and won a lot of money over the two weeks' – though his mind was fixed on a grander prize. Roche issued an ultimatum to himself for the final weeks of the 1980 season, to get a professional contract or move home. There would, he told himself, be no second year at ACBB. 'I wasn't into losing my time, no. I didn't have to be a pro, and if I couldn't do it after my first year in France, then so be it,' he says.

At the end of a season that yielded 19 wins, there was never any real doubt. When Cyrille Guimard, manager of Bernard Hinault's Renault team, offered Roche a contract for 1981, Peugeot finally felt compelled to sign him up. 'ACBB was the feeder team for Peugeot and it was expected that you'd go there, but Pascal Poisson, who turned pro the same time as me, went with Renault,' Roche says. 'So it was one of two teams – Peugeot or Renault.'

After a bout of haggling, Roche convinced Peugeot to match the salary he would have earned on the factory floor in Dublin, around £500 a month. He returned to Ireland for the winter with a professional contract in his hand and Lydia Arnaud by his side.

How to Win Friends and Influence People

As the figure in white stepped forward onto the stage, a middle-aged woman in the crowd below craned her neck sideways for a better look, as though jostling for a glimpse of a newly elected Pope. The podium ceremony atop the Col d'Èze in March hardly classes as a religious experience, and while there was wonderment in her tone, there was precious little reverence as she called out to no one in particular: 'Look, a little kid won the race!' The race was Paris-Nice; the little kid was Stephen Roche; the real wonderment was at how he had emerged from the Peugeot conclave and won it.

Peugeot had, by some distance, the strongest team at the 1981 Paris-Nice, and in the absence of Bernard Hinault, it seemed to be a question of which of their number would win the so-called Race to the Sun. The powerful Gilbert Duclos-Lassalle had triumphed the previous year. The more stylish Michel Laurent had claimed it in 1976, and now seemed primed for a resurgence. As these men vied for the right to tickle the ivories for Peugeot, logic suggested that the likes of Roche would be tasked with shifting the piano on their behalf on the week-long slog through snow and cold to the Côte d'Azur.

Before the race began, however, Peugeot directeur sportif Maurice De Muer had refused to outline the hierarchy of his team in public. If at Renault, Hinault was the Sun King around whom the entire operation revolved, then Peugeot was more akin to Napoleon's *Grande Armée*: for an inherently authoritarian man, De Muer allowed his generals some freedom just as long their actions fell within the bounds of his own, usually aggressive strategy. 'We have nothing defined for Paris-Nice,' he told *L'Équipe*. 'We'll look to make an attacking race, where Roche and Anderson could also have important roles to play.'

His words proved prescient. Although Laurent took the leader's white jersey after Peugeot won the team time trial in his hometown of Bourbon-Lancy, he lost it again the very next day, when a breakaway escaped up the road, never to be seen again. Roche was policing the move for Peugeot, and, almost by accident, he took the white jersey from Laurent that evening. On such moments do careers turn. At 21 years of age, Roche was suddenly presented with an opportunity to fast-track his way up the chain of command. Barely two months into life as a professional, he was ready for his close-up.

Eager to impress, Roche had left Dublin in early January 1981 for a week of warm-weather training at Narbonne Plage on the Mediterranean coast before linking up with Peugeot for the team's traditional preseason training camp in nearby Seillans. Roche's idea had been to shed some of his usual winter padding, but De Muer did not seem rapt by the fruits of his labours when Robert Millar, a second-year professional at Peugeot, introduced them on the first night. 'When we arrived into the hotel, De Muer was playing cards with some of the local people. He looked at me and then he turned to Millar and said, "Is your driver having dinner with us or is he leaving?"' Roche says. 'I wasn't the typical thin rider like Millar or Phil Anderson. I was fairly round, you know.'

With his receding hairline, broad shoulders and penchant for sunglasses, De Muer looked like a tough guy, and acted accordingly when he felt the occasion demanded, which was often. He had been a modest rider with Peugeot in the 1940s, but built a reputation as an imposing directeur sportif during his spells at Pelforth and Bic, guiding the fabulously erratic Luis Ocaña to Tour victory in 1973. Two years later, he returned to Peugeot as manager, and had an immediate impact, directing Bernard Thévenet to Tour wins in 1975 and 1977. Even by the severe standards of the time, De Muer was an especially demanding taskmaster. A tightly wound man, his occasional bursts of invective served almost as a pressure valve. 'Regularly, he would go absolutely livid for 15 minutes, but then he would calm down again for a long period of time,' Thévenet recalled on De Muer's death in 2012 at the age of 90.

Bernard Bourreau, who rode for Peugeot from 1973 to 1984, was among De Muer's most trusted riders, making the Tour team 11 years in a row, but even he was careful to tiptoe around the *chef*'s more volatile moods. 'De Muer knew how to get the best out of riders, but you needed to be on the right side of him,' Bourreau says. 'You couldn't have two bad performances in a row, because he knew how to let you know about it. But he was a great strategist, too.' De Muer approached tactical meetings with the zeal of a field marshal, outlining the plan of attack by unfurling race maps where the wind direction and key sectors had already been annotated in pencil, a painstaking task often performed by his wife, Josephine. Winning, by any means, was about all that counted for De Muer, and as he set eyes on the chubby-cheeked Roche, he might have wondered how precisely the Dubliner was going to help Peugeot do that.

Roche found a warmer welcome elsewhere, especially from a fellow new arrival, mechanic Patrick Valcke. A Lille native fresh from his year of military service, Valcke had joined Peugeot after winning what amounted to a competitive exam that winter. The natural order dictated that the established mechanics worked on the bikes of the team's stars, leaving Valcke to prepare those of the new recruits. 'The riders, mechanics and soigneurs who were there before us already had their habits and structures, so when I came along, it just so happened that I was designated to look after Stephen's bike,' Valcke says. Both wide-eyed neophytes, Roche and Valcke quickly struck up a rapport that would go far beyond the unspoken trust that develops between a rider and his mechanic. 'The clan was already there, so we found ourselves often on our own in the evenings and we gelled together,' Roche says.

Having a friend on the support staff was one thing, but if Roche was going to get ahead at Peugeot, he also needed to ingratiate himself with his peers. 'It wasn't a strategy,' he says now, 'but I knew that these guys weren't going to ride for me if they didn't know me, whereas if we have some kind of relationship, they might help me, which is the way it happened.' The Peugeot team had existed in one form or another since 1901, and though foreign riders had graced its ranks over the years, notably Eddy Merckx and Tom Simpson, it was a resoundingly French institution. 'In the mid-seventies, the team was practically 100 per cent French. When Thévenet won his Tour, the team was made up entirely of French riders on each occasion,' says Bourreau.

That situation started to change when Thévenet left the team in 1979. Renault had snapped up Hinault, French cycling's most bankable asset, and so Peugeot shopped abroad for a new leader, signing Dutchman Hennie Kuiper, who placed second at the 1980 Tour before moving on. Around the same time, ACBB was beginning to reap the benefits of its foreign recruitment policy, and Peugeot effectively aped the approach of its nursery team. Briton Graham Jones and South African Alan van Heerden were the first to arrive at Peugeot from ACBB in 1979. Millar and Anderson followed a year later, before Roche arrived in 1981, and the English-speaking contingent later included Sean Yates and Allan Peiper.

While Roger Legeay, who later joined the team's management, insists 'there was no jealousy between the French and English riders,' Philippa York, then known as Robert

Millar, begs to differ: 'There was very much a them and us mentality at Peugeot; the French guys tolerated your presence as long as they were higher up the pecking order. I wouldn't say it was personal, more a case of chauvinism on the French riders' part.' As at ACBB, Roche, who was settled with Lydia Arnaud and installed in Sagy on the outskirts of Paris, seemed to fall in with the French riders more readily than the other English- peakers. 'He was going out with a French girl and he spoke French relatively well from the start, so he was part of the family, really,' Bourreau says. 'Phil Anderson was a nice guy, but he didn't become a part of the group in the same way as Stephen.'

Calculated or not, Roche's assimilation into French culture certainly did no harm to his cause with the likes of Duclos-Lassalle, who viewed the more aloof Millar and Anderson with suspicion, and whose force of personality meant that he wielded considerable influence within the team. 'Duclos had a whole little clique going with the likes of [Jacques] Bossis and Legeay, so when you did things differently to them then they took exception to that,' Philippa York now says. 'We integrated as much as we could, but you always had the feeling you were a foreigner. Not all the French riders were twats: [Pascal] Simon, Laurent and Bourreau were OK, but even they were sucked into the Duclos gang now and then.'

Joining in the repartee at the dinner table each night was not in itself sufficient to climb the ranks at Peugeot. Roche realised early on that if he was going to get closer to the top of the pyramid, he would have to lean in by winning races, and the sooner the better. 'Gilbert Duclos-Lassalle, Jacques Bossis and Michel Laurent were up there, and the only way of getting in was to beat them,' Roche says. 'That's what I ended up doing, and that's how I got on so well with them so early. They either got on with me or got beaten by me. I was winning, and they got to share the spoils.'

Roche's opening races as a professional mirrored his early appearances for ACBB, with his own eagerness to get ahead coming into conflict with the preordained plans of the team. De Muer had to order him not to beat his leader Jean-René Bernaudeau when they found themselves in the winning move at the Grand Prix de Monaco, but Roche had another go at breaking ranks during the Tour of Corsica stage race shortly afterwards. When Bossis attacked on the second stage, he was surprised to turn around and find a lone rider in white chasing him: Roche. Rather than reprimand the upstart, Bossis figured he could use his help. They worked together, putting Bossis into the leader's jersey, and as a token of his gratitude, he allowed Roche the stage victory, the first of his professional career. The next day, however, Roche finished 40 seconds ahead of Bossis in the concluding time trial to take overall victory, ahead of Michel Laurent and Bernard Hinault.

The Tour of Corsica was a low-key preparation race, but it opened new horizons for Roche. Though *L'Équipe* printed the youngster's name afterwards as 'Steffen Roche', De Muer now knew what he had on his hands, and decided where Roche stood within his implicit caste system. Riders he distrusted were sent to minor races – 'He liked his riders to be big and strong, so as a small climber I had a difficult time,' York recalls – while his line-up for the major events on the calendar tended to be built around the same corps. 'With De Muer, there was an A team, but after that there wasn't a B team: it was a Y team,' Bourreau explains. 'That's what we called it, because he only had confidence in the same few riders all the time.'

Roche's Corsica win saw him fast-tracked into the A team for Paris-Nice, the most important race on the calendar before the classics. Through the opening days of the event, he dutifully fulfilled his obligations as a domestique, most notably in the stage 2 team time trial, where he impressed in Peugeot's winning effort, which saw Laurent move into the overall lead. A day later, Roche tracked a mid-stage breakaway, unaware that the Peugeot and Bianchi teams were engaged in a standoff behind. Bossis asked Bianchi to contribute to chasing the move, only for Silvano Contini to tell him cheerily that the Italian squad was only there to prepare for Milan-San Remo. The break's lead mushroomed to six minutes, and Roche, at 21 years of age, was in the white jersey of leader at Pars-Nice, ahead of a fellow neo-professional, Dutchman Adrie van der Poel.

Despite his dismay, Laurent was generous to the youngster who had usurped him, sparing his anger for Bianchi. 'Clearly there are no longer real champions in the peloton who take their responsibilities,' he complained. Behind closed doors, Peugeot were unsure if Roche could handle the responsibility of carrying the white jersey to Nice, but there was no other option. He was the only Peugeot rider still in contention. The following day's stage featured the mighty Mont Ventoux ahead of the finish in Miramas, and although the race ascended only as far as Chalet Reynard, seven kilometres shy of the haunting, exposed summit of the 'Bald Mountain', the climb was a daunting one, and the conditions were hostile.

As the pace rose on the wooded section at the bottom of Mont Ventoux, Roche divested himself of his long-sleeved jersey, a decision he would come to regret as they gained in altitude and rain turned steadily to sleet and then to snow. Van der Poel didn't need a second invitation to attack when he saw Roche's pink arms and chattering teeth. He leapt away to claim the time bonus at Chalet Reynard and continued with his attack as the road began to drop. Roche was hopelessly underdressed for the descent, but De Muer, not known for his compassion, showed little interest in his plight. 'I put my hand up and asked for the car,' Roche says. 'Maurice pulled up and I asked for a jersey for the descent, but he just said, 'When you get back on, you'll get a jersey.' I nearly broke my neck getting back on, and I was so cold – *so* cold – I nearly had hypothermia.'

Roche managed to latch back on just before the finish in Miramas, where Roger De Vlaeminck claimed the stage honours, and though he lost the battle – and the jersey – to Van der Poel thanks to the time bonus, he remained in contention to win the war. Perhaps as far as De Muer was concerned, Roche had undergone a necessary maturation ordeal. Now that he had been blooded, Roche was expected to win back the jersey. Two days later, the sinuous descent of the Col de Tanneron featured en route to the finish in Mandelieu, and, on De Muer's command, Peugeot launched a collective offensive. Anderson scrambled down the hill to win the stage, while Roche, safely tucked onto Duclos-Lassalle's rear wheel, put half a minute into Van der Poel.

Peugeot repeated the dose the following morning, when the race climbed back over the Tanneron en route to Nice. This time, and despite overshooting a corner, Roche slipped away in a four-man group with Laurent, adding another 30 seconds to his cushion over Van der Poel. As if to prove that it had been no accident, Roche smoothly turned over a 46x15 gear to win the concluding time trial up the Col d'Èze that afternoon, to become the first neo-professional to win Paris-Nice.

As at the Rás two years previously, Roche showed few inhibitions when a microphone was thrust in his direction. 'Oh, I eat a lot of potatoes,' he told *Antenne 2* in his Dublin-accented French when asked to explain his success. Regardless of the diet, Roche's weight loss had been striking: he had dropped from 70 to 66 kilos since he began at ACBB a year previously. The following morning, meanwhile, *L'Équipe* offered its first iteration of the Roche origin myth, detailing admiringly how he had slept rough in a porch on his first night at ACBB. The sports daily also chronicled De Muer's uncharacteristically rapturous praise for his protégé. 'Roche at 20 rides like he has the experience of a rider who's been a pro for 10 years,' he said, adding that he wanted to send his young Irishman to the Tour de France that very year, an idea that ultimately came to nothing.

De Muer had rather harsher words for Roche on the night before Flèche Wallonne in April, however. Having already chided him for taking a holiday after Paris-Nice, he was aghast when Roche joked during the team meeting that he had brought his camera with him to take some pictures during the race. According to Valcke's version, De Muer's rage was such that he smashed a chair, though Bourreau, for one, has no recollection of the contretemps. In the long-term, in any case, the incident did little to diminish Roche's standing with his team manager. 'Maurice came to my room later and said "Stephen, you did what those guys would love to do and haven't the balls to do,"' Roche says. 'And we had a good relationship after that, because I stood up to him.'

Indeed, if Roche was subject to any jealousy from the elder statesmen at Peugeot during his opening season, it was not so much for the races he won as for his rapport with De Muer. Or as Philippa York puts it: 'Roche winning Paris-Nice pleased and pissed off the old guard in equal measure. That De Muer then fawned over Roche certainly annoyed them.'

Roche went to win the Tour d'Indre-et-Loire and the Étoile des Espoirs before the year was out, finishing 1981 as cycling's most successful new professional, ahead even of the American Greg LeMond, who had signed for Renault amid such fanfare the previous winter. LeMond later revealed that Peugeot had been vying for his signature. 'I knew there was no way I wanted to go to Peugeot because I heard that the team was lenient about drugs,' LeMond told the American journalist Sam Abt in 1990 – the same year, incidentally, that he joined Z-Peugeot, the direct successor to the old Peugeot team.

The concerns raised by LeMond most likely pertained to Thévenet's 1978 admission that he had been hospitalised due to the damage that repeated doses of corticosteroids – which were not illegal at the time – had wrought upon his adrenal glands. Thévenet had been injected with corticosteroids since 1975 by Peugeot's then team doctor François Bellocq, who championed the practice as part of a process that he rather euphemistically described as 'hormone balancing'. Bellocq was not even qualified as a doctor when he began prescribing Thévenet and others on Peugeot with cortisone. He left the team in 1979, the year after Thévenet told the journalist Pierre Chany of his experiences at his hands, though the use of needles remained the norm at Peugeot and elsewhere.

Roche says that he began to receive injections of vitamins almost as soon as he started at Peugeot, in keeping with standard practice in the peloton at the time. In time, Roche learned to carry out the procedure by himself. 'The first year as a pro you're very quickly introduced to injections on the team under the supervision of the team doctor, and then you're outside the doctor when you're at home and you're changing teams and you have to become independent,' Roche says, continuing:

> With a rally car, you know a cam shaft will go so many miles. And I knew after Paris-Nice that I had to start taking some iron or vitamins, and so as not to overwork the stomach, I'd have an injection, a cure of iron. That's how it was. Today that's all banned because all injections are banned, but in my day, that was legal.
>
> We all had our small little suitcase, and in there we had our needles with our injections, our vitamin C, our vitamin D, our vitamin E, we had our liver extracts, products that are still not banned products. The problem was that there were some guys injecting vitamin C, but then other guys who were injecting hormones, and that was seen as normal because everybody was injecting anyway. I did regular blood tests and I knew each year where I was. I knew for example I wouldn't take any other injections until after Paris-Nice because I'd have had a good winter and stocked up on vitamins and minerals.

San Benedetto del Tronto in March has the feel of the coastal town they forgot to shut down. Thumbing through the pink pages of *La Gazzetta dello Sport* in the breakfast room of a dreary seafront hotel, Kelly didn't need to read Italian to understand that his status was under threat. A glance at the previous day's result from the Col d'Èze was enough. *Roche. Christ.* Kelly was riding the final time trial of the Tirreno-Adriatico stage race that afternoon, and if he felt moved to provide a response to Roche's Paris-Nice exploit, it wouldn't materialise here, as he finished the race in anonymity. This, his third season at the Splendor team, would tumble much like the two that preceded it. A clutch of sprint wins couldn't mask the feeling that he was failing to make the most of his considerable gifts. Kelly was spinning his wheels.

The portents had been ominous from the moment Kelly linked up with his new team for a training camp in January 1979. That week in Benidorm, the riders were forced to use their own bikes as the new, team-issue machines weren't ready. It was a small mercy: when the Splendor-branded bikes finally arrived, the tyres and brakes were of such substandard quality that the team opted out of Paris-Roubaix for safety reasons. Team manager Robert Lauwers, meanwhile, was out of his depth both as a tactician and an organiser. 'He was a little fat Belgian guy,' says Alan McCormack of his former manager. 'He used to be a truck driver.'

More pressingly for Kelly, Lauwers was a far more laissez-faire manager than de Gribaldy, preferring to leave his Irish signing to his own devices rather than micromanage his training programme. Though Kelly tried to replicate his regimen of previous years, standards inevitably slipped. Carrying extra pounds and bereft of his usual sharpness, Kelly struggled through the spring, and if a brace of stage wins in his Vuelta a España debut in May raised morale, it was a false dawn. The Tour de France was a chastening experience, as Kelly made no impact in the sprints, and he finished the season with just three wins to his name. 'I think I lost a bit of my focus and I suppose I wasn't being pushed as much in my training,' Kelly says. 'I had no one to account to for what I was doing.'

Kelly had moved to Belgium on signing for Splendor, and, as at Flandria, decided to base himself on his manager's home patch, which in Lauwers's case was Erps-Kwerps, a village tucked away between Brussels and Louvain. He would last little more than a fortnight living in a flat above Lawuers's café, his sleep constantly interrupted by the blaring jukebox and raucous laughter below. That temporary inconvenience would, at least, lead to one of the few positives to emerge from his troubled debut campaign with Splendor, as Kelly moved to Vilvoorde, a humdrum suburb north of Brussels, to live as a lodger in the home of Herman and Elise Nys. Nobody on the team could fill the vacuum left by de Gribaldy, but the Nys family at least offered some of the structure.

Herman Nys's affinity for Ireland began as a young man in the immediate aftermath of World War II, when he spent part of his military service undergoing training at an Allied base in Larne. His relationship with Irish cycling came later, at the 1964 World Championships in Sallanches, when he was shocked to discover that Liam Horner was sleeping in a tent in a campsite before competing in the amateur road race. Nys was at the event in an informal capacity with the Danish team, and he persuaded them to accommodate Horner in their hotel for the rest of the week. A friendship developed, and in time, Nys's house at 108 Breemputstraat became available to any Irish riders who came to race in Belgium, while each year, he was part of the backroom staff, such as it was, for the Irish team at the World Championships. 'He'd arrive every year with a roof-rack and a sign with "Irlande" on it and that was the team car for the Worlds,' says Kieron McQuaid. 'Herman was even with us at the Olympics in Munich in 1972.'

Kelly had first met Nys at the 1975 Worlds in Namur and four years on, at the urging of the McQuaid brothers, he now phoned to ask if he could stay in Vilvoorde. It was supposed to be a temporary arrangement, but he would end up living in Herman and Elise Nys's guest room for six years, only moving on – and then to a house around the corner – when Linda joined him in Belgium after their marriage. Years later, journalists who came to visit Kelly in that discreet back street in Vilvoorde would be taken aback by the modesty of his living arrangements. 'I went there in 1984, when he was the world number one, and he was still sleeping in this small room, with a suitcase in the corner, and that was it,' says Philippe Bouvet. 'I realised that his principal motivation was to make his money, and then go home to Ireland. He didn't think about the present so much; he didn't have material needs.'

That last trait was one that Herman Nys, a bookkeeper by profession, actively encouraged, while his insistence on a curfew would have earned the approval of de Gribaldy. It had, however, horrified Alan McCormack, who had also stayed with Nys during his spell at Splendor in 1978. 'I just felt it was like a military camp: a young person in a dark house, staying in all the time and going to bed at 8 o'clock every evening,'

McCormack says. 'Lucky enough, I had a *Lord of the Rings* book with me and some Pink Floyd albums I brought over, but it was just depressing, you know what I mean?'

McCormack barely lasted a month in the austere Nys household, before following Kelly's Belgian itinerary in reverse. He relocated to the flat above Lauwers's café in Erps-Kwerps and found a slightly more amenable environment than sleepy Vilvoorde for a young man barely out of his teens. 'It was a small village, with a church, cobbles and this one café, with all these Belgian guys who were always drunk. It was really loud but I slept through it,' McCormack says. 'It's not that I was at the bar every night drinking, but it was just more colourful. I didn't meet the love of my life over there but there were always chicks around, so I was actually talking to some girls my own age. It was a little more pleasant.'

In Vilvoorde, it took Kelly some time to adapt his training to the pancake-flat terrain in the hinterland of Brussels, having spent two years building strength almost by osmosis in the hills around Besançon. Even so, 1980 was a marked improvement on his first season at Splendor, both in ambience and results. Lauwers had been replaced by Albert De Kimpe as manager, and Kelly landed the Three Days of De Panne, five stage wins at the Vuelta a España and two at the Tour de France.

The Vuelta was a less mountainous affair in 1980 than it is nowadays, and boasted fewer top-level competitors, but it is still striking that Kelly and Splendor continued to labour under the misapprehension that he was little more than a sprinter even after he finished 4th overall, a mere 3:31 behind winner Faustino Rupérez. At the Tour, however, the early flat stages brought only frustration, and then desperation. On stage 9 to

Nantes, Kelly was first across the line but was stripped of the stage win for pushing Jan Jacobs in the finishing straight as he forced his way through a non-existent gap. 'I had to push Jacobs because he was in my way, preventing me from passing. If I hadn't pushed him, I would have fallen,' Kelly protested weakly. The rebuttal of Jan Raas, who was awarded the victory, was succinct: 'Kelly is a public menace.'

Four days from Paris, Kelly and Splendor were still without success, and anxiously exploring unfamiliar terrain in search of it. On a searing afternoon of heavy roads and melting tarmac in the Massif Central, Kelly infiltrated a mid-stage break, and was still out in front by the summit of the final climb, the Col de la Croix de Chaubouret, but had only the Spaniard Ismael Lejarreta for company and a lead of just 25 seconds over the chasers. One daredevil descent later, with Lejarreta screaming at his companion to slow down, Kelly won the two-up sprint convincingly. Like a harvest, the Tour had been saved.

'Ah, I beat him with one leg,' Kelly said playfully to the photographer John Pierce when he visited his hotel room that evening. His relief was such that he even ordered a half bottle of champagne from room service in celebration, a rare concession. 'Don't tell anybody or they'll think I'm an alcoholic,' Kelly warned Pierce as they toasted the win, only half in jest. Two days later, confidence replenished, he beat a full complement of sprinters to win in Fontenay-sous-Bois.

The dying days of the 1980 Tour marked a rare high point in Kelly's time at Splendor, but the period is perhaps best encapsulated by the farcical finish to Flèche Wallonne the following year, when he found himself in the winning move with two teammates, Claude Criquielion and Guido Van

Calster. In those days, the race finished on the flat in Mons, rather than on the vertiginous Mur de Huy, and the loose plan was to set up Kelly in the very likely event of a sprint. After Criquielion's lone attack petered out in the finale, however, Van Calster chose to ride for himself rather than lead out Kelly. Splendor spurned its winning hand, and Van Calster and Kelly could only manage third and fourth as Danny Willems scorched to a surprise triumph.

Such sloppiness would hardly have been tolerated at Flandria, where Kelly had been a special project for de Gribaldy, and where, as the lone outsider on a team divided along Franco-Belgian lines, his nationality had often been a help rather than a hindrance. At Splendor, by contrast, he was simply a gun for hire, and on a solidly Belgian team without a rigidly defined hierarchy, being an Irishman was of no benefit at all. Kelly had been signed ostensibly as the team's principal sprinter, but in his final season, he regularly found himself slipping behind locals Van Calster and Eddy Planckaert in the pecking order.

He began that year's Tour as the designated fast man, but was stripped of the role after he was beaten into second place by his old teammate Freddy Maertens on stage 1 in Nice. The new arrival Planckaert took over the reins, and though he scored a sprint win in the second week, neither he nor anyone else that July could live with Maertens, who won five stages amid a resurgence that proved as transient as it was unexpected; his career fizzled out again once he claimed a second world title in Prague at the end of the summer. Kelly, meanwhile, was condemned to leading out Planckaert in the sprints and trying to eke out opportunities for himself elsewhere, eventually snaring a win in Thonon-les-Bains in the foothills of the Alps, on a tough day when the pure sprinters were dropped long before the finish. The true range of Kelly's abilities seemed to be hiding in plain sight.

'With Splendor I was told that I would be the guy for the sprints, but then of course Planckaert came in, and there was Van Calster and a few more guys,' Kelly says. 'It was getting kind of crowded. For that reason, I wanted to get out.'

7

PROMENADE DES IRLANDAIS

Kelly and Roche were still some way off box office status in their home country in January of 1982, but a joint appearance on the *Late Late Show* shortly before the season began suggested their achievements were beginning to stoke the curiosity of a wider public. Roche sat next to host Gay Byrne and on occasion leant towards the studio audience as he held forth on his ambitions for the years ahead, while Kelly, as ever, was more guarded of body language and response. He certainly wasn't going to be so gauche as to compare himself, as Roche did, to reigning Tour champion Bernard Hinault.

'I've beaten him in time trials, I've been with him in the mountains, and I can fairly hold him or match him in a stage race. The French public, I think, are fairly browned off now with this fellow Hinault and they're looking for a successor, and I'm forced to be coming up. Whereas Sean will tell you, he's a different man altogether, he's a sprinter and he's there to win stages,' Roche said, before adding almost as an afterthought:

'And possibly the overall also.' Pat McQuaid, sitting in the audience, was invited to assess the new phenomenon. 'They're predicting he'll win the Tour de France within a year or two,' McQuaid said. 'He's going to be a millionaire overnight.'

If Kelly felt discommoded by the acclaim lavished upon the recent arrival at the top table, he wasn't going to betray those feelings before a national television audience. That night in Montrose and elsewhere, his public utterances were carefully deferential towards Roche's fine debut season and future potential. Besides, he had already expressed himself perfectly eloquently in his preferred, wordless manner a couple of weeks previously, when he lined up alongside Roche at Carrick Wheelers' traditional Hamper Race, a pre-Christmas handicap event that Kelly had been dominating since he was a teenager.

The two professionals set off in the scratch group, 10 minutes after the veterans and schoolboys who went out first. Kelly and Roche had downplayed their form beforehand, each insisting he had been training in the gym rather than on the bike, but once the flag dropped, competitive instincts overrode pre-race niceties. They worked together at first, shaving minutes off their deficit as they passed group after group, but once they caught the frontrunners, Kelly took off alone and left Roche behind. The race ended with 10 laps of a half-mile circuit in Carrick-on-Suir, and Kelly made sure to lap the chasers, Roche included, before the finish. Point duly proven in his backyard, Kelly turned his attention to reasserting his pre-eminence on the Continent.

'I was the guy who was out there and who was performing, and then Roche rocks up and he wins Paris-Nice and he wins Tour of Corsica and a few races,' Kelly says now. 'And I suppose, yeah, when there's somebody pushing in there and getting the exposure, that definitely does make you work harder and you say to yourself, "I have to get my butt out of the saddle."'

In late January, Roche took the ferry from Rosslare to attend the unveiling of the route of the 1982 Paris-Nice, and later the presentation of his Peugeot team, where he took possession of a new company car. Kelly lingered a little longer in Ireland before he travelled to link up with his new squad. Sem-France Loire, sponsored by a garden furniture concern, was a small outfit of modest means, but it held a trump card. Jean de Gribaldy was team manager.

Unlike at Flandria, where he was effectively a line manager, de Gribaldy oversaw the entire operation at Sem, and he revelled in building a subversive identity for a squad he saw as an extension of himself. His aristocratic ancestry, he claimed once, caused 'as much commotion in the cycling milieu as cyclists would in the Opéra de Paris'. If Peugeot and Renault were the teams of the establishment, routinely picking up the best young amateur riders in France as though building a stock portfolio, then Sem, de Gribaldy decided, would be a home for outsiders and the overlooked. The 1982 line-up featured several riders who had failed to settle elsewhere, including Marcel Tinazzi, who had struggled at Peugeot, and Jock Boyer, the first American to ride the Tour de France, whose vegetarianism and staunch religious faith had made him an outcast at Renault. 'De Gribaldy got incredible results with riders who were unknown or on the fringe or psychologically hard to deal with,' Boyer says. 'He had a lot of quirky riders, who nobody else wanted to take. He loved to take on underdogs. He made the most impact of any directeur I ever had.'

A team cannot run on ambience alone, of course. De Gribaldy needed a leader, and so during the 1981 Tour, he delegated Tinazzi and French champion Serge Beucherie to work on persuading Kelly to return to the fold. Viewed from the dissonant confines of Splendor, the Viscount's court seemed positively harmonious. 'We were going well at the time, Serge and me, and Sean wanted to know why. And we just said, "You know how it is with de Gribaldy, he has his secrets,"' Tinazzi says. 'At the end of the Tour, Sean finally said, "Ok, I'll come back with de Gribaldy next year."'

De Gribaldy's 'secrets' were a mix of the idiosyncratic and the common-sense, and some would even be dusted down decades later and rebranded, as though freshly discovered, under the risible neologism of 'marginal gains'. Weight remained his chief preoccupation. 'His reasoning was that in Formula 1 they have 800-horsepower motors and they still shave down bolts just to save 20 grams, so imagine what a bike rider could do if he lost three kilos,' Tinazzi says. Kelly had swayed from the de Gribaldy diet at Splendor, but in early 1982, Kelly began recouping the ground. He seemed to grow leaner by the day.

'I'd say I probably weighed three or four kilos more when I started as a professional. When I was with de Gribaldy at Flandria, I started losing that, and his plan was that I was going to lose a lot more if I stayed with him,' Kelly says. 'But instead I went to Splendor, of course, and you could say I lost a bit of time there. From the time I left Flandria, de Gribaldy kept saying to me I was carrying too much weight to get over the climbs. He threw that at me a few times.'

Despite limitations of budget, de Gribaldy had a keen eye for equipment, too, though perhaps his greatest strength was as a psychologist. He eschewed convention by refusing to hold tactical briefings at night in the hotel, believing that his riders needed to relax rather than fret over the following day's race. Rather like Brian Clough at Nottingham Forest, his instructions were instead limited to a few words on the start line. 'When you were going well, he'd come up to you there and he'd say "Today, I want you to ride with the small wheels." That's what he used to call light wheels: "small wheels". And then he'd have the mechanic pop the light wheels into the frame 30 seconds before the race started,' Tinazzi says. 'It meant that the night before we didn't lie awake dwelling on the responsibility of what we had to do.'

De Gribaldy was equally adept at soothing bruised morale. 'When you did poorly in a race, instead of hammering you, he'd just sit with you and say, "You know, you could have won if you'd done this,"' Boyer says. 'He'd give you an excuse. He could point out what you'd done wrong without making you feel horrible.'

In the longer-term, de Gribaldy was not averse to applying gentle pressure to certain riders, and he set about convincing Kelly that he could win Paris-Nice from the moment he signed his contract with Sem at the 1981 Worlds in Prague. Through the winter and early spring, de Gribaldy drilled home the twin tenets of his methodology, chiefly riding a lot and eating very little. The motivation, on the other hand, came largely from what Roche had achieved in the same race the previous year. It begs the question as to whether Kelly's mutation in 1982 and 1983, from sprinter to all-rounder, from misfiring prospect to dominant force, was moulded more by the influence of de Gribaldy or the emergence of Roche.

'If I was to tell you the truth, certainly Roche's performance did drive me on,' Kelly says. He would likely not have bought as readily into de Gribaldy's Paris-Nice project had his fellow countryman not already planted the flag on the Col d'Èze. 'It motivates you that bit more because he's Irish. If it was somebody else, it certainly wouldn't have been the same. But at the same time, I think de Gribaldy would definitely have been pushing me.'

Roche has little doubt about his role as the catalyst for Kelly's transformation. 'I feel partially responsible, without being pretentious about it, for Kelly's second wind in his career,' he says. 'Kelly was winning stages of the Tour de France and doing good things but when I came along, he changed his whole profile. Sean had himself down as being a classics rider and winning stages, and then this Dublin guy came along and started winning stage races so he said, "Gee, I'd better get my finger out here, otherwise Roche will be taking all the limelight."'

A win at the hilly Tour du Haut-Var in late February was an early vindication of de Gribaldy's grand idea, though Kelly was not considered among the main favourites when he lined up for Paris-Nice. The race organisation had that year sold the race start to the Belgian town of Luingne, but the basic premise remained unchanged, as the riders tackled increasingly rugged terrain, and wind, rain and snow en route to the Côte d'Azur. The first major selection came on the snowbound leg to Saint-

Étienne, where Kelly comfortably beat Roger De Vlaeminck in the sprint to take the white jersey, but though he reinforced his lead with another stage win two days later, it was expected that Roche's Peugeot teammate Gilbert Duclos-Lassalle would snatch it off him on the final stage up the Col d'Èze.

Duclos-Lassalle, who probably felt he had already done the hard part by beating out Roche, Anderson et al. to lead Peugeot's challenge, didn't have to wait that long to get his hands on the white jersey. The following afternoon, Kelly attacked coming down the Col du Tanneron, which had been washed all day by icy sheets of rain. Almost inevitably, both Kelly and Duclos-Lassalle slid off the road, but amid the confusion, the Frenchman clawed out a small advantage. He reached Mandelieu five seconds ahead of Kelly to move into the lead with just the final day's split stage to come.

Kelly completed his hat-trick of stage wins by claiming the sprint along the Promenade des Anglais at the end of the morning stage, before de Gribaldy dragged him away from prying eyes and distracting microphones to warm up for the Col d'Èze time trial. As Kelly sat pedalling on the rollers outside a quiet bistro near the start, Roche was already out on the course. Twelve months previously, bereft of fear or expectation, he had made light of those shallow slopes. This time around, he pedalled with the ponderous strokes of last year's man to finish 6th overall, but only 14th on a stage he was tipped to win. The lone consolation, perhaps, was that he was that he was the only man within Peugeot to realise fully the threat posed by Kelly from the outset. 'Nobody can say what he can or cannot do,' he warned presciently early in the week.

Duclos-Lassalle set out a minute after Kelly and had the apparent advantage of getting regular updates on his rival's time, and so de Gribaldy ordered his rider to set off at full speed in the hope that Duclos-Lassalle would push himself to breaking point by trying to match his pace. The gambit worked. Wearing the lurid pink jersey of points leader, Kelly was unperturbed by the blustery conditions on the lower slopes of the Col d'Èze, quickly establishing a decisive lead, with de Gribaldy cajoling him all the way. Come the summit, Kelly hadn't merely overhauled Duclos-Lassalle, he had won the stage itself, the first time in history that a rider had snared both stages on the final day. Paris-Nice victory was a calling card, both for Kelly and for de Gribaldy. Writing in *Le Monde*, the veteran journalist Jacques Augendre singled out the 'will to win' of the youthful Sem-France Loire team and its leader: 'It's a virtue that is becoming rarer and rarer in a peloton threatened by embourgeoisement.'

Working-class mores alone weren't sufficient for Kelly or Sem to make an impression in the classics in 1982. A spate of punctures ruined his Paris-Roubaix, and 12th place there would be his best showing in a disappointing April campaign. The upward trajectory resumed in July, however, where for the first time in his career, Kelly entered the Tour de France guided by a precise target rather than muddled by vague ambitions. Two years earlier, he had, almost without realising it, finished 2nd in the points classification, and now his directeur sportif wanted him to make a concerted effort to win the competition outright. De Gribaldy had cottoned on to an incontrovertible formula: to borrow from AJ Liebling, Kelly could climb better than anyone who could sprint faster, and could sprint faster than anyone who could climb better. Kelly placed second a maddening five times on flat stages, but then won from a reduced group in Pau after surviving the mighty Col d'Aubisque in the company of Bernard Hinault, who was en route to a fourth overall victory. QED.

Kelly had the green jersey of points winner wrapped up long before he reached Paris, arriving on the Champs-Élysées with almost triple the points of the runner-up, Hinault. He then spent much of August driving across France, Belgium and the Netherlands to perform in criteriums, evening exhibition races where he was able to command one of the highest appearance fees off the back of his displays at the Tour. De Gribaldy remained a parsimonious paymaster, after all, so each night, Kelly would don his green jersey, put on a show for the multitudes and pad out his yearly earnings.

On the first weekend in September, Kelly switched to a green jersey of a different hue, when he lined out alongside Roche in Ireland's two-man team at the World Championships in Goodwood. His year-long consistency meant that he figured among the favourites for the race, and though the exhausting criterium circuit was hardly the best preparation, he couldn't hide a quiet confidence on his arrival in West Sussex. 'I suppose I have never attended a World Championships feeling so strong,' Kelly conceded. 'The course is hard, but not savage.'

The Irish strategy was a simple one. Roche would shepherd Kelly throughout the day in the hope that the Italian team would control the race for their fastest finisher, Giuseppe Saronni. That, by and large, was how it panned out. The one deviation from the script came in the final kilometre, when Jock Boyer's late attack was surprisingly shut down by his fellow American

Greg LeMond. It made little material difference to the outcome, however, as Saronni ripped clear on the final rise to the finish to claim victory with a sprint that would be immortalised back home as *La fucilata di Goodwood* – 'The gunshot of Goodwood'. Kelly scarcely had the energy to return fire, and placed third, behind LeMond, who had used all his ammunition in the pursuit of Boyer. Like Saronni, Kelly's Goodwood exploits would also live on in his home country. That winter, a square in Carrick-on-Suir was renamed in his honour on the back of the medal, Ireland's first since Shay Elliott's contentious silver in Salò 20 years previously. 'If I could cut the medal in half, Stephen would get half,' Kelly said afterwards. After a trying second year at Peugeot, Roche appreciated the sentiment.

During the first week of the 1983 Tour de France, Colm Boland, Paris correspondent for the *Irish Times*, wrote a column describing how the country's two most famous cycling exports were in the process of becoming household names on the Continent. They must have been, Boland reckoned, 'the two most talked of Irishmen throughout Europe these days'. With Bernard Hinault, who won four of the previous five editions, ruled out of the race due to tendonitis, it was the most open Tour in a decade, and the 140 starters set out from Val-de-Marne without a consensus favourite among them.

Despite finishing 15th and almost half an hour behind Hinault the previous year, Kelly was deemed to be as likely a Tour champion as any, not least because his dramatic transfiguration at Sem had continued unabated through the opening half of 1983. If a second successive Paris-Nice win had seemed almost routine, victory in the considerably more mountainous Tour of Switzerland in June marked a wholly unexpected leap forward. 'I really only entered as a way of preparing for the Tour de France,' Kelly said. That Swiss triumph was even more remarkable given that Kelly had sat out most of April and May after breaking his thumb at the Tour des Midi-Pyrénées. A strong performance in the 1983 Tour's first long time trial at Nantes was sufficient for Raymond Poulidor, the 'Eternal Second' of Tour lore, to name Kelly as his pick for final overall victory, while Renault manager Cyrille Guimard, Boland reported, was moved to comment that Kelly 'had undergone one of the most remarkable metamorphoses ever witnessed in professional cycling'.

As well as recording the praise the hosts were heaping upon Kelly, Boland dutifully laid out the recurring criticisms levelled at Tour debutant Roche in the wake of his sophomore slump in 1982. 'Roche was seeing specialists and making vague medical excuses for poor performances. But some said the malady was more psychological, suggesting that early success had gone to his head – a bit of the prima donnas,' Boland wrote. 'Unlike the modest Kelly, Roche is endowed with an innocent kind of arrogance which suggests he simply assumes he will one day be a champion.' For a casual observer, Boland had a sharp eye.

Roche's initial problems in 1982 were a familiar matter of heft, as he once again reported for Peugeot's January training camp overweight. 'He always used to show up at the start of the season carrying an extra five or six kilos, and that really annoyed the directeurs sportifs,' Patrick Valcke says. Roche, however, felt that a relaxed winter was justified considering the heaviness of his racing programme the rest of the year. 'I was doing 110 or 120 race days in a season, and that took a lot out of me,' Roche says. 'Then you had receptions and so on over the winter, and even though I wasn't one for drinking, there was a lot of pressure there. So in my second year, I had a problem getting things together again. It was hard.'

Though Roche was still only 22 years of age and clearly buckling beneath the workload, Peugeot saw little need to cosset their asset for the future. Theirs was a one-size-fits-all approach to rider welfare. When Roche was riding poorly, as was the case for much of 1982, the suggested remedy was for him to race more frequently in a bid to find form. When he was riding well, as was the case in the early months of 1983, the Peugeot response was to pitch him into even more races and extract full value from that purple patch. 'Their attitude was, "You win, you race." They didn't appreciate that it took a lot out of you, and they wouldn't look to hold you back and develop you for tomorrow,' Roche says. 'If a guy was doing well, he had to race, because it was important for the sponsor. You didn't stop. You made hay while the sun shone.'

One positive aspect of 1982, a year in which Roche failed to win a single race, was that he sensibly postponed his planned Tour debut after pleading to be examined at a clinic in Cologne, Germany, 'which Peugeot used to test their riders'. At the time, Roche said he was suffering from chronic fatigue, but in his 2012 autobiography, *Born To Ride*, ghosted by Peter Cossins, he added that he had also been diagnosed with Wolf-Parkinson-White syndrome, which could cause a rapid heart rate, or supraventricular tachycardia. In the old-school environs of

Peugeot, matters of the heart had, predictably, already been blamed for Roche's travails. De Muer, Roche wrote, 'begged me to tell Lydia to take it easy'. Roche and Lydia Arnaud married in Paris at the end of the season, and their choice of honeymoon location suggested that De Muer's indelicate vision of the relationship was somewhat misplaced. The young couple went, of all places, to Lourdes.

De Muer had left Peugeot by the start of the 1983 season, following a putsch that left his one-time assistant Roland Berland in command, and though Roche had a frosty rapport with his new lead directeur sportif, his form returned to something approaching the effervescence of his debut season. Overall victory in May's Tour de Romandie was a confirmation, and Roche's stock had risen to such an extent that he lined up for his debut Tour as one of the protected riders in Peugeot's star-studded roster. Phil Anderson, fifth in 1981, was ostensibly the team leader, but without a *patron* like Hinault in the race, many others at Peugeot, including Robert Millar and Pascal Simon, were angling for some freedom of their own at this potentially anarchic Tour.

By the time the race reached Pau at the end of the opening week, Roche lay in 6th place and wore the white jersey of best young rider. That afternoon, he would be joined on the podium by Kelly, who picked up enough time bonuses on the stage to move into the yellow jersey on the eve of the race's entry into the Pyrenees, 20 years after Shay Elliott had become the first Irishman to wear the *maillot jaune*. In a race where viable contenders were scarce, it was legitimate to ask if he could hold it all the way to Paris. Taking care to adjust a headband extolling the merits of Reydel saddles while he spoke to reporters by the dais,

Kelly puffed out his cheeks before responding. 'Tomorrow, I'll be happy to keep my rivals in check,' he said. 'It wasn't my ambition to get the jersey today, but you must try for your sponsor to get the jersey. You might not ever get the chance again in your life.'

Kelly's words were prescient. The next stage was also the Tour's most arduous, a 201-kilometre leg to Bagnères-de-Luchon, by way of four mountain passes. Outsized passages of Tour history had been wrought in this pocket of the Pyrenees, a fixture in the race since 1910. It was a stage that called for poetry, but in such rarefied terrain, Kelly could only pedal prose. Already fading on the first climb, the Col d'Aubisque, his challenge dissolved atop the mighty Tourmalet, where he trailed the leaders by almost a quarter of an hour. The yellow jersey was long forgotten as he climbed the Aspin and the Peyresourde, leaden eyes focused on the metre of tarmac before his front wheel. Although Kelly cut his deficit to 10 minutes by the finish line, it was a chastening experience. The day was even worse for Roche, who was caught and passed by Kelly in the finale, and found his status at Peugeot abruptly downgraded to that of domestique. His teammate Millar soloed to stage victory, while Pascal Simon was the new race leader. 'The first mountain stage is always difficult for me. All the sprinting for points, using big gears in the flat stages, means that I can't adapt to using the little gears on the climbs,' Kelly said afterwards.

A rather different explanation was put forward by his Belgian soigneur Willy Voet in his 1999 book *Massacre à la chaine* (translated in 2001 as *Breaking the Chain*). Voet had, by that point, achieved the notoriety of being apprehended on the Franco-Belgian border behind the wheel of a Festina team car carrying a stock of performance-enhancing drugs, including

EPO, which he was driving to the start of the 1998 Tour de France in Dublin. Voet claimed that on the evening Kelly took the yellow jersey in Pau, he administered the rider with an injection of Synacthen Retard, a hormone which stimulates the production of corticosteroids. 'As the Irishman used to say, "On the Tour I don't mess with anything forbidden." In his eyes, and in all our eyes, that meant detectable products,' Voet wrote. According to Voet, the injection did not have the desired effect. 'The next day, Kelly was incapable of holding a wheel, and was left behind on the smallest hill – and there were a lot of those since the stage was from Pau to Bagnères-de-Luchon,' Voet wrote. 'This mistake earned me the nickname of "blocker".'

At the beginning of the 1983 season, de Gribaldy had outlined his distaste for doping in a television interview – 'It's imperative that you build form in a natural way. Otherwise it's the pharmacy, and I'm against that' – a stance that Tinazzi, who himself tested positive for amphetamine in 1984, insists was not merely for show. 'He never spoke about doping; he was against it. It was all about diet with him,' he says. Voet's memoir notes how de Gribaldy would fill water bottles himself for fear of tampering, while the other, preferred soigneur in his employ was Pierre Ducrot, who was opposed to doping.

Nonetheless, one of Kelly's Sem teammates, Patrick Clerc, was among four riders to return positive doping controls during the second week of the Tour, though such was the laxity of cycling's anti-doping policies at the time that all four riders were permitted to continue in the race with time penalties and suspended sanctions. At the start of the Bastille Day stage in Roquefort-sur-Soulzon, a group of riders even lobbied race director Félix Lévitan for the crackdown on doping products to be lifted, and then organised a go-slow for much of the day in protest. 'I don't have the impression that I cheated. I feel like I treated myself to do my job as a cyclist properly,' Clerc told *Antenne 2* that day.

In the same news report, a doctor associated with Roche's Peugeot squad, the Cologne-based Josef Assenmacher, was even more frank on the issue of doping. 'A rider who doesn't do a bit of anabolic [sic] to prepare the season, during the winter or something, isn't going to arrive like he should to prepare the Tour de France,' said Assenmacher. 'From my experience of twenty or thirty years, you need to take certain doping substances to improve performance.' Although Assenmacher was not formally the team medic – according to one rider, the team had no official race doctor in the early 1980s – he spoke to the camera in a red polo shirt bearing the Peugeot name. Peugeot was the team of Pascal Simon, yellow jersey of the Tour de France at the time, yet Assenmacher's comments scarcely seemed to make a ripple. Nobody in the peloton seemed to feel moved to refute them.

More than 30 years on, Roche says he has no recollection of a doping controversy on his debut Tour de France. 'I didn't even know that four guys tested positive. They were taking guys for very minor stuff as well, like caffeine and steroids. It wasn't a lot of stuff in those days,' Roche says. 'In our day, doping was a five per cent increase in performance, but we all know anybody with a bit of class had a chance of beating a guy with a five per cent increase.'

In keeping with the journalistic norms of the day, the positive tests were quickly consigned to the margins, with the headlines centred around Simon, who had broken his shoulder the day after taking the yellow jersey. Coaxed by his Peugeot teammates, Simon succeeded in defending his lead for six days before finally succumbing to the inevitable and abandoning early on the stage to l'Alpe d'Huez in the final week. Freed from his nursing duties, Roche went on the attack immediately, but was caught out by his inexperience by forgetting to eat as he climbed the Col du Glandon. 'I remember when we hit the foot of l'Alpe d'Huez, the radio was saying the green jersey of Sean Kelly was 10 minutes back, and then Sean caught me on l'Alpe d'Huez, and I finished 10 minutes down on him,' Roche laughs. 'So it was lights out.'

Roche responded quickly, performing solidly on the next mountain stage to Morzine, and then taking 2nd place in the mountain time trial to Avoriaz. He reached Paris in 13th place overall, largely heartened by his first taste of *La Grande Boucle*. Even if the winner, Laurent Fignon, was a fellow Tour debutant and almost a year Roche's junior, surrendering the weighty mantle of being the next Bernard Hinault was hardly a privation. 'That's when I realised that the Tour was going to be something for me, and that I could do an awful lot better,' Roche says. 'I started thinking there could be something in this for me. I lasted the three weeks, I was good at time trialling, and I was getting better in the climbs. Those are the three main ingredients to be good in the Tour.'

Kelly, like Roche, recovered well from his *jour sans* in the Pyrenees, and he produced his usual consistency thereafter to carry the green jersey to the Champs-Élysées for the second successive year. Simon's injury and Fignon's inexperience meant that, at least notionally, Kelly even figured among the contenders for overall victory as the third week began, though a combination of the Alps and searing heat soon put paid to that passing fancy. Even so, his disastrous day in yellow aside, Kelly limited his losses in the high mountains better than ever before, and placed 7th overall in Paris. Rather than a missed opportunity, Kelly felt his Tour showing was a confirmation that 4th place in the 1980 Vuelta had not been an anomaly. 'I produced my best form of the year to win the Tour of Switzerland,' Kelly insisted a few weeks later. 'Next season, I'll be going all out to win the Tour.'

Kelly still had miles to ride and promises to keep in the remainder of 1983, but come the third Saturday of October, he was running out of road. The Tour of Lombardy was the last opportunity to reap the fruits of his labours over the year, but seven kilometres from the finish in Como, it seemed that one of the chief targets laid out by de Gribaldy – a maiden classic victory – would again escape him. Kelly was, by reputation at least, the quickest finisher in the front selection of 18 riders, but when Spaniard Pedro Muñoz sallied clear on the climb of San Fermo della Battaglia, nobody in the group seemed minded to chase. As the sun began to dip behind the hills that pepper the western branch of Lake Como and the day died softly, another classic was ebbing away from Kelly.

Since that humbling experience in his debut Paris-Roubaix in 1978, Kelly's progress in the great classics had been fitful at best, and by no means commensurate with his aptitude for their rigours. The Tour of Flanders, with its succession of short, cobbled hills, seemed ideally suited to Kelly, but a distant 8th place in 1981 had been his best showing. A brace of podium finishes at Het Volk and 3rd place in the 1980 Amstel Gold Race were the only tangible achievements on a classics résumé blighted by the 1981 Flèche Wallonne fiasco and a regrettable 4th place at the 1980 Milan-San Remo, where Kelly was woefully under-geared for the sprint on the Via Roma. Injury had forced Kelly 2.0 to miss the 1983 spring classics and now, at 27, he risked becoming known as a big man for the small occasion.

With no Sem teammates alongside him, Kelly needed an ally of circumstance to reel in Muñoz on his behalf, but Claude Criquielion, his old friend from Splendor, didn't have the strength. The rest of the group seemed composed of rivals. Newly crowned world champion Greg LeMond had been stuck to his wheel all afternoon, racing to defend his lead in the season-long Super Prestige rankings rather than to win the Tour of Lombardy. The Italian favourite Francesco Moser was not going to tow Kelly to the line, nor was Phil Anderson. When a counter-attack ghosted off the front with five kilometres to go, none of the favourites budged.

Kelly glanced to his left and spotted a white jersey at his shoulder: Roche. Kelly turned his eyes to his fellow countryman. 'He said he would do what he could,' Kelly said afterwards. 'I knew what he meant.' Roche upped the pace on the front of the chasing group, and Adrie van der Poel and the counter-attackers were quickly brought to heel. Only Muñoz dangled off the front as they entered the rosy-hued streets of Como. Roche continued his lone effort at the head of the chasing group; to the uninformed observer, it might even have seemed like he was riding in support of his teammate Anderson.

The Tour of Lombardy would be Roche's final race for Peugeot, however, and the break-up was proving rancorous. At the end of the Tour, he had told reporters he was likely to stay put for a fourth season, but there was a surfeit of ambitious, would-be leaders on the team, and relations with Berland were already strained. 'From the moment Berland took over from De Muer, it got more complicated,' Patrick Valcke says. 'Stephen quickly understood that if he stayed, he would be blocked by a few riders and, above all, the directeur sportif. Berland didn't imagine at that point that Stephen could become a real leader for the whole season.' A contretemps over Roche's new contract for 1984 triggered the definitive rupture. 'I had a discussion with Peugeot, and we'd agreed on the conditions but we hadn't agreed a figure because the World Championships were still coming up,' Roche says. 'I said I wasn't going to put my name to a contract until after that.'

LeMond was untouchable at the Worlds in Altenrhein, Switzerland, but Roche was one of four chasers who clipped away on the final lap, and he snatched a bronze medal, Ireland's second in as many years. As at Goodwood 12 months previously, the two Irishmen in the race had dovetailed well, with Kelly policing the chasers behind Roche.

'After the World Championships, I went looking for my contract,' Roche says. 'It was bound with numbers on it, but I hadn't signed to those numbers. I'd signed the first few pages, which had the conditions about my living conditions and my car and what have you, but the financial part was still to be decided.' He elected to leave for rival team La Redoute. Peugeot prepared to sue.

As the copper dome of Como cathedral reared into view, Roche figured that he owed a greater debt to Kelly than to Peugeot. He kept riding even after Munoz was swept up inside the last kilometre, finally swinging over in the finishing straight. The sprint was a close-fought thing, but in a blanket finish, Kelly edged out LeMond, Van der Poel, Hennie Kuiper and Moser to win his first-ever classic.

De Gribaldy being de Gribaldy, meanwhile, he made sure to bury a gentle admonishment amid his blanket of praise. 'I am confident it will be the first of many,' de Gribaldy said, 'but it shouldn't have taken as long as this.'

8

THE ROAD TO LOS ANGELES

In the summer of 1981, Pat McQuaid had just completed his final race, the Grand Prix of Ireland in the Phoenix Park, when JJ McCormack, father of his old Irish teammate Alan, approached and asked if he might accompany the Irish team to the World Junior Championships in Leipzig the following month. By then, McQuaid had broadly fulfilled his ambitions as a rider. After spending 1977 at VC Metz, he raced the following two years with British professional outfit Viking, all while holding down a full-time teaching job in Ballinteer. Later, he was involved in coaching the 1980 Olympic team, but he left the set-up in acrimonious circumstances shortly before the Games, when his brother Oliver was removed from consideration for eschewing the Tour of Britain in favour of a race in Chicago. A year on, however, Pat McQuaid was willing to come back on board with the juniors. 'I was a teacher with the summer holidays off anyway; it was no bother to me,' McQuaid says.

The youngsters in McQuaid's charge formed a talented group. Martin Earley had won the inaugural Junior Tour of Ireland while still an under-16 rider. Gary Thomson had beaten McQuaid to win the Grand Prix of Ireland. David Gardiner had placed second in the Viking Trophy on the Isle of Man. A week before they travelled, 19-year-old Paul Kimmage claimed the national senior title. That last fact ought to have given the ICF selectors pause for thought: the junior ranks are for riders aged 18 and under. The ICF, however, failed to spot the discrepancy and sent McQuaid on his way to East Germany with three ineligible riders.

'It was total chaos. Thomson was the only one of them able to race because the federation didn't know the right ages for juniors. The others were disgusted and angry with the federation, and I had to calm them down,' McQuaid says. 'Martin Earley was very pragmatic and accepting and said, "Look, that's the way it is." Davy Gardiner was a gentleman, he accepted and understood as well.'

The third non-starter was less inclined to stifle his disappointment.

'Kimmage was Kimmage,' McQuaid says. 'Kimmage was fucking and blinding, fucking and blinding: what he wasn't going to do to people when he got back to Dublin was nobody's business.'

Kimmage doesn't dispute that recollection. 'That would tally – I would have been really pissed,' he says. 'We actually flew to fucking Leipzig and then we were told we were overage. They hadn't checked. Leipzig was a brutal place. We went there, found out we were overage and then flew home, which was mad.'

The return journey scarcely improved spirits. A further mix-up, this time regarding their travel arrangements, meant that the Irishmen were marooned in Brussels airport as they waited for a connecting flight home. 'I was embarrassed, to say the least,' McQuaid says. He registered his own annoyance with the ICF, and later that winter, after some deliberation, he was eventually ratified as national team director, with the task of preparing Kimmage, Earley et al. for the 1984 Olympic Games in Los Angeles.

Paul Kimmage and Martin Earley were born little more than a month apart in the summer of 1962. They both grew up in Coolock on the north side of Dublin, and both went on to become professional bike riders, yet neither man claims to have much in common with the other. Their place of birth and shared interest in cycling brought them into one another's orbit, and, for the most part, they got along, but their personalities were perhaps always too disparate for the roots of a lasting friendship to take hold.

Kimmage came into cycling because he was born into it. To his mind, he had no choice. His father, Christy, was an international rider in the 1950s and 1960s, and later a coach and masseur for various Irish teams going abroad. Even though Christy encouraged his first-born to partake in a variety of sports, not even Kevin Heffernan's revitalisation of Dublin GAA in the 1970s could dissuade Paul from following in his father's wheel tracks. 'I had no *grá* for it at all, and I even managed to get out of playing it in school,' Kimmage says. 'I never understood that culture really. It was a bit strange. I felt like a foreigner on All-Ireland final day in Dublin.' His one visit to Croke Park as an adolescent was not to cheer on Heffo's Army from the Hill, but to sell match programmes before Limerick's 1973 All-Ireland hurling win. 'I couldn't sell oil, I'm useless, so I just stood there with massive heaps of programmes, in the pissing rain,' Kimmage says. 'I felt like a complete alien.'

By then, Kimmage had already started cycling, and it's striking that, even as a child, competition felt intrinsic to the sport's attraction. After the Kimmages moved from Ballymun to Coolock, for instance, an eight-year-old Paul began organising unofficial races against his new neighbours on Kilmore Avenue. A couple of years later, Christy presented him with his first racing bike, and the following weekend Paul lined out in his first race in the Phoenix Park, too excited to dwell at any length on his father's gentle pre-race warning: 'In cycling, you will experience more heartbreak than happiness.' Finishing second last against a small peloton of older boys did little to quell his enthusiasm, and he joined Orwell Wheelers, but it was the beginning of a frustrating run. For most of his teenage years, Kimmage's ability struggled to keep step with his ambition.

'I would have regarded myself as a good rider, but I knew I wasn't a superstar. That was always engrained in me: I was no superstar. As a kid, I would have had a certain sense that I wasn't good enough, because even though I won some races, there were always better kids around,' he says. Gallingly, one of them happened to live under the same roof. Kimmage's brother Raphael – named, incidentally, after Stephen Roche's future manager Géminiani – was two years his junior but an obvious talent. 'My brother came through,' Kimmage smiles, 'and he *was* a fucking superstar.' At least the age gap meant that he didn't race with Raphael as a juvenile, and by a similar token, Stephen Roche's seniority meant that his gifts were to be admired rather than envied. With Earley, who lived barely a mile away on Glin Drive, the relationship was different. He was a direct opponent throughout their teenage years.

They were training partners before they became rivals, given that Dublin's young cyclists, regardless of club affiliation, tended to assemble outside the GPO every week before setting off for the countryside. 'That's probably how I met Martin for the first time, and we would have started chatting,' Kimmage says. Unlike Kimmage, Earley did not hail from cycling stock, and came into the sport at 12 years of age only through the influence of a schoolmate, Sean Lally. Earley already had the curiosity and the equipment – he had seen the finish of the Rás in the Phoenix Park a year or two previously, and owned a Dawes bike – so he joined the Obelisk club and started racing. 'I went through the winter just going on club rides, youth hostel weekends and that,' Earley says. 'When the start of the season came, a lot of them were talking about racing and I just sort of drifted into it, really.'

With his waif-like physique and thick glasses, Earley didn't seem an obvious athlete, but he was blessed with natural qualities of endurance, and his diminutive stature only made his margin for improvement each year all the greater. 'I've got photos from the early days and I was so small that you can see me looking up through the cables on the handlebars,' Earley says. 'I liked it from the start and I was getting results as a schoolboy – maybe not winning, but I was improving all the time. I just gradually progressed, which was a good way to be.'

That progression didn't go unnoticed down the road in Coolock.

'I remember Dad taking us out to Phoenix Park one evening and timing us on a lap of the two-mile circuit. It was myself, Martin and a son of my dad's friend, Andy Stoutt, and Martin was faster than me, which would have pissed me off,' Kimmage says, and to his mind, their rivalry superseded their friendship once they hit their mid-teens. Yet Earley insists that he was oblivious to any enmity. 'No, I wouldn't have seen us like that at all. I wouldn't even have noticed it, not at all,' he says. 'Everyone's a rival when you race, but it was nothing in particular.'

Despite his slight build, Earley blossomed sooner than Kimmage, winning the national junior title in 1978, when he was still an under-16 rider, and then adding the inaugural Junior Tour of Ireland that same July. 'Ah, I was above average, yeah,' he concedes. Run over seven stages, that first Junior Tour, the brainchild of JJ McCormack, was a remarkable event. 1956 Olympic 1,500 metres champion Ronnie Delany flagged the youngsters away from the GPO on the first stage, which saw them race out to Ashbourne before coming back into the city for a finish outside Glasnevin Cemetery. 'We were lining up for the start on O'Connell Street at 6 o'clock on a Tuesday evening. Can you imagine trying to do that now?' says Damien Long, who competed alongside Earley in that first Junior Tour. Stages at Mondello Park, Lucan, Skerries and Ballymun followed, before the concluding leg to Tullamore, where Earley soloed clear to take the stage win and snatch the yellow jersey on the final day. 'Earley and Kimmage showed a lot of promise as young riders,' Long says, 'but Martin was special.'

The first Junior Tour of Ireland included an NCA team, and later that summer, an ICF contingent, including Earley, was invited to compete in an equivalent three-day race run under the auspices of the NCA. The Novice Rás (in NCA nomenclature, under-18 riders were referred to as 'novices' rather than juniors) took place around Thurles, and was won by Earley's ICF teammate, Tony Murphy. It was a sign of the growing détente in Irish cycling, especially as the exchange seemed to pass off more peaceably than previous such attempts at senior level. By the time Earley and Kimmage reached the senior ranks, the Tripartite Committee would be in full effect.

Much to Kimmage's chagrin, Earley would continue to have the better of their exchanges as juniors in the biggest races, winning a second national championship in 1980, but Kimmage struck back by claiming the senior version the following season, outsprinting Brendan Madden and Mick Nulty to become national champion at the age of 19. In doing so, Kimmage emulated his father, who had won the Irish Championships in 1960, though his mind was already on following the path laid down by an illustrious spectator that afternoon in Waterford.

The previous year, Stephen Roche had competed in this very race. Now he was home on a short break, with Paris-Nice on his palmarès, his name on the side of a Peugeot, and a young Frenchwoman on his arm. Kimmage had finished school and was working as an apprentice plumber in Dublin airport at the time. Earley was serving as an apprentice welder. The professional peloton seemed an alluring sort of a place. 'Roche was over and that was fucking huge,' Kimmage says. 'I remember seeing him standing by the side of the road with Lydia and thinking, "Fucking hell, is this what happens?!"'

At a function in Dublin in March 1982, Pat McQuaid was finally unveiled as national coach, with the express target of preparing a team for the Los Angeles Olympics. The formal ratification had been delayed to coincide with the announcement of Raleigh's sponsorship of the new venture, which he had himself negotiated. Not for the first time, McQuaid was wearing several hats at once. 'I was connected with Raleigh from my days as a rider,' McQuaid says. 'When I came back from Leipzig, I was disgusted and I said we needed something professional. I got a group of 10 or 12 good young riders together, we got them bikes and kit, and they were called the Olympic squad and they rode races together abroad. It wasn't officially the national team but it brought them on.'

Kimmage and Earley were among the young hopefuls in attendance that night, and McQuaid's ambitious project marked a definite change from an era when Irish teams were cobbled together for each event without any overarching objective. 'It was a big deal, and it definitely did raise the level. We had nice bikes and Le Coq Sportif jerseys, instead of the moth-eaten ones with old Mars bars left over in the pockets,' Kimmage says. 'The Raleigh Olympic squad had a nice ring to it, too, it helped the old ego. And you thought, "Olympics: wow, I could be going there. This might be good."'

Had he not met his wife Ann after the final stage of the Rás, however, Kimmage might have been inclined to dismiss 1982 as an annus horribilis. After his national title and senior international debut the previous season, it marked a step backwards, the nadir arriving when he was omitted from the Irish amateur team for the World Championships in Goodwood that September. 'Raphael was there, and Philip Cassidy and all the crack guys were on that team and I wasn't, so that was a slap in the chops for me. I was very disappointed, but I couldn't argue,' Kimmage says. 'I would never had admitted it, but it made me think maybe I wasn't good enough.'

There wasn't any discernible upturn in the early part of 1983, either, and the bleak outlook was hardly brightened by the news that three of Kimmage's contemporaries – Earley, Cassidy and Dermot Gilleran – were spending the season racing in France, already a rung ahead of him on the ladder towards a professional career. Kimmage was, however, doing enough to earn selection consistently for the Olympic squad, and he was part of the six-man team for the Irish cyclist's traditional maturation ordeal, the Tour of Britain. There had been more renowned Irish riders in the race over the years, but no one, not even Kelly or Peter Doyle, had come as close as Kimmage did to taking home the spoils.

Almost unbeknownst to himself, he arrived at the start in the form of his life, and on the rugged stage to Halifax, he moved into the yellow jersey, and then distanced his rivals, the Peugeot professional Sean Yates and American Matt Eaton, on the toughest leg to Middlesbrough. 'I started with an average enough prologue, did well on the first stage, and from there it was just a little confidence, just a spark. And here I was in the yellow jersey riding out of my fucking skin and it was amazing,' Kimmage says.

It didn't last. Kimmage punctured early on the penultimate stage to Harrogate, and then crashed while chasing the bunch, eventually losing 13 minutes and dropping to 33rd place overall, while Eaton went on to win the race. McQuaid was standing at the finish line with race organiser Phil Liggett when Kimmage came in. 'I brought him down to the changing rooms and sat down with him in the changing rooms. He was completely devastated, which is understandable,' McQuaid says. 'I tried as much as I could to comfort him, but there's very little you can say in a situation like that.'

On the final day in Blackpool, reporters reminded Kimmage of the similarity with Kelly's misfortune in the same race eight years previously. 'If I end up like Sean Kelly, I won't mind so much,' he told them. There was a dual disappointment for Kimmage that day. Raleigh's sponsorship meant there was an unwritten bonus for winning the race – a contract with their Dutch professional team. 'Had I won, I would have been riding for Peter Post's Raleigh team in 1984, which would have been the worst thing that ever happened to me,' Kimmage says.

He can smile about it now but at the time it was terrible.

Earley had missed the Tour of Britain, having moved to France at the beginning of 1983 to race with the Vélo Club Fontainebleau-Avon, 50 kilometres south east of Paris. With McQuaid's consent, he returned only occasionally to race for the Olympic squad. 'I was coming and going for races, but I didn't think the Tour of Britain was going to help me get to where I wanted to go,' Earley says. Buoyed by his junior success, Earley had begun to think about going abroad even before his apprenticeship as a welder began. On its completion in the autumn of 1982, he no longer had any impediments. 'There wasn't a lot going on in Ireland at that time, the economic situation was not good. There would have been work for me but I know everyone was struggling at that time,' Earley says. 'There wasn't a whole lot to lose by going away; that's the way I looked at it.'

By living in the Paris region, Earley guaranteed himself a diet of top-level racing, but a club of Fontainebleau's modest dimensions offered a homelier environment than the talent factory of ACBB. It was as though he had cherry-picked the best elements of Kelly and Roche's respective amateur careers. 'There was a French guy who had connections in Ireland and he set up a connection for me with Fontainebleau. They were looking for an international rider and I knew the Paris region was the place to be at that time if you wanted to get recognised,' Earley says. As the lone foreign rider on the team, Earley was treated as a valued asset rather than a mere commodity, and he spent his two years in Fontainebleau living in the spare room of the club sponsor and president, Jean Rose, owner of the local Volkswagen dealership.

'It was a smaller club than ACBB but coming from Ireland it still was a huge difference,' Earley says. 'It took a lot of time to adapt to the racing because it was really hard and there was a hell of a lot more of it. Once May came and the evenings were longer, there were two or three races in the middle of the week, as well as races on Saturday and Sunday, and maybe once a month you were riding a stage race, so it was a big jump. Off the bike, I spent time trying to learn French with phrasebooks and so on. I had no choice, because I was the only foreign rider at the club, but that was good. After a few months I settled in and results got better too. I was probably lucky I didn't go to somewhere like ACBB, because I mightn't have stayed very long.'

ACBB, however, was precisely where Paul and Raphael Kimmage landed in February of 1984, having been recommended to Claude Escalon by Stephen Roche. Their journey to Paris mirrored that of their father Christy in 1959, when he briefly joined ACBB hoping to follow in the path of Shay Elliott. Deep down, his son Paul was harbouring doubts about the wisdom of the venture in the winter of 1983–84, the sharp intake of confidence from his Tour of Britain showing quickly punctured by a chastening experience at the Tour de l'Avenir. He was the only Irish finisher at the Tour de France 'of the future' for amateurs and professionals under the age of 25, but that was the lone positive from the ordeal. 'I would have always regarded myself as a climber but we went down to the mountains and I was just fucking blitzed. It was utterly demoralising. Earley missed it, and he dodged a bullet big time,' says Kimmage. 'I would have been really unsure about it all after that. As good as the Milk Race had been, that was the opposite, a real comedown. The hope I was clinging to was that I was still working at the time, so there was still a margin to improve.'

Although they had one another for company, life in Paris was trying for the Kimmage brothers, who were housed in the east of the city and felt adrift. 'We were staying on the complete opposite side of the city, away from where the hub of the team was in Boulogne,' Kimmage says. Although Raphael showed the better form initially, performing well during the opening month of racing in southern France and then placing 5th in the Paris-Izy classic, the news didn't seem to filter home, and Paul was selected more frequently than his brother for the Irish Olympic squad. A trip to the Sealink International in Britain in April offered welcome respite from life at ACBB, where the Kimmages did not share Roche's rosy view of Claude Escalon. 'It was a miserable fucking experience. I hated Escalon. He was just a pig of a man,' Kimmage says. 'It was just a conveyor belt: get them in, see how good they are, then get them out.'

Beset by persistent illness and demoralised by Escalon's barracking style, Raphael moved back to Dublin in early summer. Paul might have been minded to join him had his form not picked up. He won his first race for ACBB in Ostricourt and was confirmed as a member on the Irish team for Los Angeles. The fact that his rival Earley was faring so well on the Continent, too, can only have motivated him to stick it out. Shortly before they travelled to the Games, Earley signed a contract to turn professional with the Fagor team in 1985. 'That would have been a real fucking kick for me, but I couldn't argue with it,' Kimmage says. 'The environment helped. Martin was in a small club, staying with a family and was well looked after, with great training roads. He got lucky.'

Kimmage and Earley were joined by Gary Thomson, Seamus Downey and Philip Cassidy in the Irish squad that left Dublin airport for the United States on 3 July 1984, accompanied by manager Pat McQuaid and mechanic Jack Watson. The road race was still some three weeks away, but thanks to the funding McQuaid had wrangled from Raleigh and Coors, the team could train and race together in Colorado to acclimatise ahead of the Games. Every step was meticulously planned. McQuaid had his charges race in a pair of criteriums on arrival, before they tackled the tough Coors Classic stage race under the Killian's Irish Red banner, with US-based professional Paul McCormack, brother of Alan, filling out the roster.

'In fairness to McQuaid, this was where he was fucking brilliant,' Kimmage says. 'Our preparation had been so wrong for the Worlds the previous year, and we had no chance, but it could not have been better in 1984. At the Coors Classic, we had altitude and heat, and we rode against the top Americans.'

At the Olympics, on a broiling afternoon on a demanding course around Mission Viejo, Kimmage made what proved to be the decisive selection of 20 riders, but his progress was halted by a mechanical issue and he finished 27th, almost 12 minutes behind the winner, American Alexei Grewel. 'I broke a spoke and it wrapped around my rear mech. It cost me four minutes and that was it, I never got back on,' Kimmage says. To rub salt into the wound, Earley came home in 19th place, in what was then the best-ever finish by an Irish rider at the Olympics. 'I shouldn't say I went in with no ambition, but the ambition was to do as well as I could rather than thinking I could win a medal,' says Earley, who met his wife, the British cyclist Catherine Swinnerton, in Los Angeles. The success of

McQuaid's approach, meanwhile, was borne out by the fact that the Irish team was one of only three to finish the road race with a full complement of riders. 'We all finished and not one Brit did, so McQuaid got that absolutely bang on,' Kimmage says.

At that point, there was no trace of the rancour that would later sour Kimmage and McQuaid's relationship. For all that Kimmage would have been, in common with many young sportspeople, critical of how the elders within his federation went about their business, he viewed McQuaid as among the most progressive coaches Ireland had to offer at the time. 'He was definitely a force for good, no doubt about that. The Olympic squad was a great idea, and I got on well with Pat,' Kimmage says. 'Pat would have been one of the coaches that we'd have listened to coming through as juniors. He was good for me in '83 in the Milk Race. I would have liked him and admired him.'

Indeed, the cordial relations between the Kimmage and McQuaid clans were longstanding. 'My dad had a lot of time for Pat's father, Jim,' Kimmage says. As Pat McQuaid puts it, he knew Kimmage 'from the time he was in pram, looking at races in the Park', and the pair would compete against one another towards the end of McQuaid's racing career. 'I remember, probably in 1981, we rode the Coast to Coast, and in the middle stage I got shelled out after I'd been in the break all day. McQuaid actually pushed me across the line when I came back to the bunch,' Kimmage says. 'We got on well.'

The lone misgiving Kimmage had about McQuaid's motivations surfaced immediately after the team time trial in Los Angeles, where the Irish quartet finished 16th. 'When we went to the Games, he wanted the skinsuits off us after the team time trial. This was the bollocks that went on,' Kimmage says. 'He wanted them back. Now what the fuck he was going to do with them, I don't know. So that was the negative with him. That was always the weakness: they were always looking out for the next buck.'

McQuaid, meanwhile, employs a neat formula to describe his experience of managing Kimmage on the Irish Olympic squad. 'I didn't have a difficult relationship with Paul but he was always a difficult rider to manage because he was driven to win, and he couldn't take second place,' McQuaid says, continuing:

Paul was unique. When we'd come down in the evening, you might have Cassidy and Thomson and Earley sitting at the dinner table, and the laughs would be flying, the craic and jokes, but Paul never really took part in that, unlike his brother Raphael, who was completely the opposite.

I never had difficulty with Paul until he turned pro, other than the fact that he was a difficult rider to manage because he was so fixated on winning and couldn't accept second. In any sport, and cycling more than any other, throughout your career, even if you're Eddy Merckx or Chris Froome or whoever, you will lose more races than you win. You have to be able to accept that and understand that. Paul couldn't understand that. And that's basically what his problem was as a cyclist.

Immediately after the Games, Kimmage claimed a second Irish national title, and then arrived back to Paris to rather happier circumstances. Rather than live alone in the apartment he had once shared with Raphael, he stayed with the journalist David Walsh and his young family in Courbevoie, a north-western suburb, for the remainder of the season. Walsh lent a friendly ear to his frustrations and helped him through the final weeks of the campaign. 'I wasn't sure I was going to go back in '85, so that was kind of a critical moment,' Kimmage says. He performed strongly in August and September, most notably at the Tour du Seine-et-Marne, but even that came with a kicker. 'I went to France with a bit of momentum, rode well in that stage race – but fucking Martin beat me, Jaysis,' Kimmage laughs. 'It was kind of a demoralising end to the year.'

Kimmage came home to Dublin at season's end adamant that he would not return to ACBB and questioning whether he should go back to France at all in 1985. Amid Ireland's ongoing recession, he and Raphael spent time on the dole that winter and then signed up to a government training course in Finglas – 'We had no jobs, no prospect of getting a job and no fucking money' – before they were tipped off by Sean Kelly that Guy Mollet, manager of the Wasquehal amateur club near Lille, was interested in their services for the new season.

'We had a chance to start again and have another crack, so we went for it,' says Kimmage. A smaller club than ACBB, Wasquehal offered a more amenable environment for a foreign rider. 'Mollet was just mad. He was an eccentric fucker. But as much as I had disliked Escalon, I liked Mollet. There was a bit of decency to him. You weren't just a number there, so it went well from the get go.'

While Paul enjoyed a fine season at Wasquehal, capped by an appearance in the 560-kilometre Bordeaux-Paris classic alongside the professionals, and a stage win at the Tour of Normandy, Raphael endured only misfortune. He made the decisive break at an unusually balmy Paris-Roubaix, but when a soigneur handed him a flask of warm tea to quench his thirst rather than a bottle of water, he lost contact with the move. 'On these margins, careers are made and lost. And that was the difference, really: things went well for me,' Paul Kimmage says.

A 6th place finish at the amateur World Championships in Montello, the best-ever display by an Irish rider, would ultimately secure Paul Kimmage a professional contract for 1986, though not, as he had initially anticipated, alongside Sean Kelly at Kas. Instead, after a protracted delay, he penned a deal with a new French outfit, managed by a childhood hero, two-time Tour winner Bernard Thévenet. 'I got the call from Mollet saying, 'RMO, you're in.' I had a contract,' he says. 'It was an interesting path.'

9

THE EVANGELIST

It's a long way from Como to Carrick-on-Shannon. On the weekend that Kelly combined with Roche to win the Tour of Lombardy, *Irish Press* journalist David Walsh found himself in Leitrim reporting on the drawn All-Ireland under-21 Gaelic Football final between Derry and Mayo. At 28 years of age, Walsh was doing what he had always wanted to do, covering sport for a national newspaper, but as driving wind and spitting rain swept across Páirc Seán Mac Diarmada, it was hard to shake off the nagging sense that he should have been somewhere else.

Monday's *Irish Press* carried Walsh's match report on the back page but there wasn't even a mention of Kelly's win inside. A day later, however, Walsh reached Kelly by telephone and successfully pleaded for half a page in which to tell the story of his Tour of Lombardy victory. The subediting left something to be desired – as Jean de Bribalby was quoted – but when Walsh opened the newspaper on Tuesday 18 October 1983, he at least had the satisfaction of seeing that the first monument classic win by an Irish rider had been dutifully recorded for posterity.

'I was very conscious of Kelly being this almost superstar on the Continent but relatively unknown in his home country. I had an absolute desire to make people aware of how great this guy was,' Walsh says. 'I'd have been outraged by the lack of coverage of him. How can an Irish guy win a stage of the Tour de France and only have two paragraphs in the *Irish Independent*, two paragraphs in the *Irish Press*? The Rás would get far more coverage than Kelly winning a stage of the Tour de France. And that was my starting point with Kelly, this sense that it was unfair.'

A native of Slieverue in County Kilkenny, Walsh was not a cycling fan in his youth – 'I had no knowledge of the history of the sport, no involvement in any way,' he says – but something about Kelly and his niche pursuit stoked his curiosity. It helped that Walsh knew Carrick-on-Suir intimately. His father ran a wholesale fruit business, and twice a week brought his van to the town. 'I would often go on the lorry helping my father and brother as the gofer, so you got to know loads of people in Carrick as a result,' he says.

In 1980, Walsh's first year at the *Irish Press*, he convinced sports editor Adhamhnan O'Sullivan to send him to Sallanches for the World Championships by heavily talking up Kelly's chances of taking home the rainbow jersey. 'I wouldn't have been sent voluntarily to that, I would have really had to make my case,' he says. Largely oblivious to the rudiments of the sport, Walsh genuinely believed victory was a possibility, not understanding that the Alpine circuit was far too difficult for Kelly, at least amid his hiatus from the ascetic de Gribaldy method. During their first major interview on the Friday before the race, Kelly gently tried to disabuse Walsh of his misconceptions, but without success.

'Being positive, it is not difficult to prepare a case proposing Kelly as the 1980 world champion, while the more conservative would suggest that he should improve on last year's ninth placing,' Walsh wrote in his enthusiastic race preview. Kelly climbed off around the halfway mark, beaten, like so many others, by the 6,000 metres of total climbing, and only 15 riders even finished a race that Bernard Hinault didn't so much win as conquer, culling the peloton on each ascent of the Côte de Domancy. Undeterred, Walsh simply switched roles from analyst to confidant, highlighting the extent of his access to the star in his post-race copy. 'Sitting comfortably in his hotel, a couple of hours after the race, Kelly still refused to allow his disappointment to infect the general conversation,' Walsh wrote, bragging humbly. It was the beginning of a symbiotic friendship.

In later years, at the height of his renown for reporting on Lance Armstrong, Walsh would on occasion don the sackcloth and ashes when recalling his early career, and describe himself as having been a 'fan with a typewriter' in his coverage of Kelly and Roche, but in July of 1983, he left the typewriter out altogether. After covering the final weekend of the previous year's race for the *Irish Press*, he simply decided to take a fortnight off work to follow the Tour de France with his friend Tony Kelly. 'In 1983, I've got two young kids at home and I took my two weeks of summer holidays to go off and watch the Tour de France. I didn't write a line. It was a pure holiday, on the back of a motorbike,' Walsh says. 'I had no accreditation. I didn't *look* for accreditation. We had no access, ducking and diving with a motorbike. It was like a nightmare, but it was brilliant. I remember being in Pau when Kelly took the yellow jersey, and we drank a cheap bottle of rosé in a nondescript restaurant to toast the lads. It was great fun, joyous. I wouldn't have seen Kelly or Roche, I was there purely as a fan.'

The year 1984, Walsh sensed, was going to be a momentous one for Sean Kelly, and he was loath to spend April Sundays covering National League fixtures in empty provincial grounds, sodden notebook disintegrating in his hands, while the Carrick-on-Suir man went about the rather more glamorous business of collecting classics on the Continent. He negotiated a leave of absence from the *Irish Press* to shadow Kelly and Roche on a freelance basis. 'Basically, I wanted to write a book about Kelly,' Walsh says. 'I said to my wife, "How would you fancy going to live in France for a year?"' Mary Walsh said she would, yes.

In January of 1984, David and Mary Walsh, with their children Kate and John in tow, decamped to Paris, renting a house on Rue Kléber in Courbevoie, not far from the business district of La Défense, then undergoing the facelift that would later add the imposing Grande Arche to the Parisian skyline. 'It was a really nice area, not middle class but not blue collar either,' Walsh says. 'We used to take the kids to a lovely toy shop near La Défense and spend hours just walking around the shop.' France was experiencing a recession of its own at the time, but life in the Paris of François Mitterand's *Grands travaux* felt impossibly cosmopolitan in comparison with the austerity back home in Ireland.

Bernard Hinault's return to Paris-Nice garnered much attention ahead of the first big rendezvous of the year, but the runes from the early races on the Riviera suggested that the white jersey would once again be the preserve of the visitors from across the Celtic Sea. Hinault had abandoned Het Volk the previous weekend, after all, and in his race preview for the *Irish Press*, Walsh delighted in recounting a discussion of the Badger's prospects between the two Irish contenders. 'Roche wondered aloud to Kelly whether the Frenchman could be beaten in the Paris-Nice race which starts this afternoon,' Walsh wrote. 'Kelly turned to him and said, "Don't worry, we'll take him alright."'

Roche, now at La Redoute, was finally an outright team leader, free of the internal rivalries and politics of Peugeot. Though Kelly's team now wore the red and white candy stripes of its new sponsor, Skil, it was business as usual. He picked up a sprint win on stage 2, then broke even with Roche and Hinault on Mont Ventoux, before moving into the white jersey the following afternoon by finishing second at La Seyne-sur-Mer. The day is best remembered for the demonstration by striking shipyard workers that held up the leaders on the descent of the Col de l'Espigoulier, and Hinault's chosen means of dialogue, a right hook to the first protestor he came across. Despite his unwelcome foray into labour relations, Hinault was still competitive, just over 40 seconds down, but come the finale in Nice, only Roche remained in contention to deny Kelly a third successive overall victory. The Dubliner had attacked on the Col du Tanneron to win alone in Mandelieu on the penultimate day and slash Kelly's advantage to just 11 seconds ahead of the final time trial up the Col d'Èze.

Rather than pitch the Kelly–Roche contest as a straight rivalry, Walsh preferred to emphasise their affable relations. 'Two Irishmen locked in a grim struggle and yet prisoners of their great friendship,' he wrote, pointing to how Kelly had refused to pursue Roche on the run-in to Mandelieu as though it were proof of a deep chivalric bond. Earlier in the week, Walsh had even filed an article on the rapport between Kelly and Roche's wives, detailing how Linda, now living in Vilvoorde with Kelly following their marriage in 1982, had spent the week of Paris-Nice staying with Lydia Roche in her home on the outskirts of Paris.

Some of the phrasing scans rather awkwardly to the present-day reader – 'Lydia Roche has organised herself pretty well. She has also ensured that she got a car of her own. So there is not a mobility problem. She will visit her parents and friends and try to be around when Stephen rings' – but Walsh's half-page spread in the *Irish Press* nonetheless serves as testimony to the growing celebrity of Kelly and Roche in Ireland. Their appeal wasn't all about the bike.

Events on the Col d'Èze, meanwhile, showed that the increasing closeness between Kelly and Roche had not dampened the quiet intensity of their rivalry, and the all-Irish tête-à-tête gave this Paris-Nice a special resonance. Three kilometres from the summit of the Col d'Èze, Roche was 10 seconds quicker than Kelly and seemingly destined to divest him of the white jersey, only for the Waterford man to produce a late surge that not only saved his overall victory, but also yielded the stage win by a solitary second. 'In a funny way, it was actually more satisfying to beat him by a single second than it would have been to win by 10,' Kelly admitted in his

2013 autobiography. At the time, he would never have been as candid. It wouldn't have fitted with the narrative.

Paris-Nice finished on Ash Wednesday, but by then, Kelly was already a week into a 40-day sequence of his own. Between 7 March and Passion Sunday, he rattled off a litany of some 13 victories, with two classics among them. It was a period of *aristeia* that drew parallels with Maertens and Merckx, as *Vélo Magazine* labelled him the 'new cannibal', and Walsh was on hand to document those joyful and glorious mysteries.

On St Patrick's Day, Kelly had to settle for winning the sprint for 2nd place at Milan-San Remo, unable to match Francesco Moser's improbable effort on the descent of the final climb of Poggio, but he was back to winning ways at the following weekend's Critérium International, claiming the general classification and all three stages, including a rare solo victory on the mountainous second leg that finished atop the Col de l'Ecre. That triumph made Kelly the overwhelming favourite for the Tour of Flanders, but the tag proved a cumbersome one. Outnumbered by Panasonic and Splendor riders in the six-man winning move, Kelly won another sprint for 2nd place after the unheralded Johan Lammerts slipped away to win. 'Second in a race with 181 starters is hardly a poor performance,' Walsh, ever the optimist, wrote from Meerbeke. 'Even Sean Kelly cannot win them all.'

De Gribaldy, on the other hand, reckoned Kelly *could* win them all, and he eschewed conventional wisdom by sending his rider to race the tough Tour of the Basque Country in the week between Flanders and Paris-Roubaix. In public, de Gribaldy reasoned that Kelly was better off cloistered away at a low-key event in Spain than at home in Belgium fielding calls from journalists for the week, but in truth, the appearance fee from the organisers was the prime attraction for *Le Vicomte*. Kelly, as ever, provided bang for their buck, winning three stages and the overall in the Basque Country before boarding a flight to France for another tilt at the Hell of the North.

At that juncture in his career, Kelly was in a sort of purgatory, now recognised as a very good rider, but still not over the threshold and into the beatific realm of the greats. His status as world number one as per cycling's freshly introduced computer rankings only seemed to reinforce the point. The year 1984 may have marked the arrival of the first Apple Macintosh, but the digital revolution didn't penetrate very deeply into cycling's fusty old world. Greatness was measured in classics victories, not computer printouts. Kelly had won often in 1984, true, but now he needed to win big.

On the Sunday of Paris-Roubaix, Walsh dallied on the start line in Compiègne until the last moment, lingering to catch a few words with Kelly, before jumping into the back seat of photographer John Pierce's car, with Linda Kelly in the front. They criss-crossed the route several times on the way north, giving Pierce opportunities to photograph the race, and Walsh a chance to gauge Kelly's progress. It was a filthy afternoon of steady rain, layers of slick mud pasted across the cobblestones, and at each stop, the rate of attrition seemed to have increased. Riders were shaken into submission by the rocky road beneath their wheels, or simply slid out of contention on the glistening pavé.

Kelly only narrowly avoided falling in the Arenberg Forest, but didn't put a pedal stroke askew from there on, as though assured by that near-miss that this was to be an unusually blessed day in Hell. Normally a study in power rather than grace, Kelly now seemed to glide over the cobbles, as if their secrets had suddenly been revealed to him. Uncharacteristically, he went on the attack some 47 kilometres from home, bringing the modestly talented Rudy Rogiers with him. Inch by inch, they pegged back the early escapees, Gregor Braun and Alain Bondue, and once they caught them, Kelly was remorseless. His pace-making on the final cobbled sections burnt off everyone bar Rogiers, and they approached the gates of the famous old velodrome together.

Pierce pulled up outside only just in time for the finish, and Walsh immediately leapt from the car and dashed for the centre of the velodrome with scarcely an acknowledgement. After gathering his equipment, Pierce hurried into position inside, but Linda Kelly was unable to watch. Instead, she sat outside in the car and knitted, while barely 50 yards away, her husband thundered to the most important victory of his career.

A week later, Linda Kelly inadvertently found herself making the front page of the *Irish Press* after Walsh spotted her slipping an item into the pocket of her husband's jersey at the start of Liège-Bastogne-Liège on the Place Saint-Lambert. 'Just a sprig of blessed palm tree,' she explained. 'Every Palm Sunday, I give him a bit if he is racing, it can't do any harm.' Some 265 kilometres of Ardennes later, nine riders rode back into Liège together at the head of the race, and Kelly, inevitably, claimed the spoils. Walsh wondered whether divine intercession had really been required. 'Sean Kelly is not just the best cyclist in the world at the moment,' he wrote. 'He is the best by some considerable distance.'

At the end of his spring campaign, Kelly quipped to reporters that he was going home to Ireland on a short holiday because 'they don't have automatic telephones there'. Or at least, it seemed like a joke. A study published the previous year showed that Ireland had the worst telephone system in Europe, with just 190 phones per 1,000 people (the average was 436), and only Greece had fewer televisions per capita. If Kelly's exploits now resonated more deeply in Ireland than they had in previous years, it was partly thanks to the evangelist from the print media who had come to chronicle them.

Kelly's run of success was propitious for his future earnings, then, but also for those of Walsh. On the morning after Liège-Bastogne-Liège, a tagline in the *Irish Press* boasted that 'David Walsh is the only staff man from an Irish newspaper on tour with our cycling stars', and by the time the Tour de France came around, Walsh's client list had expanded accordingly. 'I did five or six pieces every day at the Tour, between the UPI news service, the *Cork Examiner*, the *Irish Press* and *Cycling Weekly*, as well as RTÉ radio,' he says.

Walsh was also editing a nascent magazine known as the *Irish Cycling Review*, established in 1982 by Frank Quinn, a publisher who went on to become Kelly's agent. Although Walsh availed of his Parisian sojourn to cover the French Open tennis and travel to Genoa to interview Liam Brady, then at Sampdoria, he was primarily engaged in the Sean Kelly business, as one erstwhile stablemate noted acerbically from Burgh Quay. 'Con Houlihan once wrote a line in his *Evening Press* column, basically dismissing me as "David Walsh, the man who invented Sean Kelly",' Walsh says. Offended? He was delighted. 'I thought it was brilliant.'

Kelly's 1984 Tour provided grounds for optimism: 5th overall in Paris was his best finish yet, and he delivered strong rides in unexpected locations, like on the mountain stages to Guzet-Neige and Morzine, or the final time trial, where he came within fractions of a second of beating the *maillot jaune* Fignon. There were also some familiar shortcomings: he was again undone by the heat at l'Alpe d'Huez and never came close to matching Fignon in the high mountains, where the Frenchman was imperious. He again failed to win a stage and hesitated over his true objectives. After ignoring the points competition to focus on the overall standings, Kelly changed tack in the closing days and moved into the green jersey on the final weekend, only to lose the tunic to Frank Hoste in the last gallop on the Champs-Élysées.

Even so, the final balance sheet was a positive one. Kelly's place atop the world rankings and standing as a Tour de France contender were firmly established. August would once again be the month in which to cash in on the benefits of that status at criteriums all across France, and this time around, he would have some additional company on the road. Walsh had signed a deal with Grafton Books to write Kelly's authorised biography, and to gather material, he would join him for part of the expedition.

'He had been writing about us in the papers back home and then he decided he was going to come to France for the year,' Kelly says. 'He was at all of the races, and you'd get the feedback from that, of course. You'd talk to people back home on the phone, and they'd say "Walsh is doing good reports in the paper." And then he wanted to do the book, and I said, "Yeah, why not?"'

It was a mutually beneficial arrangement. Kelly's accomplishments had given Walsh plenty of stories to sell, and the journalist had reciprocated by adding some colour to the hitherto stoic and sober characterisation of the bike rider. Until Walsh arrived in France, few appreciated that the quiet man from Carrick-on-Suir had a neat line in deadpan humour. After placing second in the Le Mans time trial at the Tour, for example, Kelly told Walsh that he had been on the phone with Linda the previous evening. 'She told me that if I didn't do a good ride, I could be divorced,' Kelly said. 'With that threat, I had little choice.'

'Kelly would tell you a lot because he would feel what you were writing wasn't going to get back to Europe. I did feel an affinity with him, and he was cooperating with the book,' Walsh says, though such collaboration came with a price. 'It was a purely money thing. The deal we had was kind of ridiculous in a way, given how much Kelly was earning and how little I was earning as a freelance journalist in Paris. Kelly had to agree to be interviewed by me; he had to give me some time. I got £8,000 for that commission and we divided it between us, 50-50. So I got £4,000 and Kelly got £4,000. With Kelly, it was another branch of his commercial empire.'

'I felt if we did the book, that would be nice, but I suppose maybe I was a bit naïve as well in regards to how much time I needed to give to do the book,' Kelly says.

Bringing his biographer along for the ride on the criterium circuit was one way of saving time, and so Walsh spent a frenetic 72 hours with Kelly, Linda and Kelly's Belgian domestique, Ronny Onghena. They departed Vilvoorde at 10pm on the evening of 1 August and drove for 800 kilometres before reaching Tulle, in central France, at 6am. After a few hours' sleep in a roadside motel, they left for nearby Chaumeil, site of that evening's criterium. That same night, they set out for the next stop on the itinerary, Concarneau, in Brittany, reaching their waypoint, an Ibis on the outskirts of Rennes, at 4am. Following the Concarneau criterium on 3 August, they again drove through the night, this time reaching Vilvoorde at 7am on 4 August. That same afternoon, Kelly had another criterium in Kortenhoef, across the border in the Netherlands. In three days, Kelly had driven 3,500 kilometres, participated in three criteriums and pocketed, by Walsh's estimate, around £6,000. It was a lucrative form of madness.

Cycling's tradition of post-Tour criteriums was (and is) a bizarre exercise in willing duplicity. The outcome of each race was determined beforehand in a meeting between the criterium manager and the riders. The bulk of the spectators on the circuit realised that they were watching a fix, yet demanded all the vestiges of a 'real' race, namely relentlessly high speed and a flurry of attacks. The stars of the peloton, already exhausted from the Tour de France and drained from their travels, essentially had to sing for their supper. The appearance fees were doled out afterwards, usually in cash. Kelly rarely turned down such opportunities to complement his annual salary, and ensured he was always paid to the last centime. It had pissed rain all night in Concarneau, and Kelly was going in to collect his money,' Walsh says, continuing:

I think his money was 20,000 French francs, which was 2,000 quid. Half of what I'd earn for the book, he'd got it in one night. And he got paid literally from the proceeds, so he got lots of small bills. His tracksuit didn't have pockets, so when he came out, he sat in the front seat and put his hand down into his crotch and took out this huge wad of money. He turns to Linda and says, 'Count that for 20,000,' and he was sitting there in the pissing rain, watching Linda counting it. Eventually she says, 'Yeah, 20,000' and only then does he drive away.

Kelly held an unashamedly capitalist view of cycling. It was a profession, *his* profession, and he conducted himself accordingly. 'I know riders who say money wasn't a big motivator at all, but I think there's a bit of a lie there,' Kelly says. 'Once I got close to turning professional, you can calculate and see what you're getting and work out what the top ones are getting. So definitely money was the motivator. At the end of your career, maybe not so much.'

Yet while Kelly knew the value of every last 20-franc bill tucked into the waistband of his underpants, his frugality could never be mistaken for stinginess. 'I remember having lunch with Linda and Dan Grant on the Champs-Élysées, waiting for the race to come in. Linda took the bill off me and said, "Sean told me: any meals, he's paying,"' Walsh says. 'Kelly used to say to me, "What I've got is hard-earned and it will be hard spent," but I didn't find him mean. I would never have said he was mean. He was good company. He never screwed me.'

Walsh flew to Milan on Friday 12 October for the grand finale to 1984. Kelly had won his third classic of the season the previous weekend, somehow conjuring a way through the mass of bodies in the final sprint at Blois-Chaville just as it seemed his path had been irretrievably blocked. He had already sewn up the season-long Super Prestige competition, and his buffer atop the computer rankings was, like his savings account, steadily accruing interest with each of his 32 victories that season. He lined out as the de facto favourite for the Tour of Lombardy.

Aboard the plane, Walsh felt a pang of wistfulness. He had recently been offered a full-time position on the *Sunday Press* and had, after lengthy deliberation, resolved to accept it. Paris had seen the arrival of his third-born, Simon, and the blossoming of his friendship with Paul Kimmage, but now, with no little regret, his time on the Continent was nearly up. A glance at the cycling page of *L'Équipe*, however, soon stirred Walsh from his reverie. A one-paragraph sidebar reported that a rider in the top three at Paris-Brussels the previous month had returned a positive test.

Kelly had finished 3rd at Paris-Brussels, and Walsh had been there. He had travelled to the start in Senlis that morning in the company of Kimmage, who was a guest on Rue Kléber for the final weeks of his spell with ACBB. Naturally, they made a beeline for Kelly as the peloton gathered in twos and threes on the start line. 'Typical Kelly, he hasn't checked his tyres, so he's bouncing on his tyres to check if there's any give,' Kimmage recalls. 'As he's bouncing, I hear this rattling. Now I'm looking at David and he's looking at me. *Did you fucking hear that?* We spoke about it that night. That was an awakening for me. I'd have never associated fucking pills with racing. There was no reason in the world to bring a pill with you. You brought rice cakes or Mars bars or cakes. That was an eye-opener, but again, you kind of thought, was it something else?'

On reaching Milan, Walsh made straight for the Tour of Lombardy race headquarters at the Castello Sforzesco, and waited outside until Kelly pulled up in a Skil team car. Kelly quietly confirmed to Walsh, the British reporter John Wilcockson and a pair of Italian journalists that he was, indeed, the rider in question, and had tested positive for the amphetamine-based product Stimul. Later that evening, Walsh visited his room at the Hotel Leonardo Da Vinci and they discussed the case for half an hour while Kelly polished his Puma cycling shoes. 'I remember him kind of denying it, saying he was innocent and that he was going to fight it all the way,' Walsh says. 'He would have been matter-of-fact but friendly. I suppose he would have regarded me as having some importance in terms of his reception back home.'

Walsh ought to have been in something of a bind. As well as the rattling pills before the start, he had also been struck by Kelly's wide eyes and drawn pallor at the finish of Paris-Brussels. 'It wasn't just that his pupils were dilated, it's that his face was white, a really strange white,' Walsh says. 'I don't know why that would happen but he just didn't look right. I wouldn't say he looked sick but he just didn't look right.'

There was, however, no mention of either incident in the near-identical stories Walsh filed for the *Irish Press* and *Cork Examiner* on the eve of the Tour of Lombardy. His bat, ostensibly straight, was clearly tilted in Kelly's favour. As well as dutifully recording the aspersions Kelly cast upon the testing procedure – '"Either something was put in my bottle before the race or the jar which should have contained my urine contained somebody else's,' he said' – Walsh was sympathetic in his analysis. 'The facts of the case are far from clear-cut.

Primarily, it must be stated that Kelly swears he did not take any illegal product,' Walsh wrote, adding that Kelly had returned more than 20 negative tests in 1984. 'If there was a prohibited substance in Kelly's system,' he continued, 'it certainly was not evident from his performance.'

Kelly, hindered by a crash, rode a low-key Tour of Lombardy, but finished his season the following day with victory in the Criterium des As, to bring his final tally of wins to 33. In later years, Walsh felt embarrassed by his tame coverage of Kelly's positive test. 'I would have loved the guy, really, so when it came to the whole doping thing, I would have listened to his explanations and believed it pretty unquestioningly,' he says. Yet by the standards of an era when team doctors publicly advocating doping scarcely merited a raised eyebrow, Walsh went further than most in at least drawing attention to the positive test. When his biography of Kelly was published in 1986, he even devoted an entire chapter to the Paris-Brussels affair, under the heading 'A Sting in the Tale', though, as in his reporting at the time, it offers a rather partial view. There is still no mention of the rattling pills or dilated pupils, and instead Walsh makes further, woolly arguments to support Kelly's innocence: 'He had enjoyed a superb season and certainly didn't need to win that race.'

After Walsh returned to Ireland, Kelly was stripped of 3rd place in the 1984 Paris-Brussels, handed a fine of 1,000 Swiss francs and given a one-month ban, albeit suspended for two years. Although Kelly appealed with the support of the ICF, the punishment was formally upheld the following year. By then, the Stimul affair had seemingly been forgotten.

10

Summit Meeting

Conjure up a scene from cycling's golden age of the 1950s and 1960s, and Raphaël Géminiani will inevitably be somewhere within that sepia-tinted picture. In an era when fact and fiction readily overlapped, Géminiani always seemed to be part of the story, or better still, telling it, true or exaggerated. He was there when Ferdi Kübler rode himself to a standstill on Mont Ventoux in 1955, calling out a warning as the Swiss bounded past. He was there when Fausto Coppi contracted the malaria that killed him on a hunting trip in Upper Volta (now Burkina Faso) in 1959, and was even stricken by the same illness. He was there when Jacques Anquetil risked losing the 1964 Tour de France on the descent of the Port de l'Envalira after a fortune teller predicted he would die during the stage. Géminiani, by then a directeur sportif, curtly told him that if he was going to die anyway, he might as well do it at the front of the race.

As a rider, Géminiani was good enough to finish 2nd at the 1951 Tour, behind the era's matinee idol, Hugo Koblet, and blessed with a personality forceful enough to earn him the nickname of *Le Grand Fusil* – literally, 'The Big Gun'. In 1955, while still a rider, he negotiated a deal with cycling's first team sponsor from outside of the bicycle industry; appropriately, Saint-Raphaël aperitifs. In retirement, though his waistline expanded and his features softened, his irascible character retained its sharp edges. He was directeur sportif for three of Anquetil's Tour victories in the early 1960s, regularly holding court for journalists in his booming voice, always insistent on having the last word.

Ahead of the 1985 season, when the then 60-year-old Géminiani was unveiled as La Redoute's new manager, the team leader, Stephen Roche, was less than impressed. Géminiani's glory days behind the wheel with Anquetil were long in the past, and nowadays he gained more notice for trenchant opinion – 'Anti-doping is a cancer on the sport,' he said in 1977 – than for directorial achievement. On the other hand, Roche had not exactly been enamoured by the management team in place during his first year at La Redoute, in 1984. 'It was different to Peugeot. It was a smaller set-up and I had more responsibility, but they were having problems with the management side of it,' Roche says.

Bernard Thévenet had the credentials, and bore the reputation, then as now, as a gentleman, but therein, at least to Roche's mind, lay the problem: 'A nice guy, but he wasn't a manager.' To compound matters, Roche's old Peugeot boss De Muer was hired as technical adviser, but soon inserted himself into the direction of affairs on the road, with his wife Jacqueline regularly undermining Thévenet to the riders. One early problem identified by De Muer, incidentally, was La Redoute's curious decision to hand a professional contract to a rider who had only been a second-category amateur the previous season: Thierry Arnaud, Roche's brother-in-law. 'I was never consulted on this matter, Roche spoke about it with the management,' De Muer told *Vélo Magazine* in March. 'In two or three months, he'll realise he's made an error and stop.' Arnaud's professional career was limited to one season.

Despite the power struggle, Roche was consistent in the early part of the season – after losing out to Kelly at Paris-Nice, he won a second successive Tour de Romandie – but his Tour de France was a disaster. Hampered by a crash at the end of the opening week, he did little more than tread water thereafter, placing 25th in Paris. Within days of reaching the Champs-Élysées, La Redoute fired both Thévenet and De Muer, and Géminiani was installed.

Roche's relationship with this big beast of French cycling followed a familiar trend. As with Wiegant and De Muer, their first encounters were guarded, if not frosty, but once the ice was broken during a full and frank exchange of views one night at the Tour of the Mediterranean, a marriage of convenience thawed into complicity. 'He was old school, in that it was all hard work and dedication, but he was also a dreamer,' Roche says. 'He always had a vision and I was always a guy with dreams, so we got on very well together.' He also quickly discovered that Géminiani's tendency to hark back to the days of Coppi and Anquetil was something of a façade. Despite an image as yesterday's man, *Le Grand Fusil* had a keen eye for innovation. 'He was hard and he had to be managed,' Roche says. 'But at the same time, he was very modern for his age.' Indeed, he repeatedly begged Roche for the loan of his Walkman.

Patrick Valcke followed Roche from Peugeot, and enjoyed Géminiani's approach. 'You might think someone of his generation would follow the old methods, but it was completely the opposite. With Géminiani, I remember we were the first in the world to use disc wheels,' Valcke says. This isn't strictly true – Francesco Moser, for one, had used disc wheels on the track and the road in 1984 – but the DiscJet lenticular wheel, developed by TGV manufacturer Alstom Atlantic, marked another stride forward in the technology. A carbon fibre disc, though heavier than a traditional, metal-spoked wheel, offered sizeable aerodynamic benefits. The DiscJet was reportedly offered first to Bernard Hinault's La Vie Claire team and Laurent Fignon's Renault outfit, but both passed on the opportunity.

Unlike their respective managers, Paul Koechli and Cyrille Guimard, Géminiani had no misgivings, or perhaps he simply felt a greater sense of urgency. With La Redoute's sponsorship guaranteed only to the end of the season, Roche and Géminiani wanted to win early and often to secure their futures. Roche placed 3rd at the Tour of the Mediterranean, and, though he won the Col d'Èze time trial, had to settle for 2nd at Paris-Nice as Kelly claimed a fourth consecutive victory. Come the end of March and the Critérium International, La Redoute needed a win or, at the very least, media attention. The DiscJet guaranteed the latter before a pedal had even been turned.

'At the Criterium International in Antibes, we used the DiscJet for the very first time,' says Valcke. 'It was a big motivation to be the first people to work with these wheels, though it made for a lot of extra work too. But for a mechanic, working with Géminiani was the top, because he was interested in every detail. He had his own ideas too. For time trials, we used to inflate the tyres with helium, because helium was lighter than air. There were always things like that with Géminiani.'

Roche, never happier than when in the spotlight, was perhaps the perfect test pilot for the new technology, and he duly rose to the occasion, winning the final time trial of the Critérium International, beating Fignon by four seconds and putting nearly half a minute into Kelly in the space of just 13 kilometres, to claim overall victory. The following morning's newspapers focused, inevitably, on Roche's curious rear wheel and Géminiani's apparent masterstroke. 'Guimard and Koechli think they're the best and I'm past it,' he said sarcastically.

Yet for all his faith in the logic behind pioneering technological accoutrements, Géminiani was also an inherently superstitious man. As Roche prepared to retire for the night after winning Critérium International, Géminiani rapped abruptly on his door: 'Roche, get ready, we're going out for a drink.' They wound up in a rather glum establishment in Cannes. 'We're sitting in this empty nightclub and this Chinese girl was there,' Roche says. 'Gem called her over and said, "The other night, I came here and she had a mouse. You pull the tail of the mouse and if the mouse squeaks, then whatever you're thinking of at that moment will happen. And I said if that was true, then on Sunday night, I'd bring in the winner of Critérium International." Gem was a man of his word, you see.'

Nothing ever seemed to be any hassle for Martin Earley. After avoiding any undue melodrama as an amateur in France, he continued in the same unfussy vein when he joined the professional peloton in 1985. He trained diligently all winter in Dublin without any specific expectations or trepidation. 'I had no idea about the pro ranks, I just knew that guys who had turned pro before me were there and doing reasonably OK,' Earley says. 'I just took it as it was. I had a two-year contract and I said I'd give it everything and that's it.'

Though Spanish-sponsored, Fagor was a predominantly French team, and Earley continued to use Fontainebleau as his Continental base. He doesn't recall any difficulties in fitting in on a team that included Jean-René Bernaudeau, and Kelly's old teammates Patrick Clerc and Marcel Tinazzi. 'I was pretty fluent in French, and there were no little groups on the team anyway,' he says. On the road, there were few teething troubles, and Earley picked up some early results, including 2nd place on a stage of the Volta Valenciana. 'I knew they weren't miles ahead of me from the training camp, and then I got good results down in Valencia, so I felt I was up to it,' Earley says.

Earley was unperturbed, too, by the demands of his directeur sportif, the 1973 Tour winner Luis Ocaña. Even by the levels of combustibility seemingly de rigueur for a team manager in the 1980s, Ocaña was a special case: during that year's Vuelta, he became so riled that he tried to crash into the car of Reynolds directeur sportif José Miguel Echavarri. 'It didn't take much to set him off. It was just the way he was. He was just a fiery character,' Earley says, matter-of-factly. 'He'd lose it over anything. It wasn't always logical, though maybe it was logical to him.' Earley, like just about everyone else, felt Ocaña's ire on occasion in the spring of 1985, but he did enough to earn selection for the Tour in his debut season, meaning that, for the first time, there would be three Irishmen seated at cycling's grandest moveable feast.

Kelly was ever more firmly enshrined as world number one come the *Grand Départ* in Plumelec, but his season to that point had been a frustrating one. Although he had taken the by now obligatory Paris-Nice victory and a second Tour of the Basque Country, and marked his return to the Vuelta by winning three stages, the spring classics campaign had been wholly exasperating. A 3rd-place finish at Paris-Roubaix and 4th at Liège-Bastogne-Liège indicated that Kelly's form was not far off that of 1984, but some of his tactical decisions went awry, most notably at Milan-San Remo, where he and Eric Vanderaerden effectively marked one another out of contention.

To Kelly's annoyance, Vanderaerden then went on to solo to a stirring victory at a rain-soaked Tour of Flanders and added Gent-Wevelgem three days later, prompting observers, at least in Belgium, to wonder whether the mantle of king of the classics had already passed to the man-child from Limburg with the frizzy blonde perm poking out from beneath his leather helmet. Unusually for a rider who won so often, Kelly ruffled few feathers and made precious few enemies over the course of his career, but Vanderaerden was a notable exception. Officially, their mutual antipathy had its genesis in a clash during a sprint at Paris-Nice during Vanderaerden's first professional season in 1983, but in truth, Kelly and an elite cadre of Belgian riders had viewed the youngster with patrician disdain before he ever entered the professional peloton.

'The root was of it was that Vanderaerden was untouchable as a junior and as an amateur in Belgium. He was the best thing since sliced pan coming out of Belgium. When he was coming to the professionals, I remember some of the older guys said to me, "We can't leave him win all the races. We're going to make it difficult for him,'" Kelly says, continuing:

> When I was coming up, there was De Vlaeminck, Moser, Jan Raas and a few more guys, and it was hard to break into that group. It's an elite club and when you're there on that doorstep, they don't make it easy for you. So now we weren't going to make it easy for Vanderaerden. I remember his first races in the south of France, they were trying to make it difficult for him on all the climbs because they knew he wasn't so good there. From the start, I think I had all that in my head from the older Belgian guys, and then it continued because he was a good sprinter. He got established quite quickly in the sprints. The fighting started there and then it spread over into the classics.

In Vanderaerden's early days, Kelly used to deploy Jock Boyer as a sweeper to prevent the Belgian from latching onto his rear wheel in sprints. Their blood feud reached its nadir in the bunch sprint on stage 6 of the 1985 Tour in Rheims. Kelly was glued to Vanderaerden's rear wheel as the peloton trundled towards the finish, but when he tried to come past, his rival veered to block his path. Kelly's response was to raise an arm to push Vanderaerden, and the Belgian responded by grabbing at his jersey. Somehow, both men stayed upright, and Vanderaerden even won the stage, while Kelly crossed the line in 4th, his hand waving in protest. Cycling's governance may have been lax in other areas in the 1980s, but then as now, the race jury took a dim view of bike-borne mixed martial arts. Vanderaerden and Kelly were swiftly relegated to the last places on the stage and the win was awarded to Frenchman Francis Castaing. Within 24 hours, Kelly's initial anger dissipated into a typically pragmatic view. 'Our contracts are based on the publicity we get,' he said. 'A finish like that and a disqualification generate more publicity than winning a race.'

Vanderaerden had spent a chunk of the opening week in the green jersey and, perhaps unsurprisingly, that seemed to coincide with Kelly's renewed interest in the competition. By the time the race reached the mountains, he had wrested the garment from Vanderaerden's back, but chasing points on a daily basis was hardly conducive to mounting a concerted overall challenge, and he proceeded to cough up more than three minutes on the road to Avoriaz, losing all hopes of Tour victory. Under normal circumstances, that might have precipitated a steady drop down the rankings, but when Kelly looked at the results sheet over dinner that evening, he was still 4th overall, and though he was now six minutes off Hinault's yellow jersey, he was only nine seconds off a podium place.

Although the rider in 3rd place was one S. Roche (Irl), Kelly dismisses the idea that his fine showing in the mountains that followed during that 1985 Tour owed anything at all to an internecine rivalry with his fellow countryman. 'I don't think it really pushed us that we were two Irish guys. It was that we were in that category where we would be finishing 3rd or 4th,' Kelly says. 'We were at that level.' Kelly won the sprint for 3rd behind Colombian duo Fabio Parra and Luis Herrera on the following day's mountainous leg to Lans-en-Vercors, and then produced one of the best climbing displays of his career on the demanding stage to Luz-Ardiden in the Pyrenees. In the intervening period, Roche gained time on the rugged stage to Saint-Étienne, and although the race for final overall victory remained resolutely an internal squabble between Hinault and his La Vie Claire teammate LeMond, the increasing likelihood of an Irishman standing on the third step of the podium in Paris saw Tour coverage gradually expand across all of Ireland's main newspapers as the race entered the third week.

'I think there was maybe a bit of undiscussed competition there. Not on my behalf because I was in front anyway, but I think it did spur Sean on. I think I can say that,' Roche says. 'It was like, "If this Dublin guy can do it, then so can I." And it spurred me on as well, he wasn't the only one benefiting. It helped both of us.'

The high point came on the final day in the Pyrenees, which saw the peloton tackle a split stage, with a short 52-kilometre leg to the top of the Col d'Aubisque in the morning. Since the unveiling of the Tour route the previous winter, Géminiani had repeatedly told Roche that he was going to win this novel stage, and, as the Dubliner had discovered in the lounge of Cannes' least glamorous nightspot, the Big Gun was not for turning. He had commissioned a special one-piece skinsuit to be made for Roche just for this the stage, as if to emphasise that this was not so much a mountain stage as a time trial. 'It was something he got made up himself, with a silk top and lycra bottoms. I didn't even want to go to the start with it on, so I put a jersey over it,' says Roche, for once eager to keep a low profile. 'I threw the jersey off near the bottom of the climb, but I couldn't be seen on the start line in this sort of one-piece skinsuit.'

Roche tracked Herrera's move on the initial ramps of the Col du Soulor and then pressed on alone before the short drop onto the Aubisque itself. The previous day, Roche had showcased his form by attacking on the Col du Tourmalet with LeMond, but the move lost momentum when the American was ordered to relent rather than put Hinault's yellow jersey in jeopardy. Now, unencumbered by company or the intramural strife of other teams, Roche had the freedom of the mountainside as he tapped out his own, metronomic rhythm. He was helped, too, by the politics of the group behind. Hinault, stricken by bronchitis, was struggling to hold the wheels and LeMond, now consigned to the role of dutiful teammate, tempered his pace accordingly and Roche's advantage stretched out beyond 50 seconds. Stage victory was guaranteed.

All the while, Kelly maintained a watching brief in the *groupe maillot jaune*, and, like Roche, he was enjoying one of his best days in the high mountains and white heat of July. When the chasers splintered in the final two kilometres and Hinault was dislodged, Kelly felt sufficiently emboldened as to make a rare mountaintop acceleration of his own. Barely a minute after Roche had rolled across the line with his arms aloft, Kelly lifted himself from the saddle to sprint home and complete an Irish one-two. 'If I hadn't gone away on the Aubisque, I don't think Sean would have taken off behind me and left Hinault behind,' Roche says. 'If I hadn't gone when I did, Sean would have waited for the sprint. Sean was gaining time here and there, and he wasn't chasing me, but I do think it spurred him on and motivated him a bit.'

Four days later, Roche and Kelly rolled onto the Champs-Élysées in 3rd and 4th overall, respectively, while Earley survived his maiden Tour, relieved simply to reach Paris alongside them. 'The Tour was a big jump, and at the end of the it, you're just dead,' he says. Kelly endured the frustration of another 2nd-place finish beneath the Arc de Triomphe – his fifth of the race – but such consistency saw him capture a record-equalling third green jersey. More important, he had also finished the Tour little more than six minutes off yellow, by some distance his most competitive outing.

At 29 years of age, Kelly still had margin for improvement, and there were other encouraging signs. Over at La Vie Claire, a clearly diminished Hinault was slouching towards retirement, while LeMond's failure to impose himself within his own team hardly suggested that the American, for all his gifts, was an unbeatable foe. Roche, four years Kelly's junior and buoyed by his first clear run at the Tour, reached Paris with a similarly buoyant outlook. 'I never thought of winning that Tour, really. The podium was the aim,' Roche says. 'But it helped seal my ambition that I could win it later.'

11

A Sort of Homecoming

In the run-up to Christmas 1983, at a reception in Dublin to mark the publication of the *Irish Cycling Review*'s end of year edition, Rás organiser Dermot Dignam was making small talk with Sean Kelly when the tenor of the conversation suddenly amplified. 'Why don't you get the Rás pro-am status?' Kelly asked. He didn't tend to deal in throwaway comments. He beckoned Stephen Roche over, and suggested they each bring their teams with them, while a couple of British professional outfits could also be invited, with one caveat: the race would have to be brought forward from late June to early May to avoid a clash with the Tour de France. 'The only people you would have to pay for would be Stephen and me,' Kelly added. Always be closing. David Walsh was listening in on the exchange, and the story ran on the back page of the *Irish Press* the following morning.

The Tripartite Committee may have been in situ since 1979, but the old federations still carefully policed their respective boundaries within its aegis. On learning that Kelly and Roche, both of ICF stock, might race the NCA's flagship event, the ICF-affiliated Tour of Ireland, which was already registered as a pro-am event with a May slot on the calendar, made its own pitch to the professionals. Roche was initially receptive, but when Frank Quinn rejected the offer on Kelly's behalf, he too opted out. 'It would be too risky before the Tour de France, that's where I'll make the money,' Roche said.

Kelly did, however, make a guest appearance at the prologue of the 1984 Rás. Though the race remained resolutely amateur and stuck to its June slot, Kelly flew to Dublin the morning after completing the Tour of Switzerland and, following the presentation of a silver coffee pot by Lord Mayor Michael Keating at Mansion House, he made it to the Eamonn Ceannt track in Crumlin in time to be the last man to tackle the one-kilometre time trial. Before a crowd of 500, Kelly clocked a mark of 1:15, a full second ahead of the quickest Man of the Rás, Dermot Gilleran. Immediately afterwards, Kelly and Rose of Tralee winner Brenda Hyland led the 123 competitors on a parade to the GPO for the official start of the Rás, before he returned to Vilvoorde to resume preparations for the following week's Tour de France.

Even before Kelly floated the idea of Rás participation, Pat McQuaid had already been working separately on creating a platform for Ireland's professional riders to compete on home roads. Although he was a full-time teacher and coach of the Olympic team, McQuaid, it seemed, could never have enough on his plate, and in 1983, his curiosity was stoked by a series of professional criteriums taking place in Britain, sponsored by Kellogg's and televised by Channel 4. The organiser was Alan

Rushton, who had been the public relations officer at Viking when McQuaid had raced for the British professional team in the late 1970s. 'I watched those criteriums and I thought to myself, "Jesus, one of them would go down well in Ireland,"' says McQuaid, who promptly rang his old contact and proposed a collaboration. Rushton was receptive, and in the winter of 1983–84, they worked together to convince Kellogg's, Dublin Corporation and RTÉ of the merits of a city centre race featuring Kelly and Roche the following summer.

On the evening of Tuesday 14 August, barely two weeks after McQuaid returned from the Los Angeles Olympics, the inaugural Kellogg's Cycling Grand Prix of Ireland took place over 30 laps of a mile-long circuit. The course was designed by McQuaid and based around Dublin Castle, though it underwent some revisions when Kelly voiced concerns following a walking reconnaissance during his flying visit for the Rás in June. Eddy Merckx was on hand to serve as the official starter and Roche, as per the custom of such events, sent the multitudes home happy by soloing to victory on Lord Edward Street, while Kelly completed the choreography by winning the sprint for 2nd place ahead of British professionals Phil Thomas and Malcolm Elliott. That same night, McQuaid added the role of television commentator to his ever-expanding list of services, performing the duties alongside Phil Liggett, and the event was enthusiastically received, with Kelly and Roche mobbed as they made their way through the finish area.

'It was a wild night altogether,' McQuaid says. RTÉ and Kellogg's quickly signalled their eagerness to add a criterium in Cork in 1985, and buoyed by that response, McQuaid decided to pitch an additional, more ambitious idea – a five-day professional stage race. 'Alan's initial intention was to organise a stage race in the UK, but it was obvious after the reaction in Dublin that Ireland was ready for it,' McQuaid says. 'The Irish public knew the Vanderaerdens and all these guys. They were ready.'

►⊙◄

Organising a professional Tour of Ireland required several overlapping elements to be underpinned by the most crucial component of all: money. To attract sponsorship, McQuaid and Rushton realised that they first needed to guarantee a minimum of publicity, and so RTÉ were involved off the bat. McQuaid's first port of call was Michael O'Carroll, who had filmed Roche's Rás win in 1979, and the idea was quickly kicked upstairs to the national broadcaster's head of sport, Tim O'Connor. 'Eventually they agreed to do it,' McQuaid says. 'If we could provide the race, the logistics, the cost of all the race, they would provide the TV.'

All through the winter, the would-be organisers canvassed potential sponsors, and, despite the gloomy economic climate, Rushton succeeded in negotiating a deal that saw the Irish arm of Nissan Motors come on board as title sponsor for the new race. McQuaid, meanwhile, had successfully lobbied the UCI for a late-season slot on the calendar, despite the concerns raised by the Étoile des Espoirs, a French pro-am event organised by the Leulliot family, who also ran Paris-Nice. 'Everything was controlled by the French, so an outsider coming in, be it from Ireland, England or outside mainland Europe, was regarded in not very friendly terms and didn't get any advantages or anything like that,' McQuaid says. His powers of persuasion seem to have sufficed.

In February 1985, McQuaid and Rushton, by now operating under the banner of Sportsplus, announced that the first Nissan International Classic would take place from 25 to 29 September of that year, with Kelly and Roche set to be the headline acts. There was, however, an element of smoke and mirrors to that announcement. The precise route, contingent on the support of local authorities nationwide, had yet to be confirmed. The budget, reported as being between £175,000 and £200,000, was in fact somewhat lower. 'It was about £110,000, of which 85 or 90,000 was from the main sponsor; the rest was from subsidiary sponsors,' McQuaid says. Most importantly, neither Kelly nor Roche had yet agreed an appearance fee.

If McQuaid thought personal relationships and goodwill alone would bring the Irish professionals home for the Nissan Classic, he was quickly disabused of the notion when Kelly sent Frank Quinn to negotiate on his behalf. A native of Enniscorthy in County Wexford, Quinn's sporting love was rugby, but behind his affable demeanour was the sharp bargaining acumen developed over the years in his day job as a magazine publisher. He would later represent Earley and Kimmage, and also work for a time with Roche, but in early 1985, Kelly was his sole cycling client. 'It was all hardball stuff. Don't underestimate it,' Quinn says of the Nissan talks. 'We said we realised there'd been a lot of effort been put into promoting the race, from Pat McQuaid and Alan Rushton, but at the same time, the main reason for having it was Kelly and Roche, so they really had to say, "This is the price," and then try to stick to it.'

Quinn had a kindred spirit in Kelly, who kept himself abreast of the state of the negotiations. 'The one thing I remember Frank saying to me was: "McQuaid is so difficult to get money out of,"' Kelly says. 'And I know from my own experience … It was like trying to get blood from a turnip. You could deal easier with Alan Rushton. Sometimes, later on, I'd speak with Alan Rushton, and to get the contract out with him was easier than with McQuaid.'

The impasse continued into the spring, even after McQuaid, now on a six-month leave of absence from his teaching job in Ballinteer, had begun to visit races on the Continent as part of his campaign to lure professional teams to the nascent event. While Kelly and Roche understood that the Nissan Classic would not be a success without them, McQuaid was sure that they couldn't afford simply to sit out Ireland's first professional stage race. Their teams had agreed in principle to participate, after all, and they were already seeking temporary Irish sub-sponsors to defray their costs.

'Well, McQuaid *knew* that we wanted to ride the Nissan, and he also knew that I had the agreement from my team that I'd get a second sponsor,' Kelly says. 'He knew I was on the bingo machine and he didn't want to give the money. He knew we wanted to ride the race and had other sponsors coming on for that, and he was just really tight with the money. When you'd do a deal with him, a deal was a deal, and that was it.'

Although much of Roche's negotiations were being carried out on his behalf by Peter Crinnion, he liaised with Kelly throughout the process, feeling that when it came to commanding a fee, it was wise to form a cartel. 'Myself and Sean were the principal actors that Pat wanted to showcase on

Irish roads, and in turn get a good paycheque from it,' Roche says. 'Sean and I were a bit upset about that, because they were using us to line their pockets and we felt we didn't get a good deal. We felt if we hadn't been doing what we were doing on the Continent, Nissan wouldn't have been getting involved in this Nissan Classic, so there was always a bit of friction there between the organisers and us. We weren't getting our share of the cake.'

All the while, McQuaid was playing the role of travelling salesman, circling the country to cajole councils and corporations into closing their roads and hosting the race. He quickly discovered that no hard sell was needed: the names of Kelly and Roche carried enough prestige to do that by themselves. No town, it seemed, wanted to miss out. 'They did everything we wanted,' McQuaid says, and by the time the route was formally presented in May 1985, there was white smoke in the negotiations with Kelly and Roche.

'Kelly was and is very slow to make decisions but when he makes the decision, it's 100 per cent,' Quinn says. 'Once we gave a commitment, right or wrong, we fixed a price and Kelly stuck with that. That would probably be the country upbringing – he wouldn't want to offend anybody – and he'd also want to get the best price. He's famous for being mean and tough and getting paid for everything, more or less. That's his criteria for everything else.'

Regardless of the fee, Kelly was hardly going to pass up on a stage finish in Carrick-on-Suir, but it was perhaps telling that he did not appear in the Kellogg's races in Cork and Dublin that August, preferring instead to race in criteriums on the Continent. He did, however, make a point of coming to ride a GOAL charity event in Dublin – a three-cornered pursuit against Roche and Martin Earley in Belfield – later that same week. 'It doesn't suit me to come to Ireland at this time, but I am pleased to be able to help the people of Africa in this way,' Kelly explained.

Kelly's charity clearly did not extend to Irish race organisers whose ambitions were deeper than their pockets, but McQuaid's disappointment was tempered by the knowledge that he had his man secured for the main event in September. And if Kelly was riding the Nissan Classic, then Roche would have to come too. 'Myself and Sean had agreed, 'You don't sign until I sign, we'll sign together,' but then all of a sudden Sean signed, he left me out there,' Roche says. 'I couldn't not do it, but I had no negotiating power now because Sean had already signed.'

Contemporary reports speculated that Kelly was commanding close to £3,000 per day to ride the Nissan Classic, though the true figure was perhaps lower, given that in 1987, Roche would complain publicly that he had only received £10,000 for the entire race despite being the world champion. 'They were small appearance fees because we didn't have a big budget,' McQuaid says, and, in time, Roche would come to accept as much. Indeed, though the budget for the first Nissan Classic was £110,000, the costs ultimately inflated to £150,000, with McQuaid and Rushton making up part of the shortfall themselves.

'We imagined Pat and Rushton were getting millions, but it was only later when I worked in management that I realised how the costs can add up, so maybe they weren't getting that much money out of it,' Roche says. 'At the time, we felt like we should have got more of the spoils and you're vocal about it then, but then later you realise the lads had their expenses too. Alan Rushton had to mortgage his house to pay his debts because he overspent. I know a lot of stuff went on there.'

It would hardly have felt like a major Irish international cycling event without some sort of a political falling-out, though for once, it was not the cycling fraternity who were at loggerheads. When Fine Gael Taoiseach Garret FitzGerald was invited to flag the inaugural Nissan Classic away from Trinity College on 25 September, Dublin Lord Mayor Liam Tunney of Fianna Fáil responded by refusing to attend and then cancelling the civic reception planned for the Mansion House on the final evening of the race. Nissan stepped in to organise an end-of-race reception of their own, while the morning after the race started, the front page of the *Irish Press* showed a photograph of FitzGerald standing alongside a smiling Kelly.

Irish cycling, on the other hand, seemed to be navigating relatively tranquil political waters in 1985. The original Tour of Ireland was quietly superseded by the Nissan Classic, while in June, the Rás had managed to persuade Kelly and Roche to come and compete against one another in an exhibition pursuit match before the race proper began, with the Dubliner winning out. Kelly and Roche's exploits in that summer's Tour had boosted their profile still further at home, and the Nissan Classic offered a window in which to maximise their then slim portfolio of endorsements in Ireland. Aer Lingus came on board as sub-sponsor of Kelly's Skil team for the week, while

John Mangan is arrested for his part in the NCA protest at the 1972 Olympics in Munich. The NCA–ICF split defined Irish cycling in the decades before Kelly's emergence. (*Irish Times*)

While back home Irish cycling seemed unable to awake from the dreary, repeated nightmare of Civil War politics, Shay Elliott operated in a different realm on the continent in the 1960s. (John Pierce)

Sean Kelly toasts victory in Sheffield at the 1975 Milk Race in the expected manner. He would be less enthusiastic about attending the official banquet that evening. (John Pierce)

Kelly grinds towards l'Alpe d'Huez on the 1978 Tour de France. His Flandria leader Michel Pollentier will be expelled from the race at the summit for cheating an anti-doping control. (John Pierce)

Pat McQuaid poses with the spoils of his amateur career. He was a cycling blueblood and a supremely confident young man. 'We were a successful family,' McQuaid says. 'We were brought up to be winners.' (John Pierce)

Stephen Roche was not short on motivation during his season at ACBB in 1980: 'I wouldn't give the Irish cycling community the pleasure of seeing me come home with an empty bag.' (Ray McManus/SPORTSFILE)

Kelly could rely on two father figures on the continent. Herman Nys and Jean de Gribaldy await the start of Paris-Roubaix in 1984. (John Pierce)

'Look, a little kid won the race!' Stephen Roche was only 21 years old when he won Paris-Nice in 1981. (Offside/*L'Equipe*)

Congratulations

FOUR FOR THE ROAD RIDE RALEIGH TO SUCCESS!

21 year old Martin Earley of Fingal Road Club.

Paul Kimmage

Gary Thomson

Seamus Downey

Martin Earley rode his Raleigh superbly to take 19th place in the gruelling 180 km Olympic road race in Los Angeles. Backed ably by fellow members of the Raleigh Ireland Team, Paul Kimmage, Gary Thomson and Seamus Downey.

That's the sort of performance you can expect from Raleigh.

Well done lads!

RALEIGH

1984 LOS ANGELES OLYMPICS

Martin Earley and Paul Kimmage were in Pat McQuaid's Olympic squad in 1984. Earley signed a professional contract before the Games. Kimmage would have to wait another year before joining him.

David Walsh, Con Houlihan said, was the man who invented Sean Kelly. Here, he quizzes Kelly on losing the green jersey on the final day of the 1984 Tour as Herman Nys looks on. (John Pierce)

Roche and Kelly pose in the white and yellow jerseys at the 1983 Tour in Pau. (Offside/*L'Equipe*)

Roche and Kelly hamming it up at the first Nissan Classic. Each drove the other to greater heights in the mid-1980s. (John Pierce)

Tensions between Roche and Roberto Visentini simmered at the 1986 Trofeo Baracchi before boiling over at the next year's Giro d'Italia. 'He's always talked bollocks,' Visentini says. 'He's not reliable.' (Fotoreporter Sirotti)

Over a decade, Patrick Valcke served as Roche's mechanic, confidant, bodyguard, rallying co-driver and directeur sportif before the relationship ended in acrimony. (Getty Images/Stringer)

Martin Earley is the first rider to congratulate Roche at the end of the 1987 Tour de France. Pat McQuaid (right) prepares to grab the first interview for RTÉ. (John Pierce)

Kelly tugs at the jersey he coveted above all others at the 1987 Nissan Classic. A month after Villach, the event was the high point of his and Roche's popularity at home. (John Pierce)

Paul Kimmage was already more journalist than professional bike rider come the 1989 Tour de France. An interview with *L'Équipe* in the first week strengthened his resolve to write *A Rough Ride*. (Offside/*L'Equipe*)

Kelly crashes out of the 1987 Tour: 'When you see Roche winning it, I suppose you say to yourself, "Shit, if he can win it, I should be able to win it."' (Offside/*L'Equipe*)

Fagor was a fiasco of a team and Roche's form was scarcely better. (Offside/*L'Equipe*)

Roche, pictured here at the Rally of the Lakes in Killarney in 1989, turned increasingly to extra-curricular activities during his time at Fagor. (INPHO)

An ill Martin Earley leaves the 1991 Tour with his entire PDM team in the wake of the Intralipid Affair. 'Acute PDM-itis', read one sceptical headline. (INPHO/ Billy Stickland)

Martin Earley, Stephen Roche, Sean Kelly and Laurence Roche on the final day of the 1991 Nissan Classic. Kelly sealed a fourth and final overall victory in Dublin. (John Pierce)

Burning the days. Roche watches yellow jersey Miguel Indurain on television during his final Tour in 1993. (INPHO/Billy Stickland)

Sean Kelly and Pat McQuaid at the 2013 Irish Championships, two weeks after an Irish Cycling EGM voted against nominating McQuaid for re-election as UCI president. (INPHO/Ciarán Fallon)

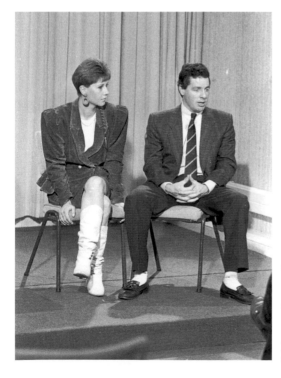

'Don't fight for the seats, lads.' Stephen and Lydia Roche announce the launch of Stephen Roche Promotions at Dublin Airport in 1988. (Getty Images/ Independent News and Media)

Kelly, the new world number one, rides towards victory at the 1984 Paris-Roubaix, mindful that greatness was measured in classics wins, not computer print-outs. (John Pierce)

Kelly, David Walsh says, 'was the kind of person that a lot of Irish people wanted to think represented your typical Irishman.' In 1990, Volkswagen built an advertising campaign around that image.

Roche, Earley and Kelly line out in a three-cornered pursuit as part of a GOAL
charity event in Belfield, August 1985. (Ray McManus/Sportsfile)

NISSAN CONGRATULATES
SEAN KELLY & STEPHEN ROCHE

ON THEIR HISTORIC ACHIEVEMENTS IN THE
1985 TOUR DE FRANCE

and look forward to welcoming them to the
Nissan International Classic,
September 25-29, 1985.
Dublin, Wexford, Carrick-on-Suir,
Clonmel, Cork, Limerick, Galway,
Tullamore, Dublin.

Nissan International Classic

Nissan (Ireland) Limited, Nissan House, Naas Road, Dublin 12. Telephone (01) 504877. Telex 30813.

NISSAN

Kelly and Roche took some time to agree an appearance fee for the inaugural Nissan Classic. Negotiating with McQuaid, Kelly says, 'was like trying to get blood from a turnip.'

Kelly as Jean de Gribaldy found him, aboard his brother Martin's tractor in Carrick-on-Suir. (John Pierce)

Roche and his La Redoute teammates Regis Simon and Paul Sherwen lined out in the grey and red of Eveready batteries for the occasion, given that their team was disbanding at the end of the season.

There were 76 starters in total for that maiden Nissan Classic, and, in comparison with the years of plenty that would follow in the latter part of the decade, the field was not of considerable depth. It included an Irish amateur selection – minus the injured Paul Kimmage – and a plethora of British professionals, but of the riders from Continental Europe on show, only two Dutchmen, Adrie van der Poel and the veteran Hennie Kuiper, seemed likely to deny the home favourites. It was doubtful, however, that either had the same motivation as Kelly. 'Kelly was determined to win it, really determined to do it. This was his home patch and he went about it in a very serious way,' McQuaid says. 'Roche was different. It depended on the year, and usually towards that time of the year, he had switched off a bit.'

The opening stage to Wexford set the tone not only for that year's event but for Kelly and Roche's respective fortunes in the Nissan Classic for the remainder of its existence. When Van der Poel joined a break as the race went through Tullow, Kelly sensed the danger and bridged across immediately. Roche, on the other hand, was wrongfooted and missed the move. He was more than 10 minutes down by the time he reached Wexford, his challenge already over. Up ahead, Kelly snuffed out Van der Poel's late attack on the finishing circuit, and then sprinted to take the stage and claim the first yellow jersey of the Nissan Classic.

Kelly would wear the garment on the following stage to Carrick-on-Suir, though the preordained script required some furious rewriting to ensure a felicitous end to the day's proceedings. It was one thing for the stage honours to fall to late escapee Teun van Vliet, but quite another for Kelly then to be beaten by Van der Poel in the sprint for 4th place in his home town. When time bonuses were factored in, the result meant that Van der Poel had drawn level on Kelly in the general classification, and they were tied, too, in the points classification. The rules stated that placings on the most recent stage would serve as the tiebreaker in such an event. By that rationale, Van der Poel was the new leader of the Nissan Classic, but after some deliberation, it emerged that the head of the race jury was employing a contorted brand of logic of his own making. Van der Poel, he reasoned, had drawn level with Kelly on the overall standings, but had not surpassed him. The yellow jersey, he ruled, would stay with Kelly. It had the feel of an Irish solution to an Irish problem. Van der Poel voiced no objection. The commissaire who overlooked the fine print of the rulebook, incidentally, was Gerry McDaid, the same man who had failed to spot Kelly and the McQuaids on the second leg of their South African trip all those years before. McDaid knew he was on safe ground as he watched Kelly step onto the rostrum in yellow to accept the acclaim of his home town. The Carrick crowd was hardly going to shout for him to bring them Barabbas instead.

The point was perhaps moot given that Kelly wore his regular Skil skinsuit for the next morning's stage, a 21-kilometre time trial that set out from the square that bore his name and followed the Suir upriver to the finish in Clonmel. In theory,

Roche was the favourite for the stage win. In practice, Kelly was unbeatable. Crouched into his aerodynamic position, teeth clenched in a half-grimace, Kelly seemed oblivious to all but the 50 metres of road in front of him as he turned over a huge gear through the early morning mist that enveloped the valley road.

Van der Poel felt he was on a good day when he caught Van Vliet, who had set out a minute before him, only for Kelly to come thundering past the two of them inside the final two kilometres at a considerable rate of knots. Kelly stopped the clock in 24:09 for an average speed in excess of 53kph. He beat Roche into 2nd place by 49 seconds, while future world pursuit champion and time trial specialist Tony Doyle was a further 25 seconds back. It was a stunning display. 'It was a combination of things: starting last man, being the yellow jersey, the support I had starting out from the square in Carrick and riding on a road I knew so well – all of that pushed me on,' Kelly says.

At the finish line, Roche was incredulous. 'I may have been wearing an Eveready shirt, but I would have needed Eveready batteries,' he told reporters as he stood alongside Kelly. 'Maybe he could have taken four or five seconds out of me, but to beat me by 49 seconds is just hard to believe. I'm still wondering if he knew of some kind of short cut.' 'Only in a speedboat,' Kelly fired back.

John Pierce was photographing Kelly from a following motorbike, and he dismisses any suspicion that the local hero had sheltered in the slipstream of race vehicles. 'Absolutely not: there was one motorbike and me, and I was on the other side of the road, literally, because it was a big wide road,' Pierce says. 'He got no helicopter draft or anything like that. He was just fast, he was like an Exocet. He had his big gear rolling and it was incredible, just incredible.'

The prospect of beating Roche in his own speciality had, Kelly admits now, only added to his motivation as he readied himself for the start that morning. 'Roche would have been one of the big favourites, probably *the* favourite, and I suppose I wanted to beat Roche also. If I tell you anything else, I'd be telling you a bloody lie,' Kelly says with a grin. The Nissan Classic was always at the more competitive end of the spectrum of their friendly rivalry. Roche may have shaded the popularity contest in Dublin – and even that was debatable – but in rural Ireland, Kelly was simply adored. That country–city dichotomy would prove part of the inherent attraction of the Nissan Classic.

'You'd be reminded a lot down the country that if you're not from Dublin, you don't get on teams so easily and you don't get as much recognition. That was the case in the club in Carrick and I'm sure all around Munster,' Kelly says. 'That probably filtered down to me and Roche, and especially when it was the Nissan, on home ground. And I was really on home soil in that time trial, so I just went out and, well, I bursted myself.'

The afternoon stage saw the peloton ride south to Cork, and witnessed the first instance of what would become a common occurrence at the Nissan Classic over the years, the go-slow. This late in the season, the European professionals had little appetite for racing flat-out over the seemingly interminable distances covered by the event, while the amateurs in the bunch were simply relieved at the prevailing mood of détente. At Molly Barry's Cross outside Fermoy, as the riders ambled along at 25kph, Gerry McDaid felt moved to issue a formal warning for lack of effort.

Shortly afterwards, Pat McQuaid dropped back in the race director's car and sought out Kelly, the de facto *patron* of the peloton. There were, he pointed out, an estimated 30,000 people already lining the streets of Cork and the race was now half an hour down on the slowest predicted schedule. It would be the first of many such conflabs. 'I was always the first guy McQuaid approached. He'd come back in the car, always crying, and he'd come to me, of course,' Kelly says. 'McQuaid would start giving out and saying we had to ride or else we were going to arrive in the dark. So I'd start talking with some of the riders and teams to get things organised and start riding at a decent pace to try to pull back some of the time we lost and the time we were down.'

The peloton compensated for its earlier lassitude by putting on a spectacle amid the hills and spires of Cork city's northside. Four times the peloton tackled the viciously steep slopes of St Patrick's Hill, with Kelly and Roche always placed near the front as they wove their way towards the summit. On the final lap, Roche slipped clear at Dillon's Cross and stayed away to win at the finish atop St Patrick's Hill. In a mirror of the Aubisque, Kelly, in yellow, placed 2nd behind him. 'Patrick's Hill was an amazing feature, although after the first year, the race got too big and we couldn't finish at the top anymore,' McQuaid says.

Roche won again in Limerick the following day, but the race belonged to Kelly and he carried yellow to Dublin, where Van der Poel captured the final stage on O'Connell Street. Although Barry McGuigan's defence of his world featherweight title in Belfast competed for the weekend's sporting headlines, the masses at the roadside and the audience figures for the nightly televised highlights confirmed that Kelly and Roche were no longer an exotic curiosity, but a mainstream phenomenon. Long feted on the Continent, they had now, thanks to the Nissan Classic, finally broken Ireland. 'I knew if we'd bring the best pros here, especially outside of Dublin, to Carrick-on-Suir or Waterford or Galway or Cork, it would be big,' McQuaid says. 'It turned out to be massive.'

Nissan immediately committed to another two years as race sponsor, and McQuaid promptly resigned from Ballinteer Community School. He threw himself full-time into race organisation, supplemented by running a bike shop and occasional moonlighting as a television commentator. That winter, he stood down from the role of national coach, though only under duress, and lamented what he perceived as the insular attitude prevalent in Irish cycling. 'Because of the NCA-style attitude of the Tripartite Committee, I don't want anything more to do with amateur cycling here,' he told the *Irish Times*. Raleigh immediately withdrew its sponsorship of the Irish Olympic project in sympathy with McQuaid.

Although Kelly's victory in the first Nissan Classic fell in the middle of his imperial phase, the bar was now set so high that the overall yield from 1985 felt a disappointment. The experience on home roads boosted morale ahead of the end-of-season classics, however, and Kelly hit his quota by mid-October, winning the Tour of Lombardy in a group sprint on the Vigorelli velodrome in Milan, a triumph that also lifted him ahead of Phil Anderson to win the season-long Super Prestige

Pernod classification for the second year in succession, and cemented his hold on the top spot in the computer rankings.

Once more, Kelly's Tour of Lombardy triumph owed something to the kindness of friends, allies, and even complete strangers. When Kelly woke for his pre-race meal at 5.30am that morning, he found the kitchen of Skil's hotel near Como was under lock and key, but he eventually sat down to a steak breakfast in the home of the 1950s professional Pasquale Fornara. On the long run-in to the finish in Milan, Kelly's old friend Claude Criquielion, a noted non-sprinter, proved a willing accomplice, though the passivity of the on-form Van der Poel, who placed 2nd in the sprint, was somewhat more surprising. An explanation arrived when David Walsh published his biography of Kelly the following year. In exchange for being allowed a free run at his Créteil-Chaville victory the previous week, Van der Poel pledged that his Kwantum team would not ride against Kelly in Lombardy. Such alliances were commonplace in the everyday workings of the professional peloton, though in this rolling hub of horse-trading and entrepreneurship, riders often preferred to deal in cash. Jan Raas once caustically noted that Kelly was 'always beatable because he always has a price', and nobody leapt forward to dispute the characterisation. 'I think Kelly sold quite a few races early on, because at that stage, his career was about making money rather than building a palmarès,' Philippe Bouvet says. 'He later understood that by winning races, he could earn even more money.'

'Sometimes it was money changing hands and other times it would be just favours,' Kelly says. 'In the bigger races, I think it would be just favours. Nobody wants to sell a Tour of Flanders or a Paris-Roubaix – it was smaller races. In bigger classics, it would be a favour. There'd be a guy and you know if you do him the favour in a classic, and you know the guys you're working with, then you can trust them. If the opportunity comes around, they'll do it for you.'

A year later, Kelly did sell the Tour of Lombardy for hard cash to Gianbattista Baronchelli and his Del Tongo team, though only after he had first been bumped in warning by race director Vincenzo Torriani's car. When Baronchelli attacked from the front group of six on the outskirts of Milan, Kelly and his teammate Acácio da Silva simply looked the other way, having already agreed a deal with Del Tongo. 'Miracle in Milan' read the headline in *Corriere della Sera*, seemingly without irony. 'With Baronchelli, that was a special one, with a race organiser who wanted an Italian to win, and Del Tongo hadn't won much on that year,' says Kelly, who won the sprint for 2nd place.

Kelly was probably more inclined to do business at that Tour of Lombardy, given that his 1986 season had been a near-replica of his stratospheric 1984 campaign. The one major difference was the colour of his jersey, with Kelly now donning the canary yellow of Kas after the Spanish soft drinks company had stepped in to replace Skil as title sponsor of de Gribaldy's team. His fifth straight Paris-Nice win was one of almost routine dominance, as he led from gun to tape and then beat Jean-François Bernard, Urs Zimmerman and Greg LeMond up the Col d'Èze to boot. The following weekend, he would again have the measure of LeMond, this time at Milan-San Remo, when he tracked the American's attack on the final climb of the Poggio with disarming ease, and then beat him convincingly in the sprint on the Via Roma.

In a mirror of 1984, Kelly placed 2nd at the Tour of Flanders, though partly because his trade deal with Van der Poel had not yet run its course. Kelly performed the bulk of the heavy lifting in powering the four-man winning break to the line and then placed 2nd behind Van der Poel in the sprint. The scenario would reverse itself in Roubaix the following weekend, when Van der Poel effectively led out Kelly in the four-man sprint for the win by shutting down Ferdi Van Den Haute. This time, the sprint was a formality. For such a modest man, Kelly had developed a rather flamboyant tic when it came to celebrating big wins, punching the air three times before stretching his arms into a long victory salute for the cameras. It would be a familiar image in a season that yielded 21 wins. That year's Paris-Roubaix finished not on the stately old velodrome, but on the drab Avenue des Nations-Unies in the centre of town. Race sponsor La Redoute, having ended its commitment to Roche's team, had piled more capital into Paris-Roubaix in return for having the race finish outside its headquarters. Kelly, never one to sacrifice commerce for romance, was wholly unperturbed by the change. 'Money is what it was all about and what it still is about,' Paul Kimmage says. 'He wouldn't give a shit.'

Frank Quinn, now firmly established in Kelly's entourage, was struck by how equable he was before and after major races. There were never histrionics in defeat, nor was there any overflow of joy in victory, save for those exuberant, almost child-like outpourings on the finish line. Quinn was in the car with Kelly and the Belgian rider Marc Sergeant on the night of that second Roubaix victory, and they had driven halfway to Brussels in near silence before the floodgates opened. 'Kelly mightn't talk, he'd just sit there, but eventually you'd get it out of him,' Quinn says. 'You'd ask him did he get a puncture or something, and – boom – you'd get the story of the race. After the event, he would be very quiet, but he'd be able to tell you every pothole on the course of Paris-Roubaix if you asked him.'

Kelly had an understated routine, too, the morning after a major victory. Herman Nys would raise an Irish tricolour in celebration outside his house, and, as if responding to the Bat Signal, a journalist from Belgian television would arrive to record an interview. 'Only one fella would come in, a fella with a beard, a lovely fella,' Quinn says. 'He'd do the sound and all, ask all the questions. Then Kelly would go training after that, like nothing had happened.'

The de Gribaldy schedule didn't allow much time for contemplation, and though the infusion of Spanish money had altered the dynamic of his team, the tenets laid down by the Viscount often dovetailed with the demands of the new sponsor. To Kas owner Louis Knorr's delight, Kelly again made the whistle-stop trip to ride – and win – the Tour of the Basque Country between Flanders and Roubaix. He then proceeded to finish 3rd overall at the Vuelta a España, his first podium finish at a Grand Tour, winning two stages and the points classification in the process. Few big team leaders provided quite as much value for money across the calendar as Kelly.

'When he started off, he rode the bike to make money and the more he rode the bike, the more money he got. And he wasn't sure when that would stop,' Quinn says. 'He rode everything he could possibly get, he rode everywhere to make money, because he thought it might stop. He didn't lay himself out to win the Tour de France or Paris-Nice or anything like that. It was one day at a time. That's hard to believe. He was racing about 165 days a year, and his training regime was just mental.'

Kelly's penchant for making hay while the sun shone seemed sage in 1986, when he missed the Tour after crashing heavily on the final stage of the Tour of Switzerland. 'My usual aim is to do better than last year, so I felt I was in with a good chance of winning it,' Kelly said forlornly when ruling himself out just two days before the start. The previous year's Nissan Classic had opened Kelly's eyes to the commercial opportunities available at home, and he made sure to return in time for the Kellogg's races in August, winning in Cork. When the second edition of the Nissan Classic rolled around in September, Guinness joined Kas on the front of Kelly's jersey for the week. 'Deals revolved around the Nissan, more or less,' Quinn says. 'The rest of the year, Kelly was away, apart from a week or two in June, so the Nissan was very important.'

Even in Kelly's absence, there were still three Irishmen in the 1986 Tour, but despite Quinn's intercession, two of them were unable to secure contracts to line out in the Kellogg's races just weeks later. Martin Earley had won a stage of the Giro d'Italia in May and then completed his second successive Tour for Fagor, and he was joined in Paris by debutant Paul Kimmage, who had struggled through his opening months as a professional at RMO, but was deemed to have enough potential as to warrant a place in the Tour line-up. They were just the fourth and fifth Irishmen to ride *La Grande Boucle*, yet, absurdly, they were deemed surplus to requirements for McQuaid's post-Tour jamboree on the streets of their home city.

'I don't remember too specifically but I would have wanted to make the people running the event pay and I certainly would have advised Paul and Martin, "If you don't get paid, don't ride", and that's it,' Quinn says. 'The people running the event are getting paid. The sponsors are benefiting. To expect the athletes to come for free is not on, basically.'

Although Kimmage was already in Dublin the week of the Kellogg's races, McQuaid insisted he could only stretch to covering his travel expenses, and could not stump up an appearance fee. On the morning of the Dublin race, the *Irish Times* reported that an unnamed sponsor had agreed to pay £1,000 for Kimmage to ride the Kellogg's events, but noted that the promoters – namely McQuaid and Rushton – 'would not agree to this'. Kimmage sat at home in Coolock while Kelly, Roche and a cast of Continental riders – including Freddy Maertens, heavily indebted and in the final weeks of his career – performed for the masses a couple of miles away.

'That pissed me off. That really pissed me off,' Kimmage says. 'Is that the glory of being a pro rider? This crit is on in Dublin and I can't even get an invite to it. I never spoke to McQuaid about it, but it would have festered.' In hindsight, it was the beginning of the end of Kimmage's rapport with McQuaid, though there had already been a mild falling-out on the eve of the previous year's amateur World Championships, when Kimmage insisted on racing aboard his own Mercier bike rather than the Raleigh machine supplied by the sponsor.

McQuaid insists that the decision not to pay Kimmage and Earley was strictly business. Just as he looked to negotiate Kelly and Roche's appearance fees downwards by pointing to the residual benefits of performing for a home audience, McQuaid felt that simply racing in Ireland should have been its own reward for the other two professionals. 'Those races were run on tight budgets. We only had a certain amount of money to spend on riders, and Kelly and Roche took a large chunk of it,' McQuaid says. 'When it came to the one or two years Kimmage and Earley rode, we would offer them their expenses and hotel to come over, the same as all the British riders, because they weren't big stars. We were already offering them a race in which they could showcase themselves in Ireland. Kimmage felt we should have paid him a chunk of money, but number one, we didn't have it, and number two, we didn't feel he warranted it.'

Earley and Kimmage would at least get to ride the Nissan Classic in October. It was Earley's first appearance, after his Fagor team had skipped the event the year before, but Kimmage was only a late addition to the line-up. When Roche withdrew through injury, he was, at the 11th hour, drafted into a composite, Eveready-sponsored team that also featured Sean Yates.

The race and the occasion – inevitably – again belonged to Kelly, who snatched overall victory from Steve Bauer on the final day. In the absence of Roche, the spotlight was trained firmly upon him. At stage starts, the crowds swarmed around the Kas team car in the hope of a fleeting glimpse of the man in yellow. In towns and villages across the country, schoolchildren were ushered outside to watch Kelly and the Nissan Classic whizz past. After the podium ceremonies each day, Kelly was cornered by reporters for half an hour or more, and then spent as long signing autographs and pausing for pictures. Heavy lay the crown of local hero in the Nissan years, yet Kelly wore the burden lightly. Besides, the four or five hours in the peloton each day provided respite from Being Sean Kelly. It wasn't always a serious business.

'One year, we had to pass the Nissan dealership in Ennis, but the only way we could do it was to come off the main road and cut across a boreen,' McQuaid recalls, continuing:

Now this boreen was about four or five kilometres long and only the width of a car. The bunch was halfway along it when Kelly puts his hand up. This was the days before radios and all that, so word goes back to the team car and the assistant manager, Christian Rumeau, starts passing cars, and he's taking trees with him and bushes and everything with him while he's trying to get up to Kelly. He finally gets to the back of the bunch and he calls out, 'What's wrong?' And Kelly just leans over and says to him: 'This is a fucking narrow road, isn't it?'

12

Sappada

Patrick Valcke was the only member of the entourage Roche brought with him from La Redoute to Carrera at the beginning of 1986. It was a lonely kind of existence, especially as Roche had picked up a knee injury after a crash during the Paris Six-Day track event over the winter, and scarcely raced in the opening months of the season as he searched for a remedy. Though this big money acquisition was a statement of global ambition from Carrera, the team, sponsored by a Verona-based jeans manufacturer, remained resolutely local in feel. Team manager Davide Boifava, star rider Roberto Visentini and the bulk of the staff all hailed from the hinterland of Lake Garda. Outsiders were few, or at least it felt that way. If Carrera was a family, then Valcke was its black sheep, viewed with a mix of suspicion and contempt. 'Carrera was a big machine, but at the same time, virtually the entire staff lived in the same town,' says Valcke. 'There I was, all alone in the middle of a team where people were looking at me and wondering, "What are we going to do with this guy here?" It was hell.'

Roche's long absences only accentuated Valcke's alien status. Without a word of Italian, he would work in silence on bikes as his colleagues jabbered merrily around him, pricking up his ears every time he heard them speak Roche's name, and straining to decipher the dark murmurings each mention elicited. 'I taught myself Italian using cassettes. For hours on end, I'd repeat words of Italian to myself, and bit by bit, I started to understand snatches of what everyone was saying. Eventually, I understood enough to get that they were constantly badmouthing Stephen,' Valcke says. 'They were saying, "He's the phantom rider, he's never here! He's paid as a leader and we never see him!" It was a complicated year.'

After initially attempting to train through the injury, Roche was eventually diagnosed with crushed knee cartilage, and though corrective surgery performed in Italy in April provided temporary respite, the consequent muscle imbalance would have knock-on effects for years afterwards. Under pressure to salvage something from a disastrous campaign, Roche competed in both the Giro d'Italia and the Tour de France, abandoning the former and finishing an anonymous 45th in the latter, and he ended the season without a win or a significant placing to his name, prompting Boifava to seek a renegotiation of his contract ahead of 1987. Carrera had, after all, made a commitment to Roche that went beyond his salary or the hiring of Valcke. As part of the settlement to Roche's contract dispute with Peugeot, Carrera had agreed to print the car manufacturer's name on its shorts for two years even though it was not contributing anything to the sponsorship of the team. Roche, however, stood firm and refused to alter his contract, punting any possible review forward to the following April. 'I said to them, "When you get married, you get married for better or for worse,"' says Roche.

The year 1987, mercifully, proved rather more promising, even if he didn't mine as many victories as he ought to have done from a bountiful seam of early season form. After he won the Volta Valenciana in February, Roche was undone by an untimely puncture at Paris-Nice, where he lost another all-Irish duel to Kelly, and he missed out to his fellow countryman again at the Critérium International two weeks later. More traumatically, Roche frittered away victory at Liège-Bastogne-Liège when he indulged in an ill-conceived game of cat and mouse with breakaway companion Claude Criquielion, and world champion Moreno Argentin stole past them on the Boulevard de la Sauvenière to snatch the win. 'Anyone would think there's a curse on me,' Roche lamented afterwards, bitterly aware that he had only himself to blame for the fiasco. 'It must be written that I'm not going to win a big race this season.'

Roche needn't have worried. He restored confidence by winning the Tour de Romandie for the third time shortly afterwards, and April passed without any further attempts from Carrera to downsize his salary. Emboldened by his spring campaign, Roche was now starting to think of how much more he could earn on another team. During the Tour of the Basque Country, Fagor had sounded him out about signing for 1988, but Roche was in no hurry to put pen to paper – not when he could bolster his price tag further by winning a Grand Tour. His condition was humming, his confidence was soaring, and the Giro was fast approaching. The was one problem: the defending champion was on his team.

►⊙◄

'When you win the Giro d'Italia, you can spend the money any way you want,' Roberto Visentini says, his voice rasping with indignation over the phone from his home above Lake Garda. The charge levelled at him through his career, by both the press and his peers, was that he would have won a lot more had his devotion to the austere life of the professional cyclist matched his reported enthusiasm for *la bella vita*. It is, understandably, a characterisation Visentini resents to this day. 'The people who say that are ignorant, *basta*. But then again, there weren't a lot of correct people in cycling. Sons of bitches.'

Given that his family's considerable wealth was derived from the gloomy business of funeral direction, it was perhaps only fitting that Visentini would be a rather morose kind of playboy. Handsome, talented, moneyed and with a penchant for fast cars, Visentini had all the trappings of a would-be superstar, but for much of his career, his light was obscured. His greatest failing was perhaps the simple fact that he was neither Francesco Moser nor Giuseppe Saronni, the men whose running battle for hearts and minds defined Italian cycling in the early 1980s. The *tifosi* have long inclined towards a binary view of the world – Binda and Guerra, Coppi and Bartali – and Visentini didn't fit into the equation. For all his prodigious talent, Visentini's exploits were met with curiosity rather than affection.

Much of the coolness towards Visentini from his fellow riders, meanwhile, stemmed from his background. Cycling is historically a working-class sport, and a man without a visceral need to make his money from racing bikes tended to be viewed with suspicion. 'He came from a rich family,' says Valerio Piva, a contemporary in the Italian *gruppo* in the 1980s. 'Clearly he had talent but he didn't have the same desire to make his living from cycling. He always seemed to have this attitude that cycling wasn't the most important thing in his life. He was a great athlete, but maybe he could have won more if he really had the desire.'

A native of Gardone Riviera, near Salò, Visentini's natural gifts were evident as a schoolboy racer, and underscored when he won the inaugural junior World Championships in Lausanne in 1975. He turned professional in 1978, but only truly began to deliver on his promise when he placed 2nd to Saronni at the 1983 Giro. The following year, however, the same race exposed the demons of Visentini's more brittle nature. When the organisers controversially cut mountain passes from the race in the final week, ostensibly due to snow, Visentini complained loudly, and justifiably, that they had done so only to favour the pink jersey Moser, a noted non-climber. His challenge collapsed in the closing days after he became discommoded by continuous abuse from Moser's fans on the roadside. Two days after that Giro, at least according to lore, an indignant Visentini took a saw to his bike and hacked it into pieces. 'I brought the pieces to Boifava in a plastic bag,' Visentini says now. 'I said, "Here's your bike. I've had enough."' In later years, the same incident came to be erroneously attached to the aftermath of the 1987 Giro, and Visentini did little dispel that impression when he spoke to *La Gazzetta dello Sport* about it in 2012. Some stories are so good they bear repurposing.

Boifava talked Visentini out of thoughts of premature retirement and he returned to wear the *maglia rosa* for nine days in 1985 before being forced out by illness, but the stars aligned in 1986. For once, Visentini's health and morale made it around Italy intact, and he saw off both Saronni and Moser to win the Giro on his 29th birthday. Finally, he was at the summit, though he remained lumbered with the reputation as a *figlio di papa* – a spoilt daddy's boy. Reading between the lines of contemporary reports, it's not hard to detect a strain of tacit disapproval towards the ever more bouffant, George Michael-esque hairstyle, or his undimmed passion for motors. 'He always treated cycling like it was a game rather than a job,' tuts Giuseppe Martinelli, who raced against Visentini and joined Carrera's management in 1988.

There were the faintest murmurs, too, about the part Giovanni Grazzi, Carrera's team doctor, had played in Visentini's success. Grazzi was a close associate of Dr Francesco Conconi, who, from his base at the University of Ferrara, had built a reputation as a guru by masterminding Francesco Moser's startling late-career renaissance that saw him smash the Hour Record and win the Giro in 1984. It was heavily suspected – and later confirmed by the rider himself – that Moser had been given blood transfusions to boost performance, a practice that was not illegal at the time. By 1986, however, the IOC had outlawed blood doping, and Visentini was careful when explaining his and Grazzi's links to Conconi immediately after his Giro victory. 'Conconi? Yes, he's given us a hand, but I don't practise blood transfusions. I'd rather lose an extra race,' Visentini said at the time.

'Grazzi was the doctor for everybody on the team,' Visentini says now. 'He wasn't a personal doctor, he was there for everybody, Roche included. Regardless of whether you were one of the stronger riders or one of the weaker riders, he was the doctor.'

In winning the 1986 Giro, Visentini had proved himself the strongest rider on the team, and, unlike Roche, had lived up to the lofty expectations of the Tacchella brothers who owned Carrera and signed his paycheques. He proceeded to emphasise his status as the team's alpha male during the Trofeo Baracchi two-up time trial at the end of the 1986 season, where he was paired with a struggling Roche. As Roche saw it, Visentini seemed to revel in putting him into difficulty. Even before their antipathy came to a head in 1987, Roche would grumble publicly about the episode to *Vélo Magazine*, though he insists now that he and Visentini were never at odds prior to that year's fateful Giro. 'We had a good relationship other than that,' Roche says. 'We were both very much into cars. I remember he had a big Mercedes 190 Turbo, and we tore around Brescia in it one night.'

'We had a normal relationship, like regular teammates, with no problems,' agrees Visentini, dismissing the notion that he had felt even remotely threatened when Carrera had swooped to sign Roche ahead of the 1986 season. Through the early part of 1987, they followed largely separate programmes, with Roche racing in France, while Visentini stayed steadfastly south of the Alps. When they finally rode together at the Tour de Romandie, Visentini shrugged off his stablemate's victory. 'I should be the captain for the Giro and Roche for the Tour. These have always been the plans,' he told *La Stampa*. 'In any case, if I realise I can't win, I'll be the first to help Stephen, even at the Giro.'

The consensus as the Giro began was that the final overall winner would come from within the Carrera team, a state of affairs which perhaps only compounded Boifava's reticence to anoint a team leader in public. At the start in San Remo, he avoided the question by stating that the road would decide.

'They set out equal, on the same level,' Boifava says now. 'We decided whoever took the *maglia rosa* in the San Marino time trial would be helped by the other.' Nobody was especially convinced, not least within Carrera. 'The team went in with two leaders but two leaders never works,' Valcke says. 'Never!'

Roche and Visentini's markedly similar characteristics as riders only exacerbated the situation. Both strong time triallists who could climb with the best, it was difficult to envisage precisely when and where they might be separated in the general classification. Visentini won the short prologue in San Remo to claim the first *maglia rosa*, before Roche responded by landing the novel – and dangerous – downhill time trial the following afternoon, which sent the riders scrambling down the twisting descent of the Poggio. When Carrera, inspired rather than impeded by the posturing of their leaders, won the team time trial to Camaiore on stage 3, Roche took possession of the pink jersey, while Visentini moved back up to 2nd overall.

Visentini carelessly coughed up seconds to Roche when he was caught napping in the finale at Montalcino, but he scored a psychological victory when the Irishman's solo attack on the climb of the Terminillo came to naught two days later. They remained locked in their positions atop the overall standings as the Giro reached its southernmost point at Bari, and the phony war continued as the race travelled back up the sun-kissed Adriatic coast in the second week. By the time they reached Rimini, Roche had spent 10 days as race leader, but the pink jerseys taking up room in his suitcase counted for little when Visentini still only trailed him by a mere 25 seconds ahead of the uphill time trial to San Marino on stage 13.

A couple of days beforehand, *Tuttosport* journalist Beppe Conti asked Boifava which rider he would drive behind during the time trial. 'The weaker,' came the gnomic response. Boifava was true to his word. He opted to follow Roche, while his number two Sandro Quintarelli accompanied Visentini. In the space of 46 kilometres, Visentini seemed to put an end to two weeks of shadowboxing with one knock-out blow. He hadn't sparkled like Roche ahead of the Giro, nor had he accelerated for show on a mountaintop finish, but he seemed on another plane to his teammate in San Marino. Roche, for his part, complained he was still feeling the effects of a crash in Termoli five days previously. Visentini beat Roche by 2:47 to divest him of the *maglia rosa*, and in the overall standings, he now led by 2:42. The road had spoken. Visentini was leader of Carrera. The Giro was as good as his.

Carrera had signed Eddy Schepers ahead of the 1986 season expressly to serve as Roche's wingman in the mountains, but unlike Valcke, his new leader's long absences from racing were no grounds for an existential crisis. At 31 years of age and after almost a decade in the peloton, the Belgian had seen everything and was fazed by nothing. As an amateur, he was gifted enough to win the Tour de l'Avenir and the Giro delle Regioni. As a professional, he was canny enough to understand he was never going to be a champion, and he carved out a niche instead as a deluxe domestique, flitting between teams in Belgium and Italy according to demand for his services. Schepers was a hired hand, and he simply got on with the job in 1986, helping Visentini to win the Giro and Urs Zimmerman to 3rd place at the Tour. 'It was a good season, even allowing for Stephen's injury,' Schepers says.

Off the bike, Schepers and Roche struck up a solid rapport. Roche spoke little Italian, and so it was a relief to be able to converse in French with Schepers, who could in turn step in as a translator if required. As Roche's roommate, Schepers found himself acting as a part-time sports psychologist in that trying first year, geeing his leader up or dispensing frank Flemish home truths as the occasion required. When they reunited at the start of 1987, however, he saw a man and a rider transfigured. 'We were always roommates at races and training camps, and I'd see that he was always heading off to extra work in the afternoons,' Schepers recalls. 'When I'd ride behind him in training, it was like riding behind a motorbike.'

Schepers was by Roche's side throughout the spring, but he was informed by Boifava that he would not be required at the Giro. The team's rationale, that he should spare himself to help Roche at the Tour, was sound, but it jarred with the harsh economic reality of a man on Schepers's modest salary. 'I needed to make money and at that time, the prize money was better at the Giro than at the Tour, especially if you were riding for a good team with a rider who could win overall,' Schepers says. He explained his predicament to Roche, who in turn went to bat on Schepers's – and his own – behalf to Boifava. 'I needed to have someone like Eddy who was the same size as me, and ideal for bike exchanges,' Roche says. 'He had good tactical sense, he was someone I could count on, and we spoke the same language as well.'

Boifava conceded the point. Roche struck a blow for his own status, and won Schepers's undying loyalty in the process. Schepers proceeded to demonstrate his commitment to Roche's cause on the mountaintop finish at Terminillo, when he found himself in a two-man escape with Jean-Claude Bagot and bartered away stage victory in exchange for help from his Fagor team later in the race – the very same Fagor team that had already begun tentative transfer talks with Roche. 'I was the only one with Stephen, but I couldn't ride for him on the flat if he needed me in the mountains too, so we chose a bit of a collaboration with the Fagor team there,' Schepers says. 'They did some work for us after that.'

At that point, Roche was in the *maglia rosa*, but after Visentini whisked it off him at San Marino, his claim on team leadership, and by extension Giro victory, seemed over. In Roche's oft-repeated telling of the 1987 Giro, Schepers played a significant part in convincing him otherwise in their hotel room that night by encouraging him to attack Visentini, even if the Belgian demurs on that point. According to Roche, the pair sat on their beds watching a television interview in which Visentini flatly dismissed the prospect of riding the Tour in his service, and decided there and then to flick through the *Garibaldi*, as the Giro roadbook is named, and pick out the most opportune place to ambush their teammate, settling on the medium mountain stage to Sappada two days later. 'That night we were upset because everyone was congratulating Visentini and nobody commiserated with me,' Roche says. 'Visentini was over with the journalists saying, "Roche will ride for me at the Giro but I'm not going to the Tour, I'm going to the beach."'

Visentini, unsurprisingly, disputes the claim. 'No, that's bollocks, complete and utter bollocks,' he says. 'I was always very professional and I was going to go to the Tour to prepare for the World Championships and the races at the end of the season. That was the way the team had planned it. The Giro d'Italia was for me and he was going to lead at the Tour de France. That was the plan.'

Roche, however, had never signed up to that agreement in the first place. Long before the Giro began, and regardless of any implied internal hierarchy, he was plotting ways to win the race for himself. The San Marino setback only served to strip away any pretence of a tacit quid pro quo with Visentini. 'We didn't know the exact moment but we knew something was going to happen,' Valcke says. 'We knew that at the first opportunity, something would happen.'

The moment arrived two days after the San Marino time trial, over the top of the Forcella di Monte Rest in the Carnic Prealps. As the name suggests, the mountains on the border between the Veneto and Friuli-Venezia Giulia regions are not the most demanding, but the gravel-strewn *strada regionale* 355 that winds across the mountainside is among the most sinuous in the area. Bagot and Ennio Salvador, neither of whom posed the remotest threat on general classification, led the race over the summit, when Roche took it upon himself to shoot after them shortly after the road began to drop, ostensibly in the name of protecting his team's interests. 'I couldn't really attack but if a group got away and I happened to be in it, Roberto couldn't really ride and I'd be seen to be defending the jersey,' Roche says, not that anyone was fooled into thinking he was killing Visentini with kindness alone.

One reckless descent later, Roche was 1:30 clear of a peloton that had scarcely computed what was happening. 'Stephen hadn't talked about it the night before. Nobody knew he was going to do that, not even me. It was just the situation of the race. He took the decision off the cuff,' says Schepers. 'He didn't come as the first leader, but he poked out an opportunity to put the team in a really good position.'

At first, Visentini didn't even notice that Roche had scrambled down the descent alone and out of sight. 'I didn't realise he'd attacked at all. We were on the descent and riders were taking a drink or eating a panino and so on, when this group slips away,' Visentini says. 'I didn't even realise Roche was in it. We let the group go and they built up a lead of four or five minutes. And that's how it all happened.'

Not quite. There were still 80 kilometres and two climbs to come before the finish at Sappada, and on the long, flat approach to the next ascent, the Sella Valcalda, Roche's lead shrank. It is easy to forget, but Carrera were not the only team in the race. Panasonic's Robert Millar and Erik Breukink were in contention for podium places, as was Tony Rominger of Supermercati Brianzoli, but before either of those teams could set about shutting down Roche's move, the white-and-blue jerseys of Carrera massed on the front. 'It was up to the other teams to chase, but the management reminded us that Visentini was the leader and told us to ride behind Stephen, though I wouldn't ride on the front of the peloton,' says Schepers.

As Carrera began to chase, Quintarelli pulled up alongside Roche in the second team car at the head of the race. Boifava was in the number one vehicle, stationed behind Visentini and the pink jersey group, but he had relayed strict instructions to Quintarelli via radio. 'We told Roche to stay with the break without collaborating. And if it stayed away, so be it,' Boifava says. 'That's normal.'

'I was in the car with Quintarelli, because he had Stephen's bike,' Valcke says. 'When Quintarelli drove up alongside Stephen, he said to him in Italian, "Hey, Boifava says that you have to stop riding."'

Moments later, Valcke rolled down his window and chipped in with some additional counsel of his own: 'I said, "Steve, if you have the balls, today is the day to show them." Quintarelli didn't speak French and he only realised that I'd given the exact opposite instruction when suddenly he sees Stephen riding flat out on the front, straight after we'd spoken. He kept riding flat out, flat out, and Quintarelli was shouting to Boifava, "Patrick's just told Stephen to keep riding!"'

Back in the main peloton, Visentini was growing increasingly flustered, driven to distraction by what he felt to be Boifava's procrastination. 'Boifava should have sent the team to the front to ride full gas and chase him down, but that didn't happen,' he says now. Boifava reckons Visentini should never have allowed himself to fall into the situation to begin with. 'He made a mistake by sitting in the middle of the *gruppo* coming up to such a dangerous descent,' Boifava says. 'And the thing is, he was actually very good on descents. A leader can't let a group like that go away. And if he wanted Roche to help him, he should have been up there with him.'

Although the Carrera contingent eventually brought the bunch back to within sight of Roche and Salvador – Bagot had punctured – at the base of the Valcalda, most of them were dropped as soon as the road climbed and a Jean-François

Bernard-powered counter-attack bridged across to the leaders. Visentini just about remained in touch on the Valcalda, and even clawed his way back up to the now-expanded Roche group ahead of the final haul towards Sappada. Physically, he still seemed capable of offering resistance, but his mental resilience had been stretched to breaking point, which seems to have been Roche's objective in the first place. 'He was very uptight and we knew if we could make him panic and blow his brains, that would be a good scenario, you know,' says Roche. Yet even at a remove of 30 years, Roche still refuses to admit that his actions constituted outright treason. 'There was no intention to attack him,' he says, not entirely convincingly.

The Cima Sappada's final ramps were its steepest, but a breathless day of racing took its toll even before the gradient kicked in, and Visentini quickly started to slip backwards as the leading group fragmented. The only Carrera rider who could offer any support by this juncture was Schepers, but he hesitated when Boifava ordered him to go to the Italian's aid. A professional to the very marrow of his being, Schepers had the sangfroid to sense an opportunity. As the 1987 Giro's most tumultuous stage reverberated around him, he blocked out the white noise and began negotiating his contract for 1988.

'I was up with Stephen at that stage, and I said to him, "Look, I don't have much of a choice here, I'm going to have to sit up and wait for Visentini unless… Well, if I help you, I'll need to be certain that we'll be riding together next season,"' Schepers says. 'And Stephen said, "Listen, Eddy. Stay here." So I stayed with him, and that's where our friendship became even closer.'

Already guttering, Visentini's hopes were snuffed out altogether once he was left to his own devices, and he slowed almost to a standstill as Roche and the Giro rode away from him. The finish came after a short, shallow descent, where Johan van der Velde won the stage, and though Roche flagged in the finale, he stayed in the leading group. Immediately after the finish, he held a brief, anxious huddle with Schepers and Valcke in a tent where journalists were watching the race on television before being ushered towards the podium. He had done just enough to take the pink jersey, five seconds ahead of Rominger.

Visentini's strength, meanwhile, deserted him completely on the stiffest section of the final climb, and he reached the finish almost seven minutes down. Roche was already being helped into the *maglia rosa* as Visentini crossed the line and wheeled deliberately to a halt in the middle of a scrum of reporters and photographers. On stepping from his bike, he cast his eyes towards the podium with murderous, doomed rage writ across his face. 'I want to come up,' he called out, pointing to his own pink jersey, before RAI television's Giorgio Martino thrust a microphone in his direction.

'It looks like you've got something to say,' Martino began.

'I've got lot of things to say,' Visentini said darkly.

'Let's start saying them then,' Martino responded.

'*Niente*, I'll tell you tomorrow, maybe it's better,' Visentini said. 'But there's going to be people going home tonight.'

Carrera Jeans, based in Caldiero on the outskirts of Verona, was established by Tito Tacchella and his brothers Imerio and

Domenico in 1965. By the mid-1980s, inspired by the success of another Veneto clothing empire, Benetton, they sought to boost their international profile by taking over the sponsorship of the Inoxpran cycling team. Although Boifava managed the sporting operations, the brothers' interest extended far beyond signing off on the team's budget each season. Tito Tacchella was due to visit the Giro when it hit the high mountains in any case, but after watching on television as one Carrera rider divested another of pink, he brought his trip forward in order to pass Solomonic judgement on the power struggle.

A helicopter was ordered to transport him to Sappada immediately, but somewhere above Treviso, Tacchella was compelled to turn back by air traffic control. Ronald Reagan was holidaying at the five-star Villa Condulmer Hotel in Mogliano Veneto ahead of the forthcoming G7 summit in Venice, and a no-fly zone was enforced over the area for the duration of the president's stay. It did little to disabuse Tacchella of the importance of his own diplomatic mission. A man didn't need to read Patrick Kavanagh to understand Homer had made the Iliad from such a local row. Tacchella's journey to Sappada became a three-hour trek by car, and it would be after 10pm before he arrived at the rather less glamorous Hotel Corona Ferrea.

Carrera's hotel was located near the finish in Sappada, and Roche had been all but shooed there by press officer Gianfranco Belleri, who hoped the Irishman would remain cloistered silently in room 14 until his bosses decided precisely what it was they would do with him. Roche had managed to speak briefly with a small group of reporters before Belleri whisked him away from the podium, however, and he later granted audiences to Angelo Zomegnan of *La Gazzetta dello Sport* and British reporter John Wilcockson at the hotel. 'Your man won't talk to me,' he told Wilcockson of Visentini. 'He just goes red in the face and walks away.'

Visentini's recollection is that Roche didn't even dare approach him that evening in Sappada, preferring to remain quarantined in his bedroom while his fate was decided. 'He was nowhere to be seen that night, he didn't show his face,' says Visentini, who seems to avoid even breathing Roche's name when possible. 'I think he stayed up in his room to eat, the same with his mechanic.'

Roche, Valcke and Schepers all feared that they would be sent home for their combined show of insubordination that afternoon, and they endured an anxious wait, first for Tacchella to arrive in Sappada, and then for the outcome of his summit with Boifava. In reality, the fact that Roche had the pink jersey meant that they need not have worried. The team would row in behind him. 'They couldn't really send me home because Roberto had lost five minutes,' Roche says.

Visentini laughs joylessly at the idea that the Carrera management ever entertained the notion of pulling the *maglia rosa* from the race. 'The directors were never going to take that decision. It didn't work like that because Carrera was only interested in winning the Giro, full stop,' he says. 'I counted for zero. And the others counted for zero. All that counted was winning the Giro. The sponsors just wanted to win the Giro above all, and they had the *maglia rosa*. They weren't going to send him home.'

Boifava confirms as much. 'No, no, no, no, no. We never spoke about sending Stefano home. Never. Absolutely not. My job was to win the Giro, *basta*,' he says. 'The main thing was that Carrera, who were spending billions of lire, won the Giro, whether it was with Roche or Visentini.' In short, it wasn't a betrayal, just business.

The following day's stage was the *tappone*, the toughest leg of the Giro, a 214-kilometre trek to Canazei by way of the Passo Sella, Passo Pordoi and the Marmolada, though Schepers does not recall being daunted by the mighty Dolomites so much as by the opprobrium directed at Roche from the roadside. 'On the Marmolada, I went and asked the police on the motorbikes to protect Stephen and keep the public out of the road, in case they tried to hit him, but he was very visible in the pink jersey. That really stands out,' Schepers says. 'I can still remember riding at his side, with Stephen staying in the middle of the road all the time so that the public couldn't touch him. It really felt like it was *la guerra* up there.'

Roche extended his lead in Canazei – Breukink was now in 2nd place, 33 seconds down – but his abiding memory from the day is of spectators calling for his head. 'On the hills, they were taking wine in their mouths and spitting it at me as I came past, and they were punching me as well,' he says. In his 1988 autobiography, *The Agony and the Ecstasy*, ghostwritten by David Walsh, Roche complained that one Italian newspaper had labelled him a 'traitor', while others were reporting only Visentini's side of the story, but a scan of the archives shows relatively few traces of chauvinism among the home media.

Indeed, in his column in *Il Corriere della Sera* the day after Sappada, the three-time Giro winner Felice Gimondi came out strongly in support of Roche. 'I know that Visentini's fans have endured a great disappointment, but it would be unsporting –

uncivilised even – if they took that out on Roche, a rider who took advantage of a certain situation and who merits everyone's respect,' Gimondi wrote. 'Let's accept the verdict of this *corsa rosa*.' Interviewed on television, Gino Bartali was equally even-handed: 'For me, it's not a betrayal.'

Their thoughts were echoed by the veteran journalist Mario Fossati in *La Repubblica*. 'You can't say that Stephen Roche betrayed Roberto Visentini,' he wrote. 'Roche behaved just as the ambiguous ethics of this old sport allowed him to do.' If the Italian press revelled in the polemics engendered by the Sappada affair, it was not due to jingoism, but simply because it allowed them to cast Roche and Visentini as a latter-day Coppi and Bartali, and dust off the Homeric allusions of old. For the *sala stampa*, the drama was simply a welcome infusion of colour in a Giro that had risked playing out in greyscale.

The fans' attacks weren't all that Roche had to fend off on the stage to Canazei, as Visentini looked to test his mettle by accelerating repeatedly when the road climbed, and by taking some erratic lines through corners when it descended. Roche later claimed that Visentini deliberately tried to cause him to crash on one of the descents that day, and for once, their respective accounts tally. 'Yeah, that's true,' Visentini says matter-of-factly. 'I went very close to him. I wanted to put him off the road.'

Despite Visentini's ongoing belligerence, the rest of the Carrera team quietly rowed in behind Roche, with an emissary visiting his room in Sappada to outline the Italian riders' point of view. 'Davide Cassani came to explain why they had chased him. It was a lot more difficult for the Italians to do what I did. They were part of the organisation and they couldn't disobey Boifava's orders in the way I was able to,' Schepers says.

In the mountains in the final days of the race, Roche found a useful ally of circumstance in the shape of his old Peugeot teammate Robert Millar, even though the climber was racing for Breukink's Panasonic team. They combined most obviously on the final mountain stage to Pila, with Millar taking the stage and moving up to 2nd overall, while Roche definitively distanced Breukink. At a time when Anglophone riders in the peloton were rare, Millar's contribution was reported in the English-language specialist media as an example of the camaraderie prevalent among the so-called 'Foreign Legion', but the truth was a little more nuanced.

'I didn't ride against Roche at the Giro would be the best way of putting it. I was there to serve [Phil] Anderson and then Breukink, so my involvement in the GC race was merely coincidental,' Philippa York says now. 'I got called up at the last minute, because it was never on my race programme so I was disinterested in being there.' The Scot was also eyeing the exit at Panasonic at the time, jaded from navigating the oscillating moods of the domineering manager, Peter Post. The informal non-aggression pact with Roche was the beginning of the process that saw both riders move to Fagor in 1988. 'I suspected I was leaving Panasonic and that Giro helped make a decision of where to go. I thought riding with Stephen would be a better choice than the other offers,' York says. 'Big mistake.'

This most explosive Giro, and the ire of Visentini's most ardent supporters, had fizzled out before Roche capped his overall triumph with an emphatic win in the time trial to Saint Vincent in the Alps on the last day, and the final standings barely hinted at the true story of a fraught race. Roche's eventual margin of victory was a generous 3:40 over Millar, and more glaringly, Visentini's name was absent from the overall standings altogether. He suffered a fractured wrist in a crash on the penultimate stage, and he didn't even start the Saint-Vincent time trial.

While Roche drove through the night with Schepers to celebrate his Giro triumph quietly at his house on the outskirts of Paris, Visentini was already at home at his villa above Lake Garda, brooding over his future in the sport. Although he lingered in the peloton until 1990, it was a flickering existence; his career effectively died at Sappada. On retirement, Visentini gladly faded out from the cycling milieu altogether to concentrate on running his family's undertaking business. In the quarter of a century since, he has never admitted to the merest nostalgia for the impalpable world he used to inhabit in cycling.

Schepers maintains Visentini is the only rider who has failed to attend any of the periodic team reunions organised by Carrera in Verona. Visentini, for his part, is bemused by the very idea that anyone might expect him to show up. 'Why would I go to a Carrera party? To see the guys who made me lose the race?' he asks. 'I'll gladly go and spend time with friends and enjoy myself, but a party with the guys who made me lose the Giro d'Italia? Come on.'

Visentini's thoughts on Roche and his account of the 1987 Giro, meanwhile, are blunt. 'He's always talked bollocks,' Visentini says, more in weariness than in anger. 'He's always said false things. He's not reliable.'

13

STEPHEN HERO

Jacques Goddet never hid his admiration for Kelly, and ahead of the 1987 Tour de France, his final edition as director after almost a half a century at the helm, he was all but willing the Irishman to win it. The Tour peloton was setting out from the *Grand Départ* in West Berlin without the retired Bernard Hinault and the injured Greg LeMond, but in an interview with *L'Équipe* on the eve of the race, Goddet preferred to focus on the presence of a man who had missed the previous year's race. 'For the first time, Sean Kelly is coming to the Tour de France aiming to win it, and that is a very remarkable event,' Goddet said. In the same newspaper, the five-time Tour winner Jacques Anquetil picked Kelly as his favourite for overall honours in the first instalment of a daily column in which he answered a mailbag of readers' questions.

For his part, Kelly must have been wondering what he had done to merit such a tag after a trying spring, though no one among the wide slate of contenders held unimpeachable credentials. Laurent Fignon had struggled with injury in the three years since his 1984 triumph. Pedro Delgado was deemed too inconsistent. Jean-François Bernard was too callow. Luis Herrera was penalised by his time trialling. Roche had won the Giro, true, but the field there was weak. Besides, the Giro-Tour double had only ever been achieved by Fausto Coppi, Eddy Merckx, Anquetil and Hinault, and nobody truly believed Roche belonged amid that august company.

Kelly, still world number one, was as safe a bet as any, and he was certainly due an upturn in his fortunes by the time July rolled around. His year had begun tragically, when Jean de Gribaldy was killed in a car crash near Besançon on the night of 3 January. Among de Gribaldy's foibles was a penchant for reckless driving, as well as a tendency to drive through the night when he felt the occasion demanded it. He was a man perpetually in a hurry. The police report suggested that he fell asleep at the wheel. At the age of 64, *Le Vicomte* was gone.

Kelly and the Kas team were at a skiing camp in Combloux in the Alps at the time, and they travelled to Besançon together for the funeral three days later. 'Above all, de Gribaldy gave me freedom,' Kelly told *Vélo Magazine* later in the spring. Though his influence remained, de Gribaldy's role had altered slightly when Kas took over sponsorship at the beginning of 1986, and the team already had a ready-made replacement as manager in the form of Ramón Mendiburu. The Basque was, Kelly wrote in *Hunger*, 'the perfect character to fill the void' because, like de Gribaldy, he rarely felt the need to raise his voice.

The opening weeks of the season delivered the usual yield, as Kelly won Paris-Nice and the Critérium International, beating Roche into 2nd place both times, but he fell short in the classics. After another 2nd-place finish at the Tour of Flanders, Kelly snapped his handlebars on the cobbles at Ennelevin during Paris-

Roubaix, where Vanderaerden's victory only compounded his distress. Worse was to follow at the Vuelta a España, where Kelly led the race with four days to go to the finish in Madrid, only to be forced out by a painful cyst on his perineum that prevented him from sitting on the saddle. Instead of feting Ireland's first Grand Tour winner, the Vuelta had its maiden Colombian champion, as Luis Herrera took the spoils.

Kelly's injury had healed by the time he arrived in Berlin for the start of the Tour, but though he evinced confidence in public, he privately harboured doubts about his form. 'If I can find the little something I'm still missing, I can still win the Tour,' Kelly said after the team time trial in Berlin, though the admission that he needed to lose a kilogram of excess weight during the opening week of the race was an ill portent. He proceeded to lose rather more than he had bargained for in the first long individual time trial at Futuroscope, conceding more than five minutes to Roche. All prospects of winning the Tour evaporated there, and worse was to follow.

The early kilometres of stage 12 saw the first sustained truce of the 1987 Tour, with the peloton content to amble along at a leisurely pace. When the rider in front of him braked abruptly, Kelly rode into the back of him, and his left shoulder bore the full brunt of his fall. Kelly knew that his collarbone was broken, but he jumped back on his bike regardless. He lasted a minute before the pain proved too much to bear, and he wheeled to a halt. Race doctor Gerard Porte administered a painkilling injection, while directeur sportif Christian Rumeau gave an on-the-hoof update to *L'Équipe*'s Jean-Marie Leblanc, who was sitting beside Goddet in the race director's car. 'We'll let him ride for a couple of kilometres and see,' he said.

Kelly set off again uneasily, and was initially pushed along by his Kas teammates Inaki Gaston and Gilles Sanders, until Goddet reluctantly admonished them from atop the sunroof of the director's car. 'Gentlemen, you can't do that, unfortunately. I'm deeply sorry,' Goddet said sadly. Roche, Fignon, Kimmage, Earley and Claude Criquielion were among those to drop back to sympathise as word spread of his plight. Kelly was unable to use his left arm to brake or change gear. A platoon of photographers' bikes plagued him like mosquitoes, waiting for the moment. After 75 kilometres, on an almost imperceptible rise, Kelly brought his Tour to a halt, sobbing openly as Rumeau draped a long-sleeved jersey across his shoulders.

As the photographers stepped in to capture the moment, Goddet emerged from his car to shake Kelly's hand and whisper words of consolation. After taking his seat once again, he took the radio mouthpiece and made a special, gravely intoned address to the Tour caravan, as Leblanc put it, 'to salute Sean Kelly'.

On the face of it, Stephen Roche's victory in the 1987 Tour de France was straightforward. He was the best time triallist in the race and surrounded by one of the strongest teams. After winning the first long time trial at Futuroscope, he remained towards the top of the general classification thereafter by limiting his losses in the mountains. He took hold of the yellow jersey in the Dijon time trial on the penultimate day and rode into Paris the following afternoon as Tour champion. So far, so simple. And yet Roche, much like the hoary old cliché about Alex Ferguson's Manchester United teams, never did things the easy way. Nothing in his career, save for his first months at Peugeot, perhaps, seemed to run smoothly. There were always complications, distractions, polemics. Sometimes the turmoil proved ruinous. In 1987, he seemed to thrive on it.

Roche's chief disturbance as he began the Tour was of his own making. Negotiations with Fagor had accelerated in the aftermath of the Giro controversy, and at one point, there even arose the prospect of leaving Carrera before the Tour began at all. 'After the Giro, Stephen was looking into the possibility of finding another team for the Tour because it wasn't certain that he'd be in the Carrera selection,' Schepers says. Having felt short-changed by Roche's 1986 showing, however, the Tacchella brothers were determined to extract full value from the remainder of his contract. Not only were Roche and Schepers sent to the Tour, but the team was arguably even stronger than the one that had accompanied him at the Giro, especially with the injured Visentini an absentee.

Even so, the tensions with Carrera's top brass had not abated by the time the Tour began. After Carrera won the team time trial, Roche was upset that the squad ignored his advice and defended Eric Maechler's overall lead for the bones of a week rather than sparing themselves to work for him in the mountains. Boifava, meanwhile, took exception to the fact that Valcke, still a Carrera employee, was actively recruiting riders for Fagor's 1988 roster on the Tour. When Valcke tapped up the ephemeral *maillot jaune* Maechler, Boifava told him to pack his bags. Only the late-night intervention of Roche kept his friend on the Tour, but the die for their future was cast. 'It wasn't going to be possible to stay at Carrera. No way. We were obliged to go elsewhere,' says Boifava. Roche's impending separation from Carrera, largely ignored in Ireland, was a source of constant chatter in the French press. At one point, *L'Équipe* even reported how the normally reserved Schepers had reputedly threatened to 'smash a journalist's face' for constantly asking about Fagor.

In the middle of it all, mercifully, a bike race was breaking out. Roche's victory in the 87-kilometre time trial in Futuroscope didn't put him into yellow, but it did effectively eliminate some dangerous rivals ahead of the first mountains. Fignon, Kelly and Herrera, who coughed up nine minutes, fell by the wayside. There was a further shake-up in the Pyrenees, where Roche held his own to emerge 3rd overall, just 1:26 off the *maillot jaune*, now held by Frenchman Charly Mottet. After carelessly losing 67 seconds when the race split on the road to Blagnac, Roche regained the same amount on Mottet the following day at Millau to remain in 3rd place overall come the second rest day at Avignon. A week from Paris, Roche was where he had wanted to be from the outset: within striking distance of the yellow jersey, but without the pressure of defending it.

When the race resumed with a mountain time trial to Mont Ventoux, however, a new rival emerged, as Jean-François Bernard thrashed his way to victory on the arid slopes. The Bald Mountain had been a forbidding place for Roche on that frigid day at Paris-Nice in 1981 and it was no more hospitable on a day of soaring temperatures in Provence six years later. Usually a stylist, Roche battled grimly to keep the damage under control, placing 5th on the stage, 2:19 behind the rampant Bernard. The Frenchman had the guile to use an aerodynamic bike for the flat opening 18 kilometres from Carpentras before switching to a regular machine for the assault on the summit, but it would be reductive to attribute his triumph to his choice of equipment. Skinsuit unzipped to the waist, headband slipping down his forehead, eyes deadened, Bernard seemed to go beyond himself as he bobbed from side to side against the gradient and rode into the yellow jersey, 2:34 ahead of Roche. In the following morning's *L'Équipe*, however, Pierre Chany sounded a cautionary note. As well as demonstrating Bernard's potential, he wrote, the manner of victory 'could suggest certain worries for his immediate tomorrows'. In other words, he may have flown too close to the sun.

So it proved. When Bernard punctured near the top of the Col de Tourniol the following day, his rivals ignored the unwritten rule forbidding attacks on the yellow jersey when he suffers a mechanical problem. Roche later claimed that he didn't realise Bernard had punctured. Pedro Delgado insisted Bernard had caught up to the rear of the peloton. No matter, neither man stood on ceremony when Fignon and Mottet's Système U team launched a pre-planned attack in the feed zone at Léoncel over the other side. An isolated Bernard chased forlornly all the way to the finish, but never regained contact, conceding his yellow jersey to Roche. 'I'm not looking for excuses: I'll simply say I lost the *maillot jaune* without being able to defend it,' Bernard said afterwards. On the final climb of the Côte de Chalimont, Delgado attacked and only Roche could follow. Over the other side in Villard-de-Lans, Delgado sprinted to stage victory while Roche donned the first yellow jersey of his career, 41 seconds ahead of Mottet and 1:19 up on Delgado.

That evening it emerged that Roche's Carrera teammate Guido Bontempi had returned a positive test for testosterone after winning the bunch sprint in Troyes on stage 7. He was later stripped of that victory, but beyond that, his punishment extended only to a 10-minute time penalty in the overall standings. The infraction was reported as a footnote, if it was recorded at all. Carrera's team doctor on the race, Giovanni Grazzi, dutifully downplayed the incident to *Il Corriere della Sera*. 'We don't use medicines with that hormone because we don't see it as being useful for a rider,' he said, presumably with a straight face.

The following day brought the Tour to l'Alpe d'Huez. Roche, having struggled there so badly in his debut Tour four years earlier, was beaten before the climb even began. He never found a satisfactory rhythm on the 21 hairpins and handed over the jersey to Delgado, who now led him by 25 seconds. The Spaniard was the eighth different rider to lead the 1987 Tour, a record at the time, but now, five days from Paris, only two men could still win it: Delgado and Roche.

On the evening of 22 July, *L'Équipe* journalist Guy Roger rapped gently at the open door of an upstairs room in the Résidence Bellecôte at La Plagne, and cautiously stepped inside. Shortly past the threshold, he was arrested by Eddy Schepers, who barked at him to turn around and get out. Before Roger could protest that he had an appointment, a muffled voice emerged from within the darkened room. 'Come back after I've had my massage,' Roche called out limply. At the start in Le Bourg-d'Oisans that morning, Roger had arranged his rendezvous with Roche for after the stage, in part to discuss the Fagor saga, but the spectacular finale to the day's stage meant that the agenda for the interview had changed. Half an hour later, Roche sat down with Roger and began recounting how he had salvaged his Tour de France at La Plagne. It was the first iteration of a tale he would find himself telling over and again for the next 30 years.

These days, Roche tends to flip into auto-pilot when asked to recount stage 21 of the 1987 Tour, not out of weariness, but simply out of habit. Besides, like the audience at a pantomime, every interviewer already knows the story. Roche, ever-obliging, trots out all the favourite lines to knowing nods. Perhaps the remarkable thing about Roche's version of events at La Plagne is its consistency over the years. This is, after all, the man whose opinions of teammates could fluctuate from one autobiography to the next, but the basic tenets of his La Plagne tale have remained steadfast since that first interview with Roger.

Roche had begun the day simply looking to stay in contact with Delgado, but he tore up the playbook on the descent of the Col du Télégraphe and launched into an ambitious offensive that saw him reach the Col de la Madeleine in a group with Mottet and a lead of 1:40 over Delgado. Initially at least, Roche's attack was intended not so much to discommode Delgado as to reprimand Café de Colombia's Luis Herrera and Argemiro Bohórquez, who had set a fierce tempo on the Galibier that had upset the grandees of the European peloton. 'I said to Herrera, "If you don't tell your cowboys to relax, we're going to get mad," Roche told Roger. 'But they kept on doing cinema stuff.'

Thirty years on, Roche picks up the same thread. In the

space of a few years, the boy from Dundrum had become a part of the Old World establishment of the peloton, as he and his rivals briefly united against the outsiders from Colombia. 'Going over the Galibier, the Colombians were attacking and there were crashes. We were saying to the Colombians, "Piano, piano, piano," because if they didn't back off, people were going to get eliminated,' Roche says. 'Once we got over the Télégraphe, I spoke with Jeff Bernard and Charlie Mottet, and we decided we'd tear down it, because if we didn't get rid of the Colombians, they'd only do the same over the Madeleine.'

On the Madeleine, Roche began to entertain the notion that he could win the Tour there and then by definitively distancing Delgado. It was a rare tactical misstep, as Delgado clawed back ground on the mountain and caught him in the valley before the final haul to La Plagne. 'That was great for the panache of the event but a bit suicidal for me,' Roche says. 'I was the strongest guy in the group and nobody helped me at all, so I was a bit cooked when Delgado came back up.' When Delgado punched clear on the lower slopes of La Plagne, Roche didn't dare follow. 'I knew if I tried going with him, I wouldn't see the top.'

As Delgado pulled away and his lead over Roche nudged north of a minute, the Tour seemed to be bending towards the Spaniard. Behind, Roche was bargaining with himself. He would try to hold Delgado's advantage at 1:20 and then empty the tank in the final five kilometres. 'But when 5k to go came, I wasn't really ready. Then with 4k to go, I shook myself up and I gave it everything,' Roche says. His cause was helped by the incomplete information available to riders in an era before radio earpieces and the use of GPS. It meant that the time gaps relayed to Delgado were already out of date when he got them.

Indeed, there weren't even live television pictures of Roche's lone pursuit, as the first television motorbike was with the leaders Laurent Fignon and Anselmo Fuerte, and the other was with Delgado.

In the television gantry at the finish line, commentators were relying on garbled information from race radio. With five kilometres to go, Roche was 1:50 down on Fignon, but this was erroneously reported as being his deficit to Delgado. When Delgado was caught and passed by Fabio Parra, however, it was evident that the yellow jersey was beginning to struggle. 'All I could think of to keep my morale up was, "If I'm suffering so badly, he's going to be going even worse,"' Delgado told British journalist Alasdair Fotheringham in 2014.

Roche, meanwhile, no longer had much idea of whether he was gaining or losing ground. 'I hadn't one bit of information as to where Delgado was. I didn't know I was coming back at him, but I knew my speed was going up,' Roche says. As Delgado entered the final kilometre, word had filtered through to the gantry that Roche had steadied the ship, but his precise whereabouts were unknown. It was only when Delgado spilled across the line in 4th place that the full extent of Roche's comeback revealed itself. The Irishman rounded the final corner just behind the car trailing Delgado, and finished the stage only four seconds down. 'When I got there and they told me it was only four seconds,' Delgado said, 'my world fell apart.'

Roche cut a confused, slow-eyed figure as he wobbled past the line, reaching out towards a television cameraman to try to keep himself upright before Valcke rushed forward to his aid, wrapping a towel around his shoulders as though swaddling a child. Without the strength to stand, Roche crumpled in a heap on the ground when he was helped from his bike, and a scrum of reporters formed around him. A panicked Valcke, later helped by a gendarme, looked to clear an opening, as race doctor Gérard Porte hurried to the scene. For the bones of 10 minutes, Roche lay on the ground, initially unable to talk or move his legs. Like Eddy Merckx on Mont Ventoux in 1970, Roche had an oxygen mask placed over his mouth and nose. All the while, Valcke was crouched alongside him, perhaps with a different Ventoux collapse in mind.

'Looking back, it seems simple. People say, "Oh, he made a big effort and he just needed to recover," but in the moment, you don't think of that. He couldn't move, he couldn't talk. I had the impression that he was going to die,' Valcke says. 'Those were long minutes. Long, long minutes. I thought he was dying. It was very complicated.'

At first, Roche could hear only white noise, but gradually he started to make out discernible sounds and then words. He blinked in response to Porte's requests before finding his breath and his voice once again. 'That was frightening. I was conscious but I had no energy going to any of my limbs,' Roche says. Once he was placed in a stretcher in the rear of the race doctor's van, Roche had located his sense of humour, too. 'One of the journalists from French television came in and said, "Stephen can you just reassure your fans that everything is ok?"' Roche says, lining up the old punchline one more time. 'And I said, "Everything's OK, but I'm not ready for a woman yet."'

Rather than to hospital, Roche went directly to the Résidence Bellecôte, where he learned that he had been handed a 10-second time penalty for an illegal feed on the final climb, stretching his deficit on Delgado to 39 seconds. It hardly tempered the psychological blow he had dealt Delgado by almost catching him on the line. He played another mind game that evening at the hotel, which Carrera shared with the Spaniard's PDM team, by refusing to have dinner in his room. 'I even walked down the steps rather than go down in the lift, otherwise Delgado would think he'd won,' Roche says. By then, he had already delivered some messages during his interview with Guy Roger upstairs, mindful that the entire Tour caravan would read his words in the following morning's newspaper. 'Medically, I think it will be just a bad memory,' Roche said blithely of his collapse, before matter-of-factly moving on to discuss his 1988 contract talks: 'Carrera didn't follow through financially.' All in a day's work.

The following afternoon, Roche put one arm inside the yellow jersey by attacking Delgado on the treacherous descent of the Col de Joux Plane that led into Morzine, gaining 18 seconds. Delgado had crashed and broken his clavicle on the same descent in the 1984 Tour, and Roche exploited his anxiety after Schepers had controlled the yellow jersey group all the way up the climb. With just 21 seconds to recoup in the 38-kilometre time trial in Dijon on the penultimate day, it was beginning to look like a fait accompli. Pat McQuaid, on hand as co-commentator for RTÉ's live coverage of the final stages, saw the Irish contingent increase as the week drew on. 'I remember being in Dijon on the Friday night and there were massive groups of Irish after arriving in,' he says. 'They'd obviously been following the Tour at home and jumped on planes to get over to France to be there for the last weekend.'

On the morning of the decisive time trial, there was little doubt in the Carrera camp. 'It's funny because the night before

I'd spoken a lot with Stephen about the material and the wind and gears, our recons were always very detailed, but on the Saturday, we were in a state of complete serenity,' Valcke says. 'Of course, he still had to go out and do the time trial, but we knew he was going to take the jersey. It was a logical result.'

Delgado seemed smilingly resigned to his part. Before the stage, he hammed it up for a television crew by holding a matador's *capote*, and allowed them to travel with him in the PDM team car as he drove to the start. Seconds before he rolled down the ramp, Delgado tossed his headband to a fan in the crowd with a playful grin. After one kilometre, he was already five seconds down on Roche. Halfway through the test, Roche was more than a minute up, and the Tour, finally, had been divested of all suspense. As rain fell softly over Burgundy, Roche eased off in the final kilometres, rather than risk a crash. He took second to Bernard on the stage, but put over a minute into Delgado to take permanent possession of the yellow jersey.

The final leg on the Champs-Élysées was a formality, despite the slender 40-second lead, then the second-smallest winning margin in Tour history. Four Irishmen – a record – had begun the 1987 Tour, but Martin Earley, 65th overall, was the only one to make it to Paris with Roche. As Roche crossed the finish line, the first congratulatory pat came from Earley. 'I can remember thinking going down the Champs-Élysées, "My God, Stephen Roche has won the Tour de France, this is like amazing,"' Earley says. 'It was a surreal situation. You can remember thoughts like that.'

The felicitations of another Irishman beneath the Arc de Triomphe were rather less understated. With McQuaid acting as a liaison with the race organisation, Taoiseach Charles

Haughey made a flying visit to the final stage, travelling in a car with his French counterpart Jacques Chirac, and then bustling his way onto the podium alongside Roche. As Seamus Martin put it in the following day's *Irish Times*: 'Charles Haughey clung to the front of the podium with the stagecraft of a Sarah Bernhardt; never once did he move out of range of the TV cameras of *Antenne 2*.'

'Did I meet him that day? I think I did,' Earley says of Haughey. Did his prime minister know who he was? 'That,' Earley smiles, 'is a good question.'

Haughey's presence at least gave Roche an inkling as to the impact of his victory back home. After toasting his win in the Lido in Paris on the Sunday night, he eschewed a criterium contract in France to fly to Dublin the following afternoon for a homecoming, where the multitudes lining the roadside drew comparisons with the visit of Pope John Paul II eight years previously. Roche travelled aboard an open-top bus at a snail's pace from Dublin airport, through Drumcondra, down O'Connell Street and across the Liffey to the Mansion House. 'On the plane home to Dublin, I thought, "Who's actually going to be out to welcome me?"' Roche says. 'Then I arrive into Dublin airport and people are jumping over barriers to get to me, and pulling at my shirt. I felt really important, you know.'

Philippe Bouvet was dispatched to Dublin at the last minute by *L'Équipe*, but having failed to secure a seat on Roche's flight, touched down after the cavalcade had already left for the city centre. 'I was very stressed because I didn't speak any English, and I didn't know where his homecoming party was going to be or anything like that. I took a taxi from the airport and while

I was in the car, I asked the driver to turn on the radio, and that way he was able to figure out where the procession with Roche was,' Bouvet says. After nudging his way through the crowds at the Mansion House, he was repelled at the last by a Garda, only for Roche to catch his eye as he walked in, and usher him through for another *L'Équipe* exclusive. 'I had the impression that the whole city had come out to see him,' Bouvet says. 'It was extraordinary.'

The Irish press seemed equally captivated by the occasion. Typical was a laudatory column from Conor Cruise O'Brien in the *Irish Independent*, which bore the heading, 'Getting the hero we badly need'. In what was a grey decade in Ireland in so many other ways, the exploits of its cyclists were a dash of colour – quite literally, in fact. 'The *Irish Times* that day had a coloured front page for the first time and you had to go six pages back to find the first bit of bad news,' Roche says. 'You kind of feel you're responsible for bringing pleasure and joy into people's lives, because generally the front page is about a bombing or killing or the economy or whatever.'

The real world was never too far away, of course. Roche's most notable endorsement in Ireland was with Galtee Foods, a deal that began in 1985. Galtee's cheese sales reputedly rose by 15 per cent in July 1987 due to the Roche effect, but two days after the Tour, the company responded to a labour dispute at its bacon plant in Mitchelstown, County Cork by threatening the 360 employees there with redundancy. By then, the party in Dublin had subsided, and Roche the émigré was back on the Continent.

►⊙◄

While Roche was being feted in yellow on the Champs-Élysées, Kelly sat in a lifeless studio in Brussels, his arm still in a sling from his crash a fortnight earlier. At the behest of RTÉ, he spoke via a live link-up to give his thoughts on this most historic day for Irish cycling. His words for Roche were generous, but his disappointment at his own fate was obvious. It was a trying afternoon.

'I went into one of the TV stations in Brussels and I was talking with Jimmy Magee on the radio or something,' Kelly says. 'From one side, I think yeah, you're happy to see it. But there's another side where you're disappointed you're not in there, in the event and getting onto the Champs-Élysées. And when you see Roche winning it, I suppose you say to yourself, "Shit, if he can win it, I should be able to win it." So there's a lot of things that go through your head at that time, in those three weeks, and especially at the very end, on the final day.'

14

More Pricks Than Kicks

Following his abandon on the road to La Plagne, four days from the finish of the Tour de France, Paul Kimmage had returned to his adopted home of Vizille and resolved to avoid any reminders of the Great Bike Race. On the day of the decisive Dijon time trial, he decided to spend the afternoon shopping in Grenoble with his wife Ann rather than sit in his living room and watch, but even among civilians, he remained a convict of the road. He found himself drawn irresistibly to the glow of a television in the window of a furniture shop, and long before the on-screen graphics confirmed as much, the outcome was obvious: Stephen Roche had won the Tour de France.

Any joy Kimmage felt at his friend's moment of triumph was smothered by disappointment at the doleful way his own Tour had played out. Roche's victory, and the accolades that followed it, would only draw Kimmage's own lowly status into ever sharper contrast. They had both grown up in Dublin, and they had both competed for Ireland at the Olympics. They had both raced for ACBB, and they had both turned professional with French teams. They had both had the same opportunities. Roche had seized his and carried on to Tour victory. But Kimmage, what had he done?

Kimmage travelled to Paris for his RMO team's end-of-race dinner the following day, and felt himself an intruder as his teammates toasted their successful completion of *La Grande Boucle*. At his hotel near Porte Maillot, he encountered Roche amid a swarm of journalists and assorted hangers on, and, after some hesitation, went and offered his congratulations. On his return to Vizille, he struggled to impose order on the riot of emotions that the weekend had stirred up.

'That was hard. Really, really hard. And it's not envy, it's not jealousy. It's just fucking hard,' Kimmage says. 'Because you've given so much to it at that stage. It's nothing to do with him. It's all about you.'

Somewhere around Chapelizod, as the watery winter sun began to dip behind them, conversation turned to matters of state. It was December 1985, and Kimmage was about to join the elite cadre of Irishmen in the professional peloton. The two Dubliners, Roche and Earley, had invited him on a relaxed training ride, an unofficial initiation ceremony into the archangelic realm of the paid ranks. Since they were teenagers, Kimmage had reverentially looked up to Roche as his superior, in age and in talent, but now, at least officially, they were equals.

For most of the ride, the talk was of the jocular kind enjoyed by young sportsmen in their prime, but the timbre changed as they pedalled back into the city. Kimmage's new RMO team contained many refugees from the defunct La Redoute outfit, and Roche ran through the names of riders and soigneurs from his former squad, listing out those to be trusted and those to be avoided. It was impossible to talk about soigneurs without talking about their needles and the strength – and legality – of what they put in them. Now that Kimmage was about to join The Show, it was time for him to learn a little more about how big-time cycling was made. 'Martin was with us, and we started talking about soigneurs, taking caffeine… That day was the first and actually the only conversation about doping I had with Roche, which seems bizarre given that we shared a room four or five years later,' Kimmage says.

It was not an indoctrination, but simply a general heads-up as to the lie of the land in the professional peloton, an overview of its culture and mores. Vitamin injections and caffeine suppositories were both legal, and a fact of cycling life. If Kimmage felt any unease at the time, he didn't recognise it. 'No, I just kind of thought: "Right." I'm not sure how I would categorise it,' he says.

The details provided were sobering rather than shocking, but having survived the French amateur scene without resorting to the needle, Kimmage set out at RMO determined that syringes would not become a part of his daily regimen now. He had encountered doping at ACBB and Wasquehal, of course, but it was usually a furtive act. At the very least, it was easily ignored. 'At ACBB, one of the guys on the team was doing something at a stage race in Boulogne, so I had a sense of it there, but we were so fucking naïve,' Kimmage says. 'At Wasquehal, I'm sure there was loads of it there. There was one guy who had a pharmacy with him. He was into all sorts of shit. But we were looking at him as a fucking eejit: "What are you doing with that shit?" So there was an awareness of it, but subconsciously you were thinking, "It's not affecting me," so you didn't pay notice to it.'

In the professional ranks, he soon discovered, it was impossible to avoid. Kimmage was six weeks into his debut season at RMO when he first witnessed the phenomenon of doping at close quarters. Milan-San Remo had taken place the previous afternoon but Kimmage instead found himself performing off Broadway on the third weekend in March, at the low-key Grand Prix de Mauléon-Moulins in Cholet in western France. He had struggled through his opening races of the season, suffering the consequences of his own injury-hampered winter. It had been a brutal reality check, and the experience in Cholet hardly lightened the neophyte's mood.

The night before the race, RMO assistant directeur sportif Jean-Claude Vallaeys casually reminded his charges that there would be no anti-doping controls after the race. Before the start, there was mirth in the peloton as riders tucked sawn-off syringes of amphetamine into their pockets. The first person that Kimmage saw handling a syringe was neither a medic nor a masseur, but a cyclist from the Fagor team. 'The first time I saw a syringe was down in Cholet in 1986. The guy who shows me how it's done is Jean-René Bernaudeau. He shows me how it's done,' Kimmage says. 'Kelly had won Milan-San Remo the day before and I'm racing in Cholet. And that was the first time I'd seen it and got a sense of how fucked up it was.'

During his opening months on the team, Kimmage raised some eyebrows among the soigneurs for his refusal to accept vitamin injections, a stance he would maintain until the end of the first week of his debut Tour de France that same year. His refusal to dope was seen as a curiosity, but such eccentricity was tolerated by his teammates and, crucially, by his manager Bernard Thévenet. The double Tour winner may have been, by Roche's reckoning, too nice a man to be an effective directeur sportif, but Kimmage was grateful for his kindness. When Kimmage struggled with his confidence on descents, Thévenet came to his room to offer advice. On occasion, even Thévenet could deliver a dressing down, but never once did he question Kimmage's reluctance to dope. After experiencing the deleterious effects of cortisone abuse during his own career, Thévenet seemed to have little appetite to send riders down the same path against their will. 'He had a great humanity about him, he was an absolute gentleman,' Kimmage says. 'And there was never any mention of doping with him. Nobody was saying, "Paul, do that or try this." It was very individual. You had to seek it out. Now if you did go and seek it out, you would find it. But I wasn't interested. For what reason? I still struggle with it. I wasn't interested.'

Only once during Kimmage's time at RMO was he expressly encouraged to dope, when the squad had to defend Patrice Esnault's overall lead on the final day of the Midi-Libre in 1987, and even then, it was a teammate rather than a manager who did the prodding. 'It was Jean-François Rault who said, "This is the job now, you've got to take this,"' Kimmage says. 'I wasn't doing it, but that was the only pressure I ever felt during my time there to dope. I wasn't dealing with a US Postal situation, where if Bruyneel saw you weren't doing it, you were fucked.' Had Kimmage signed for a different team, however, he wonders if his own resistance to doping would have been as steadfast.

'This is going to sound ridiculous, but the greatest break I ever got was signing for RMO, and not for Kas with Kelly or Carrera with Roche. That was the greatest fucking break I ever got in my fucking life,' Kimmage says. 'It allowed me to be who I wanted to be, to make my choices. Had I gone to Kas or had I gone to Carrera, I would have been juiced to my fucking eyeballs from the get go. I would have gone in there, I would have seen it. I would have seen Kelly and Roche, and I would have said, "I'm going to be your loyal lieutenant. I'm going to do whatever it takes to make sure you're winning and doing what you need to do."'

Kimmage never rode on the same trade team as Kelly, but Irishmen in the Continental peloton were wont to help one another out, and early in his professional career, he stayed with the Carrick-on-Suir man in Vilvoorde when he competed in some Belgian kermesse races. 'I cannot pinpoint exactly when it was, but I feel like it was '86 because I had a much better awareness of how the business worked in '87,' Kimmage says. Ahead of one of the races, he was among a group of riders changing upstairs above a bar while rain bucketed down outside.

'I'm sitting there, getting ready for this, and the boys start taking the stuff out of the bags: injections. Syringes. Amphetamines. I'm sitting here and I'm thinking, "Fuuuck,"' Kimmage says. 'So anyway, we ride the race. I didn't get too far, I can tell you now, after I'd seen this. We went outside and it's fucking bottling down and these guys are riding like nut jobs. I didn't get too far.'

Kimmage was shocked; not so much about the doping, but that they were doing so for such an inconsequential event.

An RMO teammate would later explain that riders occasionally took amphetamine to help them through the slog of six-hour training rides. Injections, both legal and illicit, were simply an occupational hazard. Use of corticosteroids, difficult to detect in doping controls, was rife. Anything that helped get the job done, it seemed, was fair game. 'This is the business. This is your job,' Kimmage says. 'If you weren't doing cortisone in '86, you're weren't doing *le metier*. This was part of your fucking job.'

Despite this apparent professional shortcoming, Kimmage was selected to ride the 1986 Tour, his form having improved markedly after he moved his Continental base in midseason from Wasquehal to the more mountainous surrounds of Grenoble. In the early part of the year, he had struggled on flat, windswept races in northern France and Belgium, but he fared better in hillier terrain as the year progressed. In the opening week of the Tour, Kimmage's optimism was such that he even infiltrated a break on the road to Saint-Hilaire-du-Harcouet, placing 9th on the stage, but within days, his race switched from wide-eyed adventure to dead-eyed slog. After losing eight minutes to Bernard Hinault in the first long time trial at Nantes, an exhausted Kimmage consented to his first B12 injection. Although he endured to reach Paris, 131st out of 132 finishers, it was, in hindsight, the month his ambition died. From that point onwards, he would allow himself no grander aspiration than survival. 'We got to the mountains and I was just wiped out,' he says. 'To think, a couple of weeks earlier I thought I could win a stage.'

Kimmage's 1987 campaign followed a similar pattern. After a series of nondescript displays early in the year, a strong showing at the Dauphiné Libéré in June again earned him selection for the Tour. If innocence had helped Kimmage through his maiden Tour, experience was of little benefit to him in his second. Knowing precisely what lay ahead only made the road harder. The absence of a patron made for gripping racing among the contenders for yellow, but the men at the rear of the peloton paid a price for the soaring speeds. On stage 21, already long-distanced by the bunch on the Col du Galibier, Kimmage wheeled to a halt after a kilometre of the Col du Télégraphe and abandoned the Tour. As Kimmage sat mournfully in the broom wagon that climbed slowly towards the finish line at La Plagne, Roche was riding himself to the point of oblivion on what would be his most famous day. Same race, different worlds.

Little more than two weeks after refusing a doctor's offer to administer doping products to help him through the Tour, Kimmage allowed himself to be injected with amphetamine by a fellow rider before an exhibition race where the result had already been fixed in advance. It doesn't make a lot of sense to the outsider, but then professional cycling has always adhered to a logic entirely of its own making.

On the morning of the 1987 Tour's entry into the Pyrenees in Pau, RMO team doctor Bernard Aguilanu visited the race. 'He calls me in and says, "Paul, listen, how about trying this? Take this and put it under your tongue." It was testosterone. I said, "No, I'm not doing that,"' Kimmage says. 'Don't ask me why I said no, because I don't know.'

By the time the Château-Chinon criterium came around on 3 August, Kimmage was in a rather more vulnerable state. Abandoning the Tour had been harrowing enough, but Roche's subsequent victory overall turned that trauma into something of an existential crisis. He had already agreed a deal with RMO for 1988, becoming, in his own words, a 'qualified pro', and he wondered if it might be time to start fulfilling all the obligations that seemingly entailed. In the days after leaving the Tour, Kimmage had hardly touched his bike, and drove the four hours to Château-Chinon with dread knotted in the pit of his stomach. It was the first time he had secured a contract for a post-Tour criterium, and now he risked performing so badly as to ensure it would be his last.

On arrival, Kimmage changed with his RMO teammates Thierry Claveyrolat, Bernard Vallet, André Chappuis, Michel Bibollet and Jean-Claude Colotti. Out of politeness, a rider offered Kimmage a charge of amphetamine for the two-hour race ahead, even though his abstinence was common knowledge. This Irishman had, after all, refused a charge even ahead of the final stage of the 1986 Tour, a day when there were no random doping controls and the peloton would race at 60kph up and down the Champs-Élysées. Kimmage had survived that ordeal, but now, perhaps to even his own surprise, he found himself saying yes. He was a broken man. 'Maybe going out of the Tour was the last step for me. Maybe watching Stephen Roche win the Tour de France and me going out with four days to go was the last step for me,' Kimmage says. 'Maybe that was the last step.'

With amphetamine coursing through his system and an equally potent placebo planted in his brain, Kimmage rode well in the afternoon criterium, dutifully playing his part in the preordained script and pocketing his £250 appearance fee afterwards. As he prepared to drive home afterwards, Claveyrolat, a neighbour in Vizille and his closest friend on the team, kindly padded his sharp decision to yield to temptation in some context. 'You must not blame yourself,' Claveyrolat told Kimmage as he climbed into his car. 'It's just part of the job.'

It is not difficult to understand why Kimmage doped for that criterium in Château-Chinon: he was at the lowest ebb of his career and risked running aground altogether. It is rather harder to explain why he had *not* doped before that point; he had been floundering in perilous waters for almost two full seasons by that point. Yet despite seeming out of his depth, Kimmage had refused to dope, and to this day, he can't fully explain whether it was for moral reasons, health concerns or the simple fear of being caught.

'All of the above. But I say that now. What if I'd joined Kas? That was the difference. It allowed me to make my own decisions for myself,' Kimmage says. 'And you know what, it takes courage to pump that shit into yourself. There's a certain courage with that. You could say it's a stupidity as well, but it's a fine line. I always thought it took a lot of guts. I remember seeing Kelly's ass in the Tour of Britain in the showers. Fuck, it was fucking unreal. The butt cheeks of his ass in the showers, it was unreal. Just black and blue from needles. He put some amount of shit through his system. For whatever reason, I wasn't going to go there. I didn't want to go there.'

Despite Kimmage's misgivings, he used amphetamine on two more occasions in August 1987. This time around, Frank Quinn had succeeded in securing him a contract to compete in the city centre races in Ireland, with events in Dublin, Wexford and Cork. It was one thing to struggle anonymously in a race in France, but another altogether to be dropped and made to feel like a failure in one's home town. Kimmage lined up at the Dublin race with Kelly, Roche and Earley and a number of British professionals, including Paul Sherwen. Kimmage was determined not to be embarrassed in front of his own people. Even if the British riders refused to fix the race to allow Roche to win, in other respects a criterium in Dublin followed the same principles as one in France. There was, of course, no doping control, and a fast-paced show was expected.

As the multitudes gathered on College Green and throughout the city centre to fete the Tour de France champion Roche, the competitors changed in the toilets of Trinity College. They could hear the muffled clamour of the crowds through the walls as they made their final preparations for the race. Kimmage accepted a charge of amphetamine, procured from a fellow professional rider. Another rider prepared the syringe for Kimmage and performed the injection. Showtime. Ireland against Britain. Roche won, Kimmage performed, and the masses were sated. Two nights later, the same ritual was carried out before the criterium in Cork. It was intoxicating and nauseating in equal measure.

'That was the third time, and after the third time, I'm starting to think about it now. This is pretty fucking disgusting, in a toilet,' Kimmage says:

MORE PRICKS THAN KICKS

And I remember I got another crit, it might have been down in Angers, not that long after it and I made the decision: never again. I remember taking a vitamin pill, popping it into my bottle and thinking, 'This is as far as you're going now.' And psychologically, you're fucked. So from then I settled for being a domestique. That's the end of it. I'm looking for a way out from that moment on. It's a job now to me after that, because there's no glory and no ambition.

15

The Fab Four and the Fifth Beatle

Back home, he was the young man who had been broken by Belgium, but by 1987, Alan McCormack had broken America. 'I made $100,000 in 1985. I can show you my tax return,' McCormack says from Boulder, Colorado, where he has lived for over 30 years. 'I enjoyed the lifestyle, and I wasn't beaten up like I was in Belgium. There was sunshine, I was happy and I'm still here. I've got a life here: two grown kids, a bunch of wives. I still get people recognising me from the old days, and I still make the front on the group ride.'

McCormack kept racing at an elite level well into his 50s, eventually scaling back when it emerged that he needed two stents in his heart, though he still rides every day after finishing his early morning job in cleaning. His has been a life less ordinary, but for the most part, he has been consigned to a footnote in Irish cycling history. To many, he was the talented junior who raced with Kelly and Roche, and then disappeared off the face of the known cycling world to race in the United States. Only in recent years, thanks to the power of the internet, has McCormack's status in America travelled across the Atlantic in any real detail. Grainy YouTube footage shows McCormack careering to victory at events like the Coors Classic or the Tour de Moon. Google searches show photos of McCormack receiving America's ultimate sporting accolade, his image on the front of a Wheaties cereal box.

Like every other ambitious young cyclist in Ireland in the 1970s, McCormack had set out initially with dreams of making it big on the Continent. After competing at the Montreal Olympics in 1976, McCormack left his job as an auto mechanic to join Britain's burgeoning professional scene the following year, signing for the Carlton-Weinmann team for the princely sum of £25 per week. Based in Birmingham and later in Manchester, he struggled to adapt to the demands of the professional life and to life in England in general, and he cycled to catch the Liverpool-Dublin ferry home whenever he had a free weekend. A 6th-place result in the London-Holyhead race was perhaps the stand-out performance of tenure in England, but at season's end, Karl McCarthy, the secretary of the Irish Cycling Federation, suggested to McCormack that he try his luck on the Continent in 1977.

'Karl said, "You need to go to Belgium." He had all these contacts and through one of his friends who lived in Brussels, I got on a Belgian team, Splendor, and off I went,' McCormack says. As simple and as complicated as that. Although McCormack was glad of manager Robert Lauwers's offer to live above his café in Erps-Kwerps, thus saving him from death by a thousand early nights in suburbia with Herman Nys, he was less well served by Lauwers's management skills. McCormack's racing programme at Old Lord's-Splendor made no concession to his tender years or relative inexperience.

'The racing was tough. I raced Het Volk, Paris-Nice, all the classics, Tour of Flanders, Liège-Bastogne-Liège: you name it, I raced it,' McCormack says. 'In between, I raced all the kermesses. They were 150 kilometres, really fast, and maybe harder than the classics. Lauwers had me racing every day and eventually, I was just fucked. It was intense. Jesus Christ. It just got worse and worse.'

At Splendor, McCormack raced with men like Ferdinand Bracke and Eddy Merckx's old lieutenant Roger Swerts. 'They did what they could to help me; I was only a child,' McCormack says. Rather than rest the 21-year-old at the end of the spring, however, Lauwers dispatched him to ride the Vuelta a España. Somehow, he made it through the three weeks, reaching Madrid in 55th place overall, but it was the beginning of the end of his time with Splendor. By early summer, he was back in Ireland, and working as a mechanic in Clontarf. 'I was fried, mentally and physically. My body just shut down. I didn't have any interest in riding,' McCormack says. 'I was just burned out. I couldn't recover.'

In an era when the division between the professional and amateur ranks was strictly demarcated, it took considerable time and bureaucracy before the ICF allowed McCormack to race domestically once again. The innuendo that surrounded McCormack's abrupt return from Belgium certainly didn't help his cause. There were whispers about doping. 'I always had a red flag in Ireland as an ex-pro, that I had a pocket full of pills,' McCormack says. 'It didn't matter whether it was true or not. I never made any comments or never told anybody anything about anything over there [in Belgium]. But there was definitely a big party over there when I was there. And I'm sure there's a big party over there now.'

McCormack eventually regraded to amateur level, and after placing 3rd behind Roche in the 1979 Rás, he began the 1980 event looking every inch the likely winner. He held a commanding overall lead four stages in, only to abandon due to illness, caused, he says, by a late-night yoghurt in a hotel in Donegal town. 'I had people saying it was because your back pocket was full of pills, you know, the usual,' McCormack says. 'That was the end of that.'

Not quite. After the Rás, Pat McQuaid invited McCormack to join him on a five-man Irish team for a series of criteriums in Chicago. It would prove a most auspicious journey. Unlike in Europe, American criteriums were fiercely competitive affairs. 'Every lap had a prime for $100, and I was nailing all these sprints because I had so much power and energy from my time in Belgium,' McCormack says. 'In the first criterium I did, I won $1,000 in 45 minutes and I said, "I'm fucking staying here."'

McCormack's performance in Chicago earned him an invitation to race with the AMS team at the Coors Classic, alongside Eric Heiden, the Olympic champion speed skater who was beginning a new career as a cyclist, and Davis Phinney, who would go on to win a stage of the Tour de France. McCormack stayed initially with Pat McQuaid's sister Siobhan in New York, before travelling to Colorado a month before the Coors Classic to acclimatise. 'I stayed in a house in Boulder and all the riders, men and women, stayed there too. That suited me fine, hot chicks in the same house,' McCormack says. He would make Boulder his home. By the mid-1980s, his winnings were such that he could afford to buy a house there in cash.

Racing first under the aegis of Killian's Irish Red and then for Schwinn, McCormack became something of a box office name in America's developing – and increasingly lucrative – professional scene, where criteriums offered a cheap, made-for-television spectacle. 'The money was in criteriums, so I adapted my training. I went to shorter cranks, and I used to get the bikes made with really high bottom brackets so I could pedal around corners,' McCormack says. 'But those criteriums were hard. It would take you days to recover.'

And yet, for all his renown and earning power in the United States, by the mid-1980s, McCormack still yearned for something more. What better way to prove that he was an Irish professional bike rider than by riding the professional World Championships for the Irish team? He had competed at Montello in 1985, when Motta bikes paid his way to Italy. He had lined out when the Worlds came to his own patch in Colorado Springs in 1986. And now, in 1987, he was setting off to Villach, Austria to compete in the green jersey of Ireland at the World Championships.

While McCormack was blazing his lone trail in the United States, the four other members of Ireland's World Championships team came home for five days in late August, amid the afterglow of Roche's Tour victory. The Kellogg's series took place in Dublin and Cork once again, while an additional criterium was also organised in Wexford in between the two main events. Although wearing different jerseys, Roche, Kelly, Earley and Kimmage essentially competed under the same banner that week. As Irish cycling experienced its summer of love, they were its Beatles.

It wasn't planned as such, but the week ended up as something of a team-building exercise ahead of the Worlds, particularly once battle lines were drawn with the visiting British professionals and the racing descended into an Ireland–England match. On the first night in Dublin, the Irish contingent expected that the criterium would be disputed along Continental lines: the riders would put on a spectacle, but in the end, Roche, the local idol, would cross the line first and ensure everybody would go home happy. When Kelly ran the idea past some of the British party, however, he was rebuffed. At least some of the British riders had no qualms about preparing for the city centre race in the Continental manner but fixing the outcome apparently offended their Corinthian ideals. 'The British pros turned around to Sean and said, "Stephen won the Tour. If he wants to win here, he'll have to win under his own steam,"' Roche says.

Not everybody opposed the Irish plan – Paul Sherwen and the Australian Allan Peiper were among those to argue in favour of a Roche win – but the Dublin event proved more competitive than planned, even if, according to Kimmage, £1,000 was paid out to be divided among the British riders. Roche soloed to victory in Dublin, and by the following evening in Wexford, the visitors were more willing to play ball, but were now knocked back by the Irish quartet. 'We said, "Sorry guys, you had your chance." And I remember we went out and won all the primes, and Sean won the race,' says Roche. At the zenith of his renown back home, going for a quiet celebratory pint was out of the question for Roche. 'We couldn't leave the hotel, so we sat in the corridor eating fish and chips and beer, joking about what we'd done and how we'd pulled one over on the British pros.'

The final instalment came in Cork, by which point there was little hope of a compromise being brokered between the Irish and British contingents. Far from the carefully choreographed fare of a Continental criterium, the final Kellogg's race proved a full-blooded affair. The charged atmosphere was obvious to Pat McQuaid as he surveyed the scene from a portacabin overlooking the start line. 'I said to Kelly, "Has anything been sorted?" And he said, "No, the Brits won't have it,"' McQuaid recalls. '"Fuck them," he says. I could sense the adrenaline in the bunch. Everyone was on edge. And I said to myself, somebody's going to get killed here. And I wasn't far wrong.'

The race came down to a group finish as they swung off St Patrick's Bridge, and after leading out the sprint for Kelly, Roche drifted backwards. The British rider Mark Walsham crashed into Roche as he tried to come past, bringing 10 more riders down with them. Kelly sprinted to the win ahead of Peiper, while a bloodied Walsham protested at what he felt was an unnecessary manoeuvre from Roche. 'I am categorically saying that he wiped me out, he hit me with his bike just to take me out of the race because he knew I am a good finisher,' Walsham complained afterwards.

Threats of an appeal, unsurprisingly, came to nothing, and rather than look to smooth Anglo-Irish relations, Roche played to the gallery when a group of reporters jostled around him after he walked across the finish line. 'It is stupid for anyone to say they were brought down purposely. The bike game is our bread and butter,' Roche said, and then grinned: 'Anyway, the score is Ireland three, England nil.'

The Irish quartet knocked a kick out of that one as they said their goodbyes in Cork and went their separate ways before teaming up again in Austria 10 days later. 'That was a fucking great week,' Kimmage says. 'There was a great bond there.'

Tucked away in the Gailtal Alps near the Italo-Austrian border, Villach was not the most accessible venue for a World Championships. Kimmage made the 10-hour trek from Grenoble by car in the company of Bernard Thévenet, who was moonlighting as a television analyst. Kelly and Roche, finding themselves just across the frontier at the Giro del Friuli, decided to ride the 120 kilometres from Gemona to Villach. The most arduous journey, however, was that of McCormack, who flew cattle class from Boulder to Vienna by way of Boston, and then hauled his bike box aboard a train and navigated the Austrian rail system, arriving in Villach late on the Friday before the race.

At Montello two years previously, McCormack had shared a room with Kelly, Roche and Earley, and, like a returning emigrant cousin, arrived bearing delicacies from across the water. 'I'd brought over boxes of M&Ms, shitloads of them, and they were all eating them on me,' McCormack laughs. This time around, while the Fab Four stayed at the expense of their professional teams in the friendly confines of the Hotel Piber, 15 kilometres outside of Villach, McCormack was housed with the Irish amateur team in rather less comfortable lodgings in the centre of town. 'It was a horrible place. It was like a prison,' McCormack says. 'It was hell to get there. I had all these different connecting flights and delays. By the time I got to Austria, I was just fried. I barely even made it to the start.'

McCormack's teammates might scarcely have noticed if he hadn't. 'I'd actually forgotten he was in it because he wasn't part of the group, not at all,' Kimmage says. 'I don't know if we even said hello to him, which is just mad – and wrong. Maybe we did have some contact with him, but I can't remember it.' Small wonder that when Irish reporters happened upon McCormack on the eve of the race, he told them that he was not especially inclined to ride in support of Kelly and Roche. 'I don't earn £500,000 a year. I want the highest possible placing,' he said. Patrick Valcke did, however, prepare McCormack's bike ahead of the race. 'They were very kind to me,' McCormack says of Roche and Kelly. 'They had their team mechanics with them, and they wrapped my handlebar tape and took care of my tyres.'

In the Italian or Belgian hotel on the night before the World Championships, riders vying for leadership of the team would typically pledge a sizeable bonus to be shared among their teammates in the event of victory. There were no such arrangements being discussed at the Hotel Piber, nor was there any real thought given to race tactics. The Irish team had no manager, and their roughly sketched plan was to ride in support of Kelly. He was best equipped to triumph on the Villach course, and, in any case, Roche had again been troubled by knee pain since his crash in Cork. They knew there was no point in devising a more detailed scheme when the 12-man squads from Italy, Belgium and France would inevitably dictate the terms of engagement. 'You can't talk tactics with five guys,' Earley says. 'I think the idea was just to hang on as long as possible and try to help Kelly.'

In public, Kelly and Roche were the friendliest of rivals, always ready to lavish praise upon one another, but in private, they had endured the biggest falling-out of their careers in the spring of 1987. Kelly made no concessions to their friendship at Paris-Nice in March, at a time when Roche was under pressure to produce a big win to justify his Carrera contract. Roche led overall coming into the final day, and when he punctured on the Col de Vence as Kas set the pace, Kelly showed no clemency. 'I remember Jean-Luc Vandenbroucke was riding on the front for me. He heard the puncture, and he looked around and said "*Ah, c'est Roche.*" And he just pushed the pace up by about three miles an hour,' Kelly says. 'It was almost at the summit, and there was gravel on the road. I remember we did the descent full on and when we got to the flat section, other riders started to work and Roche never made it back.' To compound matters, Kelly's directeur sportif Christian Rumeau reportedly drove alongside Roche's chasing group and bumped a photographer's motorbike out of the way, lest they avail of its slipstream.

Roche won the Col d'Èze time trial that afternoon, but to no end. Kelly had his sixth consecutive Paris-Nice title, and his fellow countryman made no secret of his displeasure. 'There were sparks at the finish,' Kelly laughs. Although they trained together on the Riviera the week after the race, and ostensibly talked through their differences, the tensions lingered for much of the spring. 'I think it festered for a while, and it festered real badly for the first week or two,' Kelly says. 'Slowly, but it was there. You could feel it when we spoke to each other, and it was still there for quite a few weeks.'

By September, however, the animosity had subsided, and they served as natural foils at the Worlds, on and off the bike. On the afternoon before the race, while his roommate Roche held court for a retinue of journalists in the hotel lobby, recounting all over again the story of his famous Giro-Tour double, Kelly enjoyed a nap. During the race itself, they would each act as the other's decoy, though for most of the day, as rain cascaded over the 12-kilometre circuit, Roche was marshalling the Irish effort in support of Kelly, even if it was all rather ad hoc.

'Roche did come back one time and grab me to bring me the front: "Come on, get on my wheel." So I did that. That was my claim to fame,' McCormack says. 'He came back and got me, dragged my little ass up to the front of the peloton: "Come on, get the fuck on my wheel." But there was no "We want you to cover the early breaks." There was no "Alan, if you do this, we'll give you this."' McCormack lasted 19 laps before he wheeled to a halt and watched the finale from the Irish tent near the finish line. 'I had a hard time with the distance. Seven hours on the bike, no training can simulate that.'

With two laps remaining, as the rain finally subsided, McCormack was joined in the pits by Earley, who had put in a mammoth turn at the head of the peloton to peg back a dangerous break featuring the pre-race favourite Moreno Argentin of Italy. His job done, Earley peeled off the front and then climbed off the bike. 'When you're spent, you're spent,' he says.

Kimmage was also prominent in a supporting role in the closing laps in what, in hindsight, was arguably his finest outing as a professional cyclist. Once the decisive selection formed in the final two laps, his work was done, and he finished in 43rd place. 'A group went away and the Italians had one in it, so nobody was chasing it,' Kelly says. 'So we said, "Fuck, this is not good here." It was a break that could have stayed away, so we told Kimmage and Earley to ride. Credit where credit is due, they rode really well for Ireland. They closed that break down, or almost closed it down.'

As at Goodwood and Altenrhein, it came down to Kelly and Roche on the final lap, and with only 13 riders left in contention, numerical inferiority was no longer a pressing issue. Only the Dutch, with three riders, outnumbered the Irish pair, but Argentin no longer had any blue jerseys alongside him. With no team able to control the group, there was just one viable tactical approach amid the inevitable flurry of late attacks. 'I said to Stephen, "Look, the only thing to do here is one of us goes with one attack and the other goes with the next attack,"' Kelly says. 'I went at least two or maybe three times with attacks. I'd get a little bit ahead and then I'd be closed down, and then Roche would go with the next one. Roche went with one. They looked at each other behind, and that was the one.'

In the finale, Kelly had endured the misfortune of being man-marked by the on-form Argentin when he bridged across to an Erik Breukink attack with three kilometres to go. When Roche tracked Teun van Vliet and Rolf Gölz shortly afterwards, only Rolf Sørensen and Guido Winterberg came with them, and a gap yawned open. By the time this leading quintet reached the base of the final descent, they had a winning margin and fanned across the road, no one daring to seize the initiative. Mindful of his own weakness in a sprint, Roche looked repeatedly over his shoulder, scanning the road for a sight of Kelly, but there was a similar deadlock in the group behind. Nobody wanted to drag Kelly and Argentin to a sprint finish, and the two favourites were certainly not going to help one another.

It was up to Roche. In contrast to his dithering at Liège-Bastogne-Liège, he looked to anticipate the sprint. With 400 metres to go, as the road began to kick up towards the line, he accelerated from fourth wheel, squeezing between Sørensen and the left-hand barrier. He would not be caught. The Kelly group was closing in, but only to contest the medals. The rainbow jersey was Roche's so long as he could keep his gear turning over. Five metres from the line, he threw his arms into the air. World champion. Instinctively, Kelly flung his arms skywards at the same time. Rather than continue his attempt to battle for a medal, he freewheeled across the line in 5th place, punching the air three times as he did so. 'That's genuine. Absolutely genuine,' Kimmage says. 'You can't fake that.'

'No matter what anybody might say, no matter what doubt anybody would have about our relationship, that says it all,' Roche says. 'Because if Sean was unhappy for me, or jealous, he wouldn't have done that. That was spontaneous. That was from the heart: "I'm happy for this guy."'

Kelly was the first person to embrace Roche after the finish, clasping him in a hug even before he had wheeled to a halt. A tearful Valcke was next, followed by Herman Nys, and then Roche was wrapped in a swirl of microphones and cameras. McCormack stood stage left, surveying the scene. He had been part of one of the greatest performances by an Irish international team in any sport, yet somehow removed from it. 'I was at the tents and everybody was excited,' McCormack recalls. 'I remember one of Roche's mechanics, some little guy, was crying.'

As Roche was ushered towards the podium, Kelly held court for the gaggle of Irish reporters who had assembled in Villach expecting him to be crowned world champion. Like Roche's Tour victory, it was a bittersweet occasion. Kelly had been Ireland's standard bearer for a decade, and now in the space of one summer, Roche had carried off cycling's three biggest prizes, a treble that had been achieved only by Eddy Merckx.

Kelly was magnanimous in his praise for Roche, but honest about his own feelings. 'Naturally I'm a bit disappointed, I would have liked to have won,' he admitted. Had the cards fallen differently, the rainbow jersey might have been his. 'It could have been the other way. It could have been that I was in the move that stuck – it would have been with Argentin, of course, because he was on my wheel all the time,' Kelly says now. 'But that's the way it goes.'

Back at the Hotel Piber, the proprietor produced a bottle of champagne and Roche's world title was toasted by the Irish entourage, but that gathering was merely a prologue to a lengthier period of festivity. 'If only Charlie was here now,' Roche quipped to one reporter. Two days later, having raced a Monday night criterium in Brittany in the rainbow jersey of world champion, Roche duly posed with Haughey for a photo opportunity at

Leinster House, after a delegation led by Minister for Sport Frank Fahey had formally greeted him at Dublin airport.

The popular homecoming celebration, meanwhile, took place at the Nissan Classic three weeks later. On the eve of the race, an estimated 15,000 people gathered on College Green for a ceremony that saw Roche made a freeman of Dublin city, the first time the honour had been bestowed upon a sportsperson. At a Dublin Corporation meeting the following week, councillors complained that they had not all been able to line up and shake Roche's hand one by one. As the Nissan Classic made its way around the country, it seemed every provincial town and local councillor also wanted to get in on the reflected glory. All of Ireland's Continental professionals were included. 'I think I'm a freeman of Tralee,' Kimmage says. 'The Nissan in '87 was the height of it.'

The crowds at the roadside for that year's race were of the kind reserved for a Papal visit, and the by-now traditional go-slow in protest at stage distances and Roche's public dissatisfaction at his £10,000 appearance fee did little to dampen the national mood. Kelly, of course, won the race for the third time in a row. 'It was wild altogether,' Pat McQuaid says. 'We had something like 85,000 people on a five-mile finishing circuit in Limerick, and the population of Limerick at the time was only 60,000. On the last day in Kilkenny, the crowds were so big that the bunch went off in two different directions in the confusion at the start. We were on the radio trying to find them – "Where are you, where are you?" – and we eventually got ourselves sorted out two or three miles down the road. It was huge.'

There had never been an Irish sporting phenomenon quite like the cycling boom. This was before the Irish football team had ever qualified for a major tournament and long before the Irish rugby team's appeal moved beyond a small caste of private schools. Olympic gold medallists like Ronnie Delany and Dr Pat O'Callaghan had been respected, but competed before the advent of television in Ireland, and thus were neither as well known nor as adored. By the mid-1980s, Kelly and Roche could be seen competing in colour on Irish television screens. Their faces and accents, their quirks and foibles were familiar to an entire nation. No contemporaries in other international sports, not even Barry McGuigan, commanded the same level of adulation across the country.

'Oh, this was much bigger,' David Walsh says, continuing:

Roche winning the Tour de France was huge and Irish people just really liked Kelly. He was the kind of person that a lot of Irish people wanted to think represented your typical Irishman. He was understated, very unaffected, down to earth, all that stuff. He was a hard man, tough, out there in the big bad world of professional cycling, getting into sprints and not backing off. People liked that about him. They liked the fact that he was so straightforward.

Over the top as it may have been, an *Irish Independent* editorial on the eve of the Nissan Classic summed up the prevailing mood: 'Poor little Ireland is crippled by debt, riddled by unemployment and weighed down by a blood-sucking black economy. But this speck of green in the North Atlantic is rich with one commodity … sporting gold.' Even within that shrinking economy, Kelly and Roche cashed in on their success to some degree in the late 1980s, even if, as Roche points out, 'there weren't that many opportunities for endorsements in Ireland'. All the same, Guinness and Cidona built advertising campaigns around Kelly, and he lent his name to a cycling-based board game. Roche starred in a television commercial for Galtee cheese, and his likeness adorned promotional tea towels that seemed to make their way into almost every home in the country. Together, Kelly and Roche were the faces of Bank of Ireland's new Pass cash machines.

In the autumn of 1987, Roche's every move on his intermittent trips to Ireland was reported upon in the national media. There was speculation that he would attend Paul and Ann Kimmage's wedding on 23 October, and the newlyweds emerged from Balscadden church to find half of North County Dublin perched along the walls, waiting for a glimpse of the VIP on the guest list. Roche obliged by signing autographs. In a quieter moment during the reception that evening, he slipped a package into Kimmage's hand.

'We opened the envelope when we got to the hotel, and it was a grand in cash. The card with it says, "Paul, I just wanted to say thanks a lot for helping at the Worlds,"' Kimmage says. 'I didn't even think about money before the Worlds, and I'm looking at that, more money than I'd ever seen in my life. It was fucking great. But there was no mention of money or bonuses before the race. We didn't give a shit.'

Despite the inscription, Roche's gift was a wedding present rather than a Worlds bonus. None of the other Irish riders received payment for their efforts in Villach. 'It cost me $5,000 to get there in the first place. Jesus,' laughs McCormack, who didn't even get to share in the celebrations that followed. Not only did the Dubliner miss the Nissan Classic and the freedom of Tralee, he didn't so much as share a glass of champagne with his teammates in Villach.

'Afterwards, I just went back to my little dungeon hotel where I was staying by myself, and I left early the next morning to get the train,' McCormack says. 'I had to go and get a train to get my passport stamped for my visa to get back into the US, and then I got the plane from Vienna.'

McCormack spent the day shoehorning his bike box onto trains and lugging it behind him around Vienna, before boarding a flight to Chicago and the US Pro Criterium Championships. To the outsider, it might have seemed like a comedown after competing against the world's best in Austria. To McCormack, it was the ultimate confirmation that he had chosen the right path.

'Trudy, the Schwinn girl, picked me up in the airport in Chicago and brought me to the Hyatt hotel, top notch.' he says. 'The criterium championships were on there. I got second place, won $1,200, five days after the World Championships that Roche won. I thought, yeah, that makes sense. After all that travel, all those planes, trains, crappy hotels and Austria, which I hated, I was back where I truly belonged.'

16

A LITTLE CLOUD

Kelly being Kelly, he is reticent even now to expand greatly on the conflicting feelings conjured up by Stephen Roche's 1987 season and, in particular, his Tour de France triumph. Paul Kimmage can hazard a guess. 'Kelly would have been fucking gutted when Roche won the Tour,' he says. 'Up until then, he was the man, but when Roche won the Tour, it altered the terms of his legacy. It meant that what Roche had achieved would always be greater than what he did. Do people think about who was world number one at the time? No, winning the Tour de France is your place in history. Kelly understood that more than anybody when Roche won the Tour. That would have been really fucking tough.'

Just as Roche's Paris-Nice win in 1981 had nudged Kelly towards his reinvention as an all-rounder, his Tour victory seemed to encourage Kelly to redouble his own efforts to prove himself over three weeks. After the disappointment of the previous year, Kelly vowed 1988 would be different, even if it began in familiar fashion. A seventh straight Paris-Nice victory came as a matter of routine. 'Kelly would have disgusted

Hitchcock,' *Vélo Magazine* grumbled playfully. Jean-François Bernard saw the funny side: 'I even said to him, if you let me win Paris-Nice one day, I'll give you my Porsche.' Kelly, benign dictator and man of the people, seemed happy enough to keep his Citroën G5.

It was, on the face of it, a spring like any other for Kelly, who quietly amassed victories and refused to loosen his grip on the top spot in the FICP computer rankings. Since Kas had taken over sponsorship of his team in 1986, however, there had been a subtle shift in his habits, with an increasing emphasis placed on racing in Spain. Following de Gribaldy's death and Mendiburu's absorption of his former duties, that trend only intensified. Kas owner Louis Knorr used to joke that Belgians drank beer rather than soft drinks, and hence the northern classics were not a priority. Although Kelly did manage to pick up Ghent-Wevelgem victory, beating Gianni Bugno in a sprint, the Vuelta a España was the all-encompassing target of the first part of his season, particularly given his near miss the previous year.

'The boss of Kas said to me from the beginning, "For me, the Vuelta is the most important race on the calendar,"' Kelly says. In 1987, he had set out from Benidorm among the favourites, aiming to put time into the climbers in the two flat time trials, and then limit his losses in the mountains. He duly won the Valencia time trial in the opening week and then farmed the yellow jersey out to Reimund Dietzen. Luis Herrera took over the lead on the mountaintop finish at Lagos da Covadonga, but Kelly snatched it back from him in the Vallodolid time trial in the final week. With just four days remaining, Kelly held a lead of 43 seconds, and though some rugged terrain awaited in the

Sierras around Madrid, few were betting against him becoming Ireland's first Grand Tour winner.

A mere 14 kilometres into the next day's stage to Avila, however, Kelly dropped to the rear of the peloton, stepped off his bike and climbed into Ramón Mendiburu's team car. For reasons known only to Kas management and some resourceful Basque journalists, the *maillot amarillo* had abandoned the Vuelta. A full explanation arrived only when Mendiburu pulled up at the team hotel in Avila: for four days, Kelly had been suffering in silence with a cyst on his perineum, caused by an ingrowing hair. He could take no more. 'I was struggling to follow the pace of the peloton the day before the time trial,' Kelly told the waiting reporters. 'Pedro Delgado was the only one who spotted what was happening. He came over and asked me what was happening, so I told him, but I asked him not to tell anyone.'

Martin Earley, riding the Vuelta for Fagor, was also aware of Kelly's problems, though his discretion is hardly as surprising as that of Delgado, from the rival PDM team. 'I knew he was struggling – not to the extent that he was going to stop, but I knew he was in a bad way,' Earley says. On the eve of the time trial, the Vuelta's race doctor Fernando Astorqui came to the Kas hotel to lance the boil and stitch the wound. The makeshift remedy got Kelly through the time trial and back into yellow, but the stiches reopened during his effort. At the start of stage 19 in Barco de Avila, Kelly tried to maintain appearances by posing for photographers with a plate of beans, a local speciality, but he already knew his race was run. Unable to sit on the saddle, he left the Vuelta, and the overall victory went to Herrera.

Bad luck had not been the sole chink in Kelly's armour at the 1987 Vuelta. From his days at Sem, the team around him had tended to be replete with men to help him in sprints or the classics. Climbers were in short supply. 'When I got close in 1987, we started to talk about what we needed to do for the next year, and I said we needed to get riders who could work in the mountain stages,' Kelly says. 'I had Martin Earley in mind. I'd have known him pretty well. We'd always have talked a lot together at races, and he was performing really well.'

It helped that Earley had already shone on Mendiburu's home turf at the Tour of the Basque Country, winning stages in 1986 and 1987 during his time at Fagor, and the shorter climbs in Spain tended to suit him better than the higher passes of France and Italy. 'If I had mountain after mountain I wouldn't be strong enough, but on small mountains, up to 10k or so, I would be ok,' says Earley. Cohabitation with Kelly was seamless; neither man was given to complaining about his lot. 'I found him fairly easy to get on with,' Earley says. 'I did spend a lot of time with him, but we weren't always on the same races either because I wouldn't do the cobbled classics.' Earley's account of Kelly's leadership matches Jock Boyer's recollections from Sem and Skil: 'Sean was never outspoken as a leader.'

Kelly was the favourite to win the 1988 Vuelta, but on the day before he travelled to Tenerife for the start of the race, Mendiburu called with news that he had returned a positive test for codeine on the final day of the Tour of the Basque Country earlier that month. It was the second time that Kelly had failed an anti-doping control, after the Paris-Brussels incident of 1984, but it seems there was never any question that he would miss the Vuelta as a consequence. Indeed, when Kelly was cornered by Spanish reporters on landing in the Canaries, his principal concern seemed to be for the delay in informing him of the positive test. 'I didn't get any official communication to say that I'd tested positive,' he said. 'I took cough medicine to treat a cold that I had. It's certainly not an injection of morale before a Vuelta where I've come to win, but after 11 years as a professional, I'm used to everything.'

The cough medicine, Kelly said, was procured from a pharmacist near his home in Belgium, and he was unaware that it contained the banned codeine. According to Kelly's version of events, outlined in *Hunger*, he 'took a swig' from the bottle between finishing the final stage and heading to doping control. 'The pharmacist was a friend of mine and he was involved in cycling on a regional level, so I trusted him to know what I could take safely when I was racing,' Kelly wrote. Mistake or not, the lenient nature of the punishment for what was, regardless of intent, a second infraction demonstrates the reticence of cycling – and sport at large – to confront the issue of doping in the 1980s. As in 1984, Kelly was, months later, quietly handed a fine and a suspended ban by the Spanish cycling federation, and was also docked 10 minutes from his time at the Tour of the Basque Country, dropping him from 4th to 17th on the official overall classification.

In the Irish media, the positive test and Kelly's explanation were dutifully and dryly reported, and then seemingly forgotten about as soon as the race began. It was, as Kelly acknowledged later, a different era: 'There wasn't a big controversy. It certainly wasn't like it is today.' Five months ahead of Ben Johnson's positive test at the Seoul Olympics and a full decade before the Festina Affair, the wilful suspension of disbelief continued unabated, in Ireland and elsewhere. It's perhaps telling that Kelly always seems more anxious when discussing his positive tests now, three decades after the fact, than he ever did at the time. 'I suppose the first thing is if you look at the two positive tests I had, cough medicine and Stimul, you couldn't really say they're performance-enhancing,' he says. 'Like nowadays, if you look at it, they wouldn't be really performance-enhancing.'

Another curious formula was concocted for the start of the 1988 Vuelta, with organisers Unipublic deciding to split the peloton into five groups of 36 riders for the opening stage. Each group competed in a separate heat on a 17-kilometre circuit, with the first yellow jersey awarded to the winner of the fastest heat. 'It didn't affect GC much, but it was nonsense. It was just a nonsense,' Earley recalls. Kelly, with an eye to the long game rather than his old day-to-day existence in Grand Tours, worked on the front to ensure his heat was the fastest, rather than sparing himself to cross the line first.

The remainder of the Vuelta's early spell in the Canaries was a minor disaster for Kelly, whose Kas team allowed the dangerous Laudelino Cubino of BH to slip up the road on stage 2 and then conceded more ground in the team time trial the following day after losing strongman Thomas Wegmüller to dysentery. By the time the race reached the mainland, Kelly was more than two minutes down on Cubino and compelled to start pegging back seconds by competing for time bonuses at intermediate sprints – precisely the kind of approach that had proved so draining over the years at the Tour de France. Kelly succeeded in clawing back a clump off his deficit during the opening week, only to hand it back again on the first mountain stage to Brañillin, where the BH cohort was dominant. Álvaro

Pino won the stage, while his teammates Cubino and Anselmo Fuerte put almost a minute into Kelly and now occupied the top two positions overall. Kelly, now 2:40 behind, would have to start all over again.

The fightback began in earnest on the mountain time trial up the Alto del Naranco the next day, where Kelly placed 2nd – ahead of no less a climber than Luis Herrera – and put half a minute into both Cubino and Fuerte, and it continued as the Vuelta proceeded through the Sierra de la Demanda and into the Pyrenees. At the Vuelta, temperatures were lower and gradients were gentler than in France in July, and Kelly even claimed a mountaintop finish, winning the group sprint at Alto Valdezcaray on stage 11. 'The climbs weren't as big as the Tour, and it wasn't even like the Vuelta is now,' says Earley. 'They're climbs, but they don't go on forever. They're hard, but they're not the Alps. Sean would get over them and get back up to a group. Spanish racing just suited him and the way he was.'

Like Roche at the Giro the previous year, Kelly was blessed with the good fortune to find a willing ally in Robert Millar, now riding for Fagor. Were it not for Millar's help at Brañillin, Kelly's Vuelta challenge would likely have ended there and then, and the Scot later aided Kelly to limit his losses to Fuerte – and put time into Cubino – on the tough Pyrenean leg to Cerler in week 2. Morale on Fagor, where Roche was absent with injury for most of the year, was low. Millar, also a client of Frank Quinn, was not going to withhold assistance to Kelly, especially when it helped to pave the way to a 6th-place finish in Madrid.

'Did I help Kelly more than I had helped Roche? Yes, probably, but I only rode when it was in my interest as well, when I had my position on GC to chase or defend,' Philippa York says. 'I think the guys in our team car wanted to see Kelly lose and if that meant we lost all our chances as well, then so be it. They had this whole schadenfreude thing going on, which even involved their own personnel and riders. It was messed up. If I had listened to the advice from the team car, then Kelly would probably have lost that race but I would have missed out too.'

As the race reached flatter terrain in the final push towards Madrid, Kelly drew closer to the *maillot amarillo*, when a crosswind-buffeted stage to Albacete saw Cubino slide out of contention and cede the jersey to Fuerte. That left Kelly in 2nd place, just 21 seconds behind Fuerte, a weaker time triallist than Cubino, going into the penultimate stage of the Vuelta, a 30-kilometre time trial that finished in Villaba. In the final week of the Vuelta, RTÉ began broadcasting nightly highlights in anticipation of what was to come. Live coverage was rolled out for the final weekend, and Kelly duly won the time trial to move into the yellow jersey with a day to go. Fuerte collapsed completely, slipping to 3rd overall, with the German Raimund Dietzen moving up to 2nd.

The following afternoon Kelly rolled across the finish line outside the Estadio Bernabéu as the winner of the Vuelta, while Earley, the most reliable Kas domestique throughout, recorded his best-ever Grand Tour finish of 19th overall. Cycling's three major tours, the rainbow jersey and the status of world number one all belonged to Irish riders. In hindsight, it was the high water mark for Irish cycling, but at the time, the expectation was that the tide might rise still higher. On descending from the dais on the Paseo de la Castellana, Kelly's thoughts turned immediately to July. 'I've proved I'm not just a rider for the classics. I'm a serious candidate for the Tour de France now,' he said, with unusual candour. The subtext was clear: he wanted to emulate Roche. The positive test that preceded the Vuelta, meanwhile, was scarcely mentioned in contemporary reports, in Spain and in Ireland.

In the days immediately after the Vuelta, Kelly and Earley were feted at receptions in Cork, Carrick-on-Suir and Dublin, including the obligatory photo call with Charles Haughey at government buildings, but his own celebrations were low-key. His old Irish teammate Kieron McQuaid came to watch the finish in Madrid, and was toasting Kelly's win in the Kas hotel with a group of Irish journalists when the newly crowned Vuelta champion drew up a chair. 'He reaches for a glass, and I think he's going to have a few drinks now. He's won the first big tour of his career, so we'll knock a bit of crack out of him and get a few stories,' McQuaid says. No chance. 'He gets the glass, takes a bottle of Evian and pours himself a glass of fucking water. That's Kelly for you.'

Such self-denial yielded no reward at the Tour, where he was so desperate to match Roche's achievement. His race would prove little short of calamitous. Touted again as a consensus favourite before the start, Kelly endured a wretched July and made no impact. Unlike in 1987, there were no mitigating circumstances beyond cumulative fatigue. 'I went to the Tour with the idea of winning it. That was always the objective and especially after I won the Vuelta,' Kelly says. 'After the Vuelta, I just took a little time and rest, but in the beginning of the Tour I felt I hadn't recovered, and immediately in the early part I could feel I wasn't at the level.'

On the second day in the mountains, Kelly conceded 24 minutes on the road to l'Alpe d'Huez, and he laboured through the rest of the Tour to reach Paris in 46th place, more than an hour down on winner Pedro Delgado. At 32 years of age, Kelly would never contend again. He knew it and he said as much at the finish at l'Alpe d'Huez, even if he still wasn't quite ready to accept it.

'I went a long way into my career always thinking I could do it,' Kelly says. 'De Gribaldy always kept convincing me that I could win the Tour, and after he went, I still had it so much embedded that I was always thinking, "Yes, if I can get it right for the Tour and if I get a year where it's not too warm, I can win the Tour." And that went on until the time I moved to PDM really.'

Roche felt that Kelly's travails in the high mountains, allied to his insistence on expending energy to compete for the green jersey, meant that he was always pushing against a glass ceiling at the Tour. Even before 1988, Roche never believed his fellow countryman was a true challenger for the *maillot jaune*. 'I think it was probably a little too much to ask him to go for yellow, because I don't think he would have won the yellow. He won the Tour of Spain but the climbs and the race weren't on the level of the Tour de France,' Roche says. 'Sean in the third week would go down a bit. He was always having to dig in on the high climbs and you can only dig so deep and after a while everything just goes. I don't think Sean was really a genuine contender for the Tour and it would have been unfair to have expected him to win the Tour, but he was always a podium contender.'

And yet the Tour's roll of honour is also studded with winners who were less obviously gifted than Kelly. More limited climbers have succeeded in wearing yellow into Paris. Perhaps if Kelly had awoken to his possibilities over three weeks earlier in his career, he might have developed the armoury needed to win the Tour by the time he reached his physical prime in the mid-1980s. Instead, he was almost in his 30s before he truly committed to trying to win a Grand Tour, by which time his inhibitions and doubts had already calcified; Kelly never dared to risk his spring by building a season around the Tour in the manner of a LeMond or an Hinault.

Looking at the list of opponents he faced during his best years at the Tour, however, it's difficult to shake the feeling that Kelly missed his best chance of wearing yellow into Paris without even realising it. Had Kelly approached the 1983 Tour with a different mindset – namely, had he not left his best form at the Tour of Switzerland – could he have scaled Everest four years before Roche? 'Who won the Tour in 1983? Fignon? Then, yes, Sean could have won that one,' Marcel Tinazzi says. 'To be frank, if Hinault had been there, then no, not a chance. But against Fignon, he could have won at that point, even if Fignon became a great champion afterwards. Sean wasn't a great climber but he was very hard to drop, and he could get inside people's heads that way.'

Kelly himself maintains that his greatest impediment at Tour was neither the depth of the competition nor the altitude of the mountain passes, but simply the reading on the thermometer. There is an implied admission, too, that racing too often in the other 11 months of the year left him short when it came to the white-hot French July. 'The combination of hot days got to me,' Kelly says. 'And when you go back in the '80s, the Tour de France seemed to be much, much warmer compared to what we see in the last 10 or 15 years. I think that was where I was getting caught out. Having raced so much in the beginning of the year, if you're a little bit fatigued and you get real warm weather, then it just hits you more.'

The 1988 Tour was a bitter disappointment, but in time, Kelly, stoical to the last, made peace with the simple fact that most riders' careers, even great ones, must come and go without Tour victory.

17

KITCHEN SINK DRAMA

When Stephen Roche arrived back at the Piber Hotel after winning the Worlds in 1987, he threw his bike into the outdoor swimming pool and shouted out '*Fini!*' while the watching journalists fell about laughing. Well, it was probably funny at the time. For much of the four years that followed, Roche's career seemed to have ended there and then, as though he had struck a Faustian bargain in order to carry off cycling's three most prestigious prizes.

The auguries were foreboding from the outset of Roche's year in the rainbow jersey. Fagor's 1988 roster gathered in San Sebastian on 4 January for the official photo shoot, only for the entire team, bar the Spanish riders Pedro Muñoz and Gaxento Oñaederra, to refuse to have their pictures taken and go home. The impromptu strike was called by Roche and Valcke, who were in dispute with the sponsors over the precise role of Philippe Crépel, the French former professional who had helped negotiate their passage to the team. Roche had pushed for Crépel, part of the management set-up during his time at La Redoute, to be installed as a sort of general manager, and during the contract talks, Agustín Mondragon, Fagor's head of marketing and the man who oversaw the team, had seemed willing to accede to the request. By the eve of the new season, however, he had changed his mind. Pierre Bazzo had already been sidelined to a PR role to make way for Valcke's arrival as a directeur sportif, and Mondragon now had misgivings about handing the keys to the team – which boasted a reported 400 million peseta budget, among the highest in cycling at the time – entirely to Roche's acolytes.

What had begun as a transfer coup was beginning to feel like a hostile takeover, and Mondragon preferred to retain his influence by keeping his existing right-hand man Miguel Gomez in situ, leaving no room for Crépel. Mondragon complained to *L'Équipe* that in Crépel's short time working with the team to that point, he had overspent and negotiated certain deals 'first and foremost because they served his personal interests'. Mondragon wanted Crépel out, and so as the photographer readied himself in a hotel conference room to immortalise the 1988 Fagor team for promotional postcards, Roche led the revolt. Many of the riders had been signed that winter on Roche's recommendation, and they had little option but to follow suit.

'I can't remember clearly what the argument was about, but there was an obvious lack of comprehension and a communication problem between the management and the technical staff, which would have included Stephen. We riders stood up and said we were going home,' Eddy Schepers recalls. 'It started badly.'

If Schepers had had his way, he would never have left Carrera, but his future was tethered to Roche's after Sappada. From a purely sporting standpoint, the Belgian maintains that leaving Carrera after his golden 1987 campaign was a fateful error on Roche's part. 'In my opinion, it wasn't the right call because it meant leaving the best team in the world for a team that needed to be built again from scratch,' he says. 'I think Stephen made a bit of a mistake there, but the decision was made.'

Though he would hardly have admitted it publicly at the time, Roche nurtured similar doubts. Towards the end of the 1987 Tour, he approached Boifava and showed him the contract he had been offered by Fagor, all but pleading with the Italian to match the figure. 'I said, "Stefano, I'm terribly sorry, but I can't ask Carrera for that kind of money. My role as a directeur sportif, beyond managing the team, is to keep the sponsor in the sport for as many years as possible. They can't increase the budget like that,"' Boifava says. 'I told him I could improve his contract but I couldn't match Fagor's offer. And he said, "Davide, do everything you can, because I don't want to leave."'

Roche maintains Boifava's reticence was due to the presence of Visentini rather than the Tacchella brothers' tight grip on the purse strings. 'Visentini still had a contract for 1988, and not signing me helped them to avoid a storm,' he says. On the night Tour victory was secured in Dijon, Roche signed with Fagor, as did Valcke, Schepers, Millar and Crépel. Roche's initial influence at Fagor was such that he was in a position to veto the team's attempts to acquire Jean-François Bernard in late summer, but by the time the 1987 season had ended, the Basque domestic appliance manufacturer had reservations about the number of chefs it was allowing into its kitchen. Speaking to *Vélo Magazine* in November, Crépel admitted that his position was already under threat, though when Roche set off on holiday to Saint Lucia following further discussions with Mondragon, he declared himself 'relieved on all levels'.

The uneasy truce lasted all of four days into 1988 before the underlying tensions escalated into full-blown mutiny, and Mondragon's response was to threaten to pull the plug on the team altogether. A week later, Roche returned to San Sebastian, without Crépel and Valcke, but accompanied by two lawyers, and they spoke with Mondragon until late into the evening. They agreed that Crépel's role would be limited to that of 'consultant' and that he would not oversee the team's budget, though he would be permitted to arrange travel and logistics. The riders, meanwhile, would not be disciplined for their mass walk-out, but Roche would make an apology on their behalf. Despite the peace accord, the tension never dissipated.

Speaking to *Mundo Deportivo* after their tête-à-tête, Roche looked to make light of the difference of opinion with Mondragon. 'I think Basques have a very similar character to the Irish. I'm looking forward to being with Fagor,' he said, turning on the charm, though his comments on Crépel's consultancy role hardly suggested a lasting détente. 'It's simply a formula to avoid using the word "manager". He'll have a lot more responsibility than it seems on paper.'

It was hard to shake off a feeling of déjà vu. To have one high-profile contract dispute in a career may be regarded as a misfortune; to have two looked like carelessness. This Fagor situation, however, risked being even more acrimonious and more damaging than the divorce from Peugeot at the end of

1983. Roche hadn't yet pinned on a race number for his new team and his relationship with the sponsor was already irremediably strained. It was difficult to see how their association could possibly end well, but at least a sticking plaster of sorts had been applied to the very open wound.

More troublingly, no remedy seemed to be available for Roche's ongoing knee problems. After undergoing a third operation on his left knee in November 1987, he had scarcely touched his bike all winter and his waistline had expanded accordingly. Standing in a suit on the podium at Fagor's team presentation on 19 January in San Sebastian, Roche's double chin gave him the appearance of a manager rather than an active bike rider. He admitted that he was limited to riding his bike for an hour at a time, and, deep down, he already sensed he was about the become the poster boy for the curse of the rainbow jersey.

Perhaps the most remarkable thing about the knee injury that ruined Roche's first season at Fagor and had such a deleterious effect on his career thereafter is that he was already managing it during his year of years in 1987. The problem seemed to have its genesis in what had seemed a routine crash during the Paris Six on the track in Bercy in the winter of 1985, where Roche was partnered by British track star Tony Doyle. Roche was able to complete the event, and noticed no ill effects during his winter break, but he was struck by knee pain from the moment he resumed training at the start of the 1986 season. In

April of that year, he was diagnosed with crushed cartilage and underwent surgery in Italy. A second operation was carried out at the end of the season in Paris by Dr Jean-Baptiste Courroy, who identified fibrosis of the tendon and removed part of the meniscus. This intervention proved more successful, and Roche wasn't unduly troubled by knee pain again until his crash in Cork shortly before the 1987 World Championships.

'Straight after the Worlds, I couldn't ride a bike. I managed to get through the Nissan but it was always very painful. I was always nursing it. I had an operation that November and got back on the bike but it was still painful,' Roche says. As well as the repeated surgeries, Roche had treated recurrences of the injury between 1986 and 1988 in a manner typical for a professional cyclist of the era. 'I had one or two cortisone injections at the time, but they weren't even improving it,' he says. 'I had operations and they didn't help.'

The start of Roche's season, initially slated for the Volta Valenciana in February, was pushed back to Paris-Nice in March. That year's race was preceded by an exhibition team time trial race that didn't count towards the general classification, and after struggling in Fagor's 5.7-kilometre effort, Roche decided to opt out of the race proper. Much to Mondragon's dismay, he still wasn't ready by the time the Tour of the Basque Country came around in April. Under increasing pressure to justify his £400,000 salary, Roche eventually made his competitive debut in April at the low-key Boucles Parisiennes, where he lasted 100 kilometres. He fared slightly better at Paris-Camembert, managing 174 kilometres, but a crash at Liège-Bastogne-Liège stopped the tenuous comeback in its tracks. On 18 May, three weeks after Fagor had insisted that Roche be examined by a doctor of their choosing in Barcelona, it was confirmed that he would not be fit to defend his Tour de France title.

The formal announcement was made by Pierre Bazzo, who in Roche's absence had nudged his way back into the managerial structure. Valcke was squeezed out. 'Pierre Bazzo dreamed of one thing and one thing only – getting his job back off me,' Valcke says. 'Mondragon and Gomez were on my back looking to get Bazzo his job back, so it was a lost cause from the outset, because Stephen was never there. It was a catastrophe.'

Roche was unable to race for large tracts of the spring and summer of 1988, but found ways to occupy his time. In February, he served as a co-commentator on French television when Ireland played France in the Five Nations at the Parc des Princes. The following week, he and Lydia were guests of honour in Dublin when French president François Mitterand made a state visit, and the next day's *Irish Times* couldn't resist making the link between the rainbow jersey Roche and the man who ordered the sinking of the *Rainbow Warrior*.

In early May, Roche attended the Eurovision Song Contest in Dublin and held a press conference on arrival at Dublin airport, ostensibly to discuss his fading prospects of competing in the Tour, but, more pressingly, to announce the establishment of his new business venture, 'Stephen Roche Management, Promotions-Consultants'. If the near-empty room left Roche feeling like last year's man, he wore his disappointment lightly. 'Don't fight for the seats lads,' he quipped. Later, as he presented his management company, it seemed that even with the Tour, Giro and Worlds to his name, he couldn't help but measure himself against Kelly: 'Sean Kelly wants to be a farmer when he retires. I want to go into sport management.'

The company was fronted by Roche's former mentor, Peter Crinnion, and Roddy Carr, son of the golfer Joe Carr, and the first clients were Roche and Lydia, who was attempting to launch a media and modelling career. The first external client, swimmer Gary O'Toole, was signed the following month. Roche was, like his fellow Irish professionals, represented by Frank Quinn at the time, though this development essentially signalled the end of their collaboration. 'I didn't really like it because he cannot go to a sponsor to sell them Sean Kelly and then go the next day saying he's selling Stephen Roche for the same product,' Roche says.

Quinn took Roche's decision to change tack in his stride. 'I worked with Roche during '86, '87 and '88, and then he moved on,' says Quinn. 'If an agent represents too many players, then there's a conflict of interests among the players about who is he giving the good stuff to, and that's fair enough. I had three years with Stephen and it was very enjoyable.' Kelly, Kimmage and Earley were still Quinn clients, and would remain so for the duration of their respective careers. 'It says a lot for Kelly that he would hitch his wagon to Frank, who wasn't a spoofer. But then Kelly was shrewd and he'd have known this guy was genuine,' says Kimmage, who took a dimmer view of Roche's various arrangements over the years. 'Stephen, the amount of assholes he had…'

No matter, it was telling that Roche, still only 28, was now thinking very seriously about his life after cycling. For all that his upbeat public persona remained resolutely intact throughout the year, he was already beginning to realise that he might never return to anything approaching the heights of 1987. Unlike the relentless Kelly, his career had followed a curious pattern in which he seemed to alternate good seasons with bad. The successful campaigns of 1981, 1983 and 1985 had each been followed by subdued years. A perception existed, perhaps unfairly, that Roche tended to ease off in the first year of a new and improved contract, and that sequence seemed to be playing out on a grand and very public scale in 1988. This time, Roche's knee injury simply made it impossible to compete, but he could sense rolling eyeballs all around the cycling milieu. More gallingly, he barely raced 10 days in the rainbow jersey in 1988, and never came close to honouring it with a victory.

'I didn't get to ride all year, and then when I did wear the world champion's jersey, I had to wear a size over my normal size because I was so heavy, you know. I wasn't really presentable in the jersey,' Roche says. 'The only really good photographs I have of myself in the jersey are from the Worlds and the Nissan in 1987. I look like a bike rider in those pictures, but in the Fagor ones, I look overweight.'

Roche did at least manage a sustained block of racing in the final weeks of the season, donning the rainbow bands at the Tour of Britain, putting up an aggressive if doomed defence of his title at the World Championships in Ronse and then placing 8th in the Nissan Classic. That sequence was made possible, Roche maintains, by a chance encounter with Dr Hans-Wilhelm Müller-Wohlfahrt while he was in Germany in May to perform publicity duties as part of a sponsorship deal with Opel. Müller-Wohlfahrt was Bayern Munich's team doctor from 1977 to 2015, and Roche was introduced to him after attending a game against VfB Stuttgart at the Olympic Stadium.

The mystique surrounding Müller-Wohlfahrt and his unusual methodology was neatly summed up by a line from ESPN writer Mike Fish in a 2011 feature on the doctor: 'Healing Hans, as Müller-Wohlfahrt is affectionately known, ranks as either the greatest healer since Hippocrates or is a quack with a hyperactive syringe, depending on whom you believe.' Roche, certainly, views him as the former, and *Born to Ride* features a fawning five-page paean to the healing powers of Müller-Wohlfahrt, whose varied list of clients over the years includes Usain Bolt, Paula Radcliffe, Luciano Pavarotti, Ronaldo and Boris Becker.

According to Roche, Müller-Wohlfahrt deduced that he had not rehabilitated correctly from his initial knee surgery, and hence his left kneecap had been displaced. His solution was logical: Roche needed to build up the muscles around his knee to correct the imbalance. His methodology, however, was highly unorthodox. For his initial treatment, Roche spent 10 days at Müller-Wohlfahrt's Munich clinic, receiving injections of what he described as a glycerine gel in his knee. Roche wrote that he surreptitiously had the mystery substance analysed by a doctor in Paris, where he learned that it was a calf liver extract – in other words Actovegin, a substance later placed on the banned list in 2000, only to be removed the following year due to uncertainty over its performance-enhancing properties.

'I met Müller-Wohlfahrt and he just changed the whole thing. Even after just two months of treatment, I was riding the bike with no pain and it's been fine ever since,' Roche says now, crediting the German for ensuring that he would not require a fourth knee operation. Indeed, Roche would remain a Müller-Wohlfahrt patient for the rest of his career, even stopping to see him in Munich en route to his final race, the 1993 World Championships in Oslo.

'Müller-Wohlfahrt came along and identified the problem with my knee. The others hadn't identified it, they just operated on the tendon and then said it can't be anything else, it has to be in the mind. Or else they'd treat it with cortisone,' he says, adding: 'But that was with one doctor, just a couple of times.'

The 1989 Fagor team presentation took place aboard a fishing boat in the port of San Sebastian. Miserable as things were, somebody at the team must have had a sense of humour; after the previous year's mutiny, most of the Roche-Valcke faction had already decided to jump ship. Roche himself only remained aboard because he hadn't secured a lifeboat. Only six of the 1988 roster remained in place, with the British trio of Robert Millar, Sean Yates and Malcolm Elliott among those who had had their fill of the poisonous prevailing atmosphere and left. 'Fagor was dreadful, a team of individuals that just happened to be in the same jerseys kind of sums it up. The Spanish guys hated the French, the French tolerated the other foreigners, and with Valcke never really being in charge, the whole thing was a nightmare,' says Philippa York.

Fagor had been pitched as a sort of 'Roche and Friends' set-up, which, of course, had never really materialised. Even allowing for the injury that sidelined him for much of the year, York takes a jaundiced view of how Roche responded to the problems that beset the team. *His* team. 'Roche as usual had some kind of problem with his contracts or whatever, and though the idea was that it was his team, he never took any responsibility in how the team developed,' York says. 'Up until then, I had given him the benefit of the doubt when he was in disputes with various people because I considered him a friend, but after '88 that goodwill was used up. I doubt things would have been any better even if he had been healthy, as wherever he went there was some kind of scandal.'

It can't have helped morale among his teammates that Roche's eye seemed to be drawn increasingly towards extracurricular activities. Like many professional riders, Roche had always been fascinated by fast cars, but most limited themselves to ogling them or owning them. In December 1988, Roche went as far as to start participating in rallying events, including the Rally of the Lakes in Killarney, with Valcke as his co-driver. The duo placed 28th overall in Kerry, with Roche driving, of all things, a Peugeot 205.

Mondragon was hardly impressed, though he had, by that point, made it plain to Roche that he would not be able to extricate himself from the second year of his contract with the team. In the summer of 1988, Roche made very public overtures to Bernard Tapie, backer of the Toshiba team, and he even claimed that the entrepreneur was willing to buy out his 1989 contract. The sincerity of the notorious M. Tapie's interest is unclear, however, given that he was already switching his priorities from cycling to football, and investing heavily in Olympique de Marseille.

While Roche was trying – and failing – to find a way out of Fagor, Kelly briefly entertained the prospect of joining him there, though the approach was made by the Basque faction of the team rather than by Roche himself. When Kas announced it was pulling out of the sport at the end of 1988, Ramón Mendiburu was hired to join Fagor's already overstocked management team, and his first order of business was to try to bring Kelly with him. There had already been fanciful talk in the French media of Kelly and Roche teaming up on a new, Guinness-sponsored outfit in 1988 – it seems that Guinness's temporary sub-sponsorship of Kas during the Nissan Classic had been misinterpreted – but this time, the possibility was real, albeit faint. The chaos at Fagor was the talk of the peloton.

'Well, it was in a mess and we would have seen that was the case because Stephen didn't race at all that year,' Kelly says. 'Mendiburu was going to Fagor and he told me they were going to change a lot there, that he was going to change a lot of things. He was the guy who approached me, and I did negotiate with him, but I couldn't come to a deal. Financially, we couldn't make a deal.'

The prospect of joining Fagor remained in play until the end of November, but only because Kelly needed a back-up plan as he waited on a berth to open at PDM. The Dutch squad's signing of Kelly – and Earley, who now came as part of the same package – was contingent on off-loading Greg LeMond to the lowly ADR outfit. 'It took a long time for Greg to negotiate his deal with ADR so it was late enough,' Kelly says. 'Fagor was also pushing and the deal with them was a deal we were happy with, but the preference was to go to PDM if I could.'

More surprising was another Irishman's decision to reject Fagor's advances. Roche's younger brother Laurence had progressed through the amateur ranks in Ireland, raced with ACBB in 1988 and was now ready to make the step up to the professional peloton. He turned down the chance to join his brother at Fagor, however, preferring instead to try his luck at, of all places, Carrera. It was partly a desire to succeed under his own steam, but also a question of aesthetics.

'I loved the colour of their jerseys and the colour of their bikes, it was that simple,' Laurence Roche laughs. 'When I met Boifava, I said I'd sign as long as they didn't change their bikes or their jerseys, and they changed both! They had those lovely Battaglin bikes, they looked great, but then in 1989 they brought out these Carrera bikes, made by Battaglin, and they were the ugliest things ever. They changed the material on the jerseys too… I also kind of wanted to do it on my own, but it was a mistake. I should have gone to Fagor because Carrera was too big of a team, too strong.'

One fellow countryman did join Stephen Roche at Fagor in 1989. Paul Kimmage was deemed surplus to requirements at RMO after a disastrous season and feared the worst, only to be handed a lifeline by Roche at the World Championships in Ronse. Roche was glad to have an additional ally for company; in 1989, his team within a team was down to the bare bones. Crépel was gone. Only Kimmage, Valcke and Schepers could be counted on for unflinching loyalty. To Kimmage's delight, he was handed the same racing programme as Roche, and shared a room with his leader throughout. 'I'd probably have been pissed off if I was Schepers. I don't know what the nature of their relationship was,' Kimmage says. 'I thought Schepers was a smashing guy, and a great rider. I can't explain why I would have been rooming with Stephen instead of him, but it suited me.'

Valcke and Pierre Bazzo were rather unhappier bedfellows. Bazzo's return midway through the previous season had seen

Valcke effectively fired before the Tour, but he was reinstated, this time as Bazzo's number two, at the start of 1989. In an interview with *Vélo Magazine* that spring, Roche found a most tasteless way to say that he and Valcke would not be pushed around by the sponsor. '*Nous ne sommes pas pédés*,' he said – 'We're not poofs.' In a bid to avoid further conflict, the team was essentially riven in two in the early part of the year, with Valcke overseeing the Roche group. The trial separation was an untenable arrangement, but one that somehow held until July, when the pent-up acrimony was unleashed with such fury at the Tour that it sealed the inevitable final divorce. The fall-out saw Fagor withdraw sponsorship at the end of the year, and the team disbanded.

'Patrick was a bit mad but he wasn't a bad fella. He was passionate and he loved Stephen to death, and we got on. Bazzo would have known I was one of Stephen's guys, so I'm sure he'd have thought I was a right cunt, and I'd have thought he was an even bigger cunt,' says Kimmage, who found himself sitting alongside Bazzo on the Champs-Élysées in 2013 during celebrations for the 100th edition of the Tour. 'We both had a great laugh, which was lovely. But at the time, there was an internal war going on and you're loyal to your man and that's it. I was part of Stephen's gang.'

Roche's performances in the early part of the season gave reason for guarded optimism. He won on the Col d'Èze to place 2nd overall at Paris-Nice, where in Kelly's absence, Miguel Indurain was the first non-Irish winner of the decade. Buoyed by overall victory at the Tour of the Basque Country in April, Roche made a late decision to return to the Giro d'Italia, and rode well for the first 10 days, moving up to

2nd overall after the Riccione time trial. That same night, Müller-Wohlfahrt flew in to treat a nagging back complaint, which seemed to develop just as the German had apparently resolved Roche's knee issues. Roche struggled as soon as the race entered the high mountains, shipping time on the Dolomite leg to Auronzo di Cadore, and he continued to do so thereafter. He slipped backwards through the final week, settling in 9th place overall by the finish in Florence in a race won by Laurent Fignon.

In public, Roche put a brave face on his Giro, reasoning that it marked forward progress after his truncated 1988 campaign, and he even dared to posit himself as the third favourite for the Tour de France, behind Delgado and Fignon, in a column in the *Irish Times* the weekend before the race started. In private, however, he had already accepted that he was never going to win the Tour again. 'I was more or less resigned even then,' he says. 'When my knee problem came right, I had problems with my back, so I was only getting out 80 per cent of my fitness then. I had two slipped discs in my back, which affected my sciatic nerve and I could never get my full force out again.' While Schepers and Kimmage held out the faintest of hopes that Roche might yet stage a resurrection, Valcke was well aware that he was only going through the motions as a contender to win the 1989 Tour. 'We knew already that he was dead,' he says. 'There was no chance.'

Roche's gloomy outlook ahead of the Tour was hardly helped by Fagor's insistence that Bazzo serve as lead directeur sportif in Valcke's place. It was Bazzo, not Valcke, who followed Roche in the team car during the opening prologue. 'Bazzo really is little more than a team chauffeur. He hasn't got a clue about anything else,' Roche complained in his *Irish Times* diary, where, among other grievances, he blamed Bazzo for forgetting to bring his aerodynamic helmet. The kitchen was ablaze, and none of the chefs seemed minded even to try to put it out.

The first week laid bare Roche's own deficiencies. Off the pace in the Rennes time trial, he trailed by more than five minutes at the foot of the Pyrenees and promptly lost another 12 on the first day in the mountains after injuring his left knee when it banged against his handlebars. Roche could barely walk to dinner that night in Cauterets, and he decided not to start the next day's stage. It was an absurd way to be forced out of a Tour de France, but an utterly appropriate note on which to bring the curtain down on a two-year farce.

On leaving Fagor, Roche might have assumed things could only improve. He was wrong. The saving grace of his time there was that the intense media interest in the ongoing soap opera at least reassured him that he was still one of the peloton's box office attractions. Gallingly for a man who so craved the spotlight, the year that followed saw him begin sliding into irrelevance at Belgian squad Histor. 'They gave me the vision of having a better team, but in fact there was no money there, or at least not enough to satisfy their ambitions,' Roche says. 'That was an error, but the big teams were worried about my knee.' Roche's entourage had downsized in tandem with his salary. Although Valcke joined him as a directeur sportif, Schepers decided to take a better offer from the Tulip team.

'That caused quite a lot of strain between us. It was very difficult at the time, though we made up later,' says Schepers, who maintains Roche was overly beholden to Valcke in those years. 'I think Stephen was led astray a little bit by Patrick Valcke, in the sense that he took decisions with Patrick that he might not have taken if he'd been acting for himself alone. Patrick wanted to profit from the great rider that Stephen was, and Stephen followed him with his eyes closed a little bit.'

Valcke, on the other hand, disputes the characterisation that he had set out expressly to build a career as a directeur sportif on the back of his relationship with Roche, claiming it was Schepers himself who had first suggested he step into the role at Fagor. 'I didn't set the idea in motion. I never had personal ambition,' he says. 'I was always in the service of Stephen.' At Histor, Valcke's sole remit was Roche, and team manager Willy Teirlinck, whose interest lay in the spring classics and sprinter Etienne De Wilde, left him to it.

Roche's year began encouragingly enough. For the second successive season, he placed 2nd behind Indurain at Paris-Nice, and then won the Four Days of Dunkirk in May, though the limitations of the supporting cast around him were obvious. 'We won the team time trial at Paris-Nice, but with all the fat Belgians we didn't have the team to defend the jersey in the mountains so I felt a little bit guilty,' says Brian Holm, a teammate at Histor. The Dane smiles at the recollection of Roche's popularity with fans, and one demographic in particular. 'I remember meeting a lot of cougars; he loved cougars,' Holm laughs. 'He was very friendly, almost too friendly. After races, he'd have to sign every bloody signature for everybody, so we were always the last team to leave.'

Though Roche's days as a Tour contender were already behind him, Holm and his comrades set out from the Grand Départ in Lyon convinced they were chaperoning a potential winner. 'Honestly, you always believe you're going to win,' Holm says. The illusion didn't last long. Hampered by back problems, Roche slouched towards Paris in 44th place overall, a shadow of himself. At year's end, neither he nor Histor saw any reason to continue the relationship.

Valcke threw himself into negotiating Roche's passage onto a new team for 1991, though he had misgivings about the wisdom of prolonging a career bedevilled by chronic injury, particularly against such diminishing financial returns. Their relationship, already fraying in the latter part of the Fagor era, ruptured completely by the time Roche signed terms with another lowly Belgian team, Tonton Tapis, for 1991.

In Roche's telling, the break came when Valcke insisted on participating in a rally at a particularly sensitive moment in the Tonton Tapis negotiations, namely the collapse of a 2 million franc deal with Look bikes, which was to finance their contracts. Valcke's recollection differs. 'I was the one who put together the contract with Tonton Tapis and I was the one who negotiated a lot of the sponsorship deals, including with Gios bikes,' Valcke says. 'But we knew it would be complicated. Roger De Vlaeminck was manager, and he had more authority than me, so I understood it wasn't going to work and I pulled out straight away.'

Both agree that their friendship was never the same again. 'Yes, it was a bit complicated for the personal relationship after that,' Valcke says. 'He didn't appreciate some of the professional reproaches I made to him. When it needed to be said, I said that he should stop instead of continuing to go downhill.' Valcke returned to cycling with the ill-fated Le Groupement team in 1995, then spent a decade as a radio analyst, before moving into football to become press officer for RC Lens, where he remains to this day.

Opinion is divided among those who observed the Roche-Valcke dynamic over the years. For Holm and Schepers, Valcke was an opportunist. 'Nice but a bit of a weird guy: I think he was interested in himself, not in Roche,' says Holm. Paul Kimmage and Philippa York, on the other hand, take a more sympathetic view. 'I think Valcke would have been a decent DS given the chance, but he, like many, was drawn in by Stephen's charm and took the heat when he didn't have to,' York says.

No matter, Roche was alone, and it was hard to shake the feeling that maybe it really had all finished in Villach.

18

RIDER ON THE STORM

One last lap and then goodbye to all that. On the last Friday of August 1989, as Paul Kimmage soft-pedalled over the Côte de Montagnole in the company of Kelly, Earley, Laurence Roche and John Brady, a Dubliner based as a professional in the United States, it was hard to ignore the occasional pang of regret. Kimmage still looked the part in his Fagor kit but he was already in the process of stepping off the field of dreams. Two days after Roche's abandon at the Tour the previous month, he had climbed off his bike on the road to Montpellier, demoralised by the internal bickering at Fagor. After finishing the Giro, Kimmage had made up his mind that he was in his last season as a professional bike rider, but without Roche to ride for, he saw no point in going on even that far. He retired there and then. Now, as he rode with the Irish team as they reconnoitred the World Championships course in Chambéry, just 50 miles from his base in Vizille, he wondered if he hadn't been too hasty. There would be no raging against the dying of the light as part of Kelly's big push for the prize he most coveted. 'That is kind of a regret. I wish I'd gone on and finished that Tour and ridden that World Championships in Chambéry. It would have been a nice way to finish,' Kimmage says. 'But there was a poisonous atmosphere at Fagor, so I just said, "Fuck it." But then, I do stupid things spontaneously…'

Two days later, Kimmage watched from the sidelines as Kelly endured the greatest disappointment of his sporting life. At 33 years of age, Kelly was running out of chances to be world champion, but he rode sagely and bravely on a wet afternoon in the Alps to stay in the hunt, only to be betrayed by his sprint, of all things, in the finishing straight. Greg LeMond took the rainbow jersey, a happily ever after coda to his fairy-tale comeback win at the Tour de France that summer. An ashen-faced Kelly stood on the podium alongside the American, his head anchored downwards by the bronze medal around his neck. No other defeat punctured his stoicism quite like this one. As a friend and admirer, Kimmage felt compassion for Kelly's distress; as a nascent sportswriter, he felt inspired by the pathos the occasion inspired. But before he could expound on others from the press box, he had another, plaintive tale to piece together: his own.

Kimmage was an accidental journalist. When David Walsh interviewed him on his debut Tour for *Magill* magazine in 1986, he found the transcript so compelling – or perhaps his deadline so tight – that he turned in a 5,000-word first-person account. Over the next two years, Kimmage contributed occasionally to the *Irish Cycling Review*, but his big break came, ironically, when he was not selected for the 1988 Tour. Walsh had planned to co-write a book on the Tour with Kimmage, but now proposed he write a piece on the race each week for the *Sunday Tribune*. Active sportspeople's columns tend to be bland, ghostwritten and humourless, but Kimmage's were colourful and darkly comic. At the end of 1988, *Sunday Tribune* editor Vincent Browne offered him a job. Kimmage declined, but he would pen a column throughout the following season for the newspaper. By the time the Giro came around, it was clear that he was extracting more pleasure from moonlighting than he was from his day job. Ahead of the Tour, he decided to retire from cycling to concentrate on journalism.

In the months between abandoning the Tour and moving back to Dublin to start work with the *Sunday Tribune* in February 1990, Kimmage wrote *A Rough Ride* – it would lose the indefinite article by the time an updated edition was published in 1998 – on a Honeywell laptop computer given to him by Browne. Through Walsh, he had signed a contract with the publisher Stanley Paul, who planned to release the book in the run-up to the 1990 Tour de France. In his newspaper columns, Kimmage had pierced the glamorous veneer of professional cycling by writing about the back-stabbing within teams or providing details like the time he urinated on his hands to keep them warm on a snowy descent at the Giro. In the book, however, Kimmage felt it beholden upon him to peel another layer from the onion and talk about a topic he had neglected in his columns. The response from his peers to an interview he gave to *L'Équipe* during his final Tour gave Kimmage the encouragement he needed.

'The book had been in my head, and then Philippe Brunel interviewed me, and the story ran with a photograph of me in my Fagor jersey with a little electric typewriter,' Kimmage says. 'I spoke about the doping problem, how it needed to be addressed, and that I was going to do it. And what was amazing was that one of Kelly's old teammates, Dominique Garde, came up the next day and said well done. It got a very good reception, which was strange given the omertà. So it was definitely in my head, this awareness of the need to write something about the problem in the sport, and to do something about it. It was the easiest book I ever wrote.'

Kimmage's fellow Irish professionals had an inkling that he was writing a book, but little notion of what it might contain. Come the spring of 1990, however, when Kimmage covered Paris-Nice for the *Sunday Tribune*, Roche's antennae were picking up blips. 'I spent a couple of days with him at Paris-Nice, and he asked me about it then: "What are you going to be saying?" And that was the first sense that I was a bit wary about it,' Kimmage recalls. 'I'm pretty sure I'd have said, "Look, you'll have nothing to worry about."'

By then, the manuscript had been submitted, and though cycling's doping culture was the central plank of the book, there was not a single accusation levelled against Roche, Kelly or Earley in its pages. The references to Roche, Kimmage readily admits, were obsequious. His admiration for Kelly was more restrained, but just as obvious, and while Kimmage admitted his lingering resentment towards Earley, the depiction of his one-time rival was ultimately a flattering one.

Kimmage described the prevalence of needles in cycling, the haphazard nature of anti-doping controls and the unwillingness of the authorities to do anything about it, all refracted through his own bid to get by in the peloton without recourse to doping. He confessed to using amphetamine at the Chateau-Chinon criterium in 1987, but, mindful of the outrage it would provoke in Ireland, he was very careful not to specify that the two other criteriums at which he had doped were in Dublin and Cork, respectively. He did, however, explicitly name some of his RMO teammates in his accounts of doping practices, though they are depicted empathetically as victims of a poisoned culture rather than sensationalised as cheats. Cycling's ecosystem was the target, not those who dwelled within it, but it was green of Kimmage to think that such nuance would be appreciated by the likes of Thierry Claveyrolat and Jean-Claude Colotti, particularly when the book was never translated into French.

A month before publication, the Roche camp was growing more anxious. In April, Kimmage fielded a call from Peter Crinnion, and began to realise that *A Rough Ride* might not be received to universal acclaim. 'I remember getting a call from him before it came out, saying he'd heard there was stuff in the book, and me telling him basically to fuck off,' Kimmage says. 'My hackles were getting up at this stage. But I was very naïve. In the book, I was going to set out what was wrong with the sport. I naïvely thought that the public would see it for what it was, that the lads would see it for what it was, and that it would be well received.'

A Rough Ride was published in May 1990, and Kimmage's initial sample audience was his own family. His wife Ann and David Walsh apart, none of Kimmage's family or friends knew anything of his experiences of doping. Years later, Kimmage came to the belated epiphany that the driving force behind his cycling career had been a deep-seated desire to impress his father – 'It had fuck all to do with wanting to win the Tour de France or winning everything. It had everything to do with pleasing him,' he says – even though the equable Christy Kimmage was the very antithesis of a pushy parent. Christy sat down, read *A Rough Ride*, and offered his support in the most Irish way possible: he said nothing. 'My father had no clue I had doped until he opened the book and started reading. No clue,' Kimmage says. 'My father, mother and family had no clue. I'd never spoken to them about the decisions I'd made, and what I had or hadn't seen, in any way, shape or form. And they read it and never commented on it at all to me. Which seemed bizarre.'

Outside of Coolock, the response was less contained. Extracts published in the *Sunday Tribune* created a stir but it was his appearance on the *Late Late Show* that brought the book and its author their greatest notoriety. Gay Byrne, like everybody else, spotted the paradox at the heart of the book: *A Rough Ride* showed the prevalence of doping in cycling and the seeming impossibility of being successful without it, yet there was no accusation that Kelly or Roche had doped. 'What about the lads?' Byrne asked. Kimmage refused to say yes and he refused to say no: 'This is my story, it has nothing to with them.'

Roche begged to differ, and the campaign against Kimmage's book was immediate and sustained. The following day's *Evening Press* carried the banner headline, 'Roche may sue over *Late Late*'. At the Dauphiné Libéré the following week, he gave an interview to *L'Équipe* in which he denounced the book, though Kimmage was grateful at least that the journalist, Jean-Michel Rouet, gave him a chance to respond. On the weekend before the Tour began, Roche wrote a column in the *Irish Times* reiterating his distaste for the book. 'I learned things in Paul's book that I never knew,' Roche wrote. (There was a certain irony, mind, in Roche's inference in the same piece about Pedro Delgado's positive test from the 1988 Tour. 'Two years ago Delgado was tested positive after taking a product used for wiping out the traces of hormones – well those hormones could be traced now,' he wrote. In his *Irish Times* column during the 1988 Tour, however, his stance was different. 'I doubt very much whether Pedro was stupid enough to take any kind of hard drug,' Roche wrote then, in a piece calling for a rather drastic show of solidarity from the peloton. 'Until there is some kind of secrecy in the test procedure, I think the riders should boycott the Tour's medical controls.')

Roche's indignant and public response contrasted with Kelly and Earley's radio silence on the matter. Although it wasn't to be confused in any way with tacit support, Kimmage was grateful enough to thank them in the preface of the second edition. 'There was no contact with them at all,' he says. 'That support was just the fact that they said nothing.' Even now, Earley claims not to have read the book. 'No, I don't read books. I haven't read any autobiographies, I read textbooks and stuff like that,' Earley says. 'I'm not saying there are more important things in life… I didn't have feelings about it either way, really. That was his story. You could go on. But it is what it was, and that's it.'

At the time, Kelly limited himself to telling reporters that he would read the book before he commented on it. More than a quarter of a century on, he professes not to have read it in its entirety. 'There was a lot of stuff in the book that was true and it came out later. Some of the stuff was maybe a little bit spiced up because he wanted to have a real good book, a real good read, and that's what I said in the beginning,' Kelly says. 'But

I didn't really start picking out stuff and getting into the nitty gritty. I felt that it wasn't for me to do it. It was Kimmage's book and that was his version.'

Kelly was advised to hold his counsel by Frank Quinn, though it's very likely that he would have arrived at the same conclusion under his own steam. 'His attitude was, "The journalists get paid to write and I get paid to ride the bike. If we differ, that's fine,"' Quinn says. 'I read the book and basically in these situations, the reaction is no reaction. We took that route straight away. Stephen took a different route to the one we took.'

Roche claims that he would not have responded so harshly to the book were it not for Kimmage's appearance on the *Late Late Show*, when he refused to dismiss the possibility that Ireland's first Tour winner had doped during his career. 'I understood that he couldn't really get involved in the conversation and put one down and not the other one down. We all know that Kelly had a problem and I hadn't had a problem,' Roche says. By 'problem' he means a positive test. 'But if he's going to go on and knock one and not the other, that wouldn't look very good either. You understand that with maturity.'

Kimmage had heard pills rattling in Kelly's pocket at Paris-Brussels in 1984 and witnessed him injecting himself a couple of years later, but in his time sharing a room with Roche at Fagor, they had never so much as discussed doping. 'He knew that I knew,' Kimmage says when asked why they never spoke about the topic. 'I was four years a pro at that stage. I never asked anyone, "What are you doing, what are you taking?" You made your own decisions. If it was in front of you, you saw it, and if it wasn't in front of you, you didn't. And you didn't ask any questions.'

For that reason, Kimmage was unwilling to draw attention to Kelly's two positive tests in *A Rough Ride* or on the *Late Late Show*. A false equivalence would have been drawn with Roche. 'Kelly had already tested positive twice at that stage and Gay Byrne was saying to me, "Well what about the lads?" I could have said, "Ok, Gay, there's fucking Kelly, he's been done twice. Why are you surprised about this?"' Kimmage says. 'But if I'd said that, then it means the shining fucking man here, Mr Angel Roche, would be different, and that wouldn't be fair. So that was the reason for that.'

Although the book became a bestseller, it remained contentious within the confines of the Irish cycling community. Only years later, when he was sent the newspaper cuttings in the mail, did Kimmage learn that an illustrious predecessor had already denounced cycling's maladies in a strikingly similar fashion. In a series of ghostwritten articles in the *People* newspaper in 1966, Shay Elliott had spoken in detail of the use of syringes and doping products in cycling, and the ways riders circumvented controls. 'What really pissed my father off was that I was being accused of having invented all of this by people he had raced with, Crinnion included, who had gone to France, read those Elliott pieces, seen it first-hand themselves,' Kimmage says.

Kimmage recalls sending a copy of the book, with a letter of explanation, to Roche's father Larry, after the *Late Late* appearance, and given the furore that it provoked, he harbours mild regrets that he hadn't informed Roche, Kelly and Earley of its contents before publication. 'In hindsight, I should have sent a copy off to Kelly and Roche a month before it came out so they could have a read of it and be ready. That probably would have been fairer,' he says. 'I was finished at that point, but they weren't, so I could have handled that a bit better.' He smiles, however, at the idea of what might have happened had he shown Roche the manuscript any earlier than that. 'He would have got a fucking injunction. He'd have got the lawyers out to stop this. He wouldn't have been able to do that, but he would have tried.'

Although Roche didn't stop *A Rough Ride*'s publication in Ireland, his *L'Équipe* interview had helped to disseminate a skewed synopsis of its contents in France. Kimmage had enjoyed some respite from the controversy while covering the 1990 World Cup in Italy, but he travelled onwards to report on the Tour for the *Sunday Tribune* filled with trepidation about how he would be received by his former RMO teammates, specifically his friends Colotti and Claveyrolat. 'That was really hard because Roche had fucked me with all of them, absolutely fucked me,' Kimmage says. 'I remember I called Colotti on the night before the first stage. And he told me to fuck off, basically. So I knew I was fucked then, and I just felt it was pointless trying to explain myself to them. I didn't put myself in a situation where I'd walk up to them and ask how they were getting on. My attitude was if they want to approach me and have a go, they can, but I'm not going to go up and explain this. I can't. I felt under siege. I was there, but still hiding.'

And yet, whether he perceived it or not, there was some admiration for Kimmage's book within the cycling world. Patrick Valcke winced to himself as Roche denounced *A Rough Ride*. 'I wasn't in agreement with Stephen because I thought what Paul did was courageous. Courageous is the first word I'd use, and the second word is right,' Valcke says. 'By 1990, Stephen had come into a certain system. He wasn't the same Stephen of 10 years previously. But it's normal that when you've done 10 years as a pro, you see things differently.'

As Kimmage settled into life as a sportswriter over the following year, diplomatic channels with Roche opened once again. A truce was called, and they cleared the air in, of all places, Roche's Porsche on the motorway between Lille and Paris. When required, Kimmage would cover Roche, Kelly and Earley for the remainder of their careers, availing of the privileges afforded to a former comrade. 'They behaved as if it had never happened and I wrote as if it had never happened. I enjoyed the access I got with them,' says Kimmage.

Considering the rancour that followed, the speed with which Kimmage and Roche drew a line, however temporary, under the *Rough Ride* falling-out is remarkable. Perhaps both men simply needed each other. Kimmage was building a new career and Roche was always eager for exposure in his home country. 'You could be riding Stephen's wife in front of him as a journalist and then say, "Any chance of a quick word?" and such was his love of the microphone, it wouldn't matter what you did, he would go to the microphone,' Kimmage says.

19

PILLS, DRUGS AND MEDICINE

S ean Kelly didn't change teams – they changed around him. Sponsors, riders and managers came and went, but from 1981 through to 1988, Kelly was the kingpin at Sem, Skil and Kas. Signing to become one of many leaders at PDM in 1989 ostensibly marked a demotion, but as he closed in on 33 years of age, Kelly wasn't unhappy at the prospect of riding for a team whose success was not defined solely by his achievements, a feeling only reinforced after observing Roche's travails at Fagor. It helped, too, that the two-year deal Kelly signed with the Dutch squad was the most lucrative of his career.

Kelly's win rate slowed dramatically in his three years on the team – he claimed just two victories per season – as the focus switched from quantity to quality. PDM signed him expressly for the classics, and so Kelly rode Tirreno-Adriatico as training in 1989 rather than try to extend his sequence of Paris-Nice victories to eight. Kelly was now thinking of his legacy almost as much as he was thinking of the bottom line. 'In those last number of years, the money is not the thing,' Kelly says. 'You want to chalk up a big palmarès.'

In late April, Kelly won his second Liège-Bastogne-Liège, a victory that showed both the pros and cons of no longer being his own boss. With Steven Rooks and Gert-Jan Theunisse in the team alongside him, Kelly had two foils the likes of which he had never had before, but the Dutchmen were also rivals for the role of leader. 'PDM had a lot of chiefs, but I thought for the classics it was going to be a real good team. At that point I was thinking I could definitely win more classics,' Kelly says. He countered Rooks and Theunisse's claims on leadership by tracking the unheralded Fabrice Philipot on the Côte de Chambralles with over 50 kilometres to go. When they were joined by Pedro Delgado, Robert Millar and Phil Anderson, it developed into the winning move. Rooks and Theunisse were forced to sit on their hands behind as Kelly sprinted to victory. Although he lost top spot in the FICP rankings for the first time that summer, Kelly finished 1989 by winning the inaugural World Cup, a season-long series comprising the major classics.

Martin Earley also joined PDM at the start of 1989, arriving on the initial two-year Kelly ticket negotiated by Frank Quinn. Earley had been over-raced for much of his career to that point, and PDM's targeted approach to the calendar offered a welcome change of pace. 'They had a far better approach to planning a season, and there was a lot more advice for training,' Earley says. 'The season was more structured, rather than just riding until you broke. There was more structure in terms of using races to build up and then there'd be a break around May for a few weeks for riders who were possibly riding the Tour.'

Such a regimen, common today, aroused considerable curiosity at the time, but seemed to pay dividends at the Tour. Kelly carried the green jersey to Paris for a record fourth time, Theunisse won the King of the Mountains, while PDM placed four riders in the top 10 overall. Theunisse took 4th, Rooks 7th, Raul Alcala 8th and Kelly 9th, even if they were never truly in the shake-up for final victory in a tumultuous race that saw Greg LeMond beat Laurent Fignon by just eight seconds. 'The idea was that these were the guys for GC, but all the eggs weren't in one basket,' Earley says. 'Some of the guys were capable of winning it, but it depended on how things panned out.'

Earley enjoyed the best day of his career at the end of the first week of that Tour when he infiltrated a four-man break on the road to Pau. Opportunities for a dedicated team man like him were infrequent over the course of a career, and he had snapped up the first that came his way at the 1986 Giro, soloing to a hilltop victory at Sauze d'Oulx, but had been unable to capitalise on the two chances that had fallen to him on the Tour. In 1986, he was part of the early break that fought out stage victory on the Puy de Dôme, but had to settle for a battling 4th behind Eric Maechler. Earley was in the winning move at Blagnac a year later but finished 3rd in a three-man sprint as Rolf Gölz took the honours. 'There were five or six chances every year on the Tour for riders like me,' Earley says. 'I wasn't confident, but I was hopeful that a chance would come again.'

As the break approached Pau, the peloton had closed to within 20 seconds. He may not have been a prolific winner as a professional, but Earley was always a rational thinker. Where many would have panicked, he broke down the percentages and jumped with a kilometre to go, catching out Eric Caritoux and Michael Wilson. 'I could see the bunch coming up behind, but I knew if I attacked and got a gap, the others would start to look at each other, because whoever chases me at that point is basically giving up his chance to win,' he says.

Earley won the stage by four seconds, just ahead of the peloton. Even amid the excitement of his finest hour, he, typically, had the perspective to realise precisely what he had achieved. 'I knew there and then how important it was,' Earley says. 'I knew by that point roughly where I was, and I knew that would be pretty much as good as it would get.'

The year 1989 was also as good as the Tour would get for Kelly during his tenure at PDM. In 1990, after a broken collarbone at the Tour of Flanders ruined his spring campaign, Kelly arrived at the Tour buoyed by a surprising victory at the Tour of Switzerland, but sacrificed his own ambitions to work for his teammate Erik Breukink. Worse was to come.

PDM was an acronym for Philips Dupont Magnetics, manufacturer of chrome cassettes, but within cycling, the letters would later take on another significance. *Prestaties Door Manipulaties* went the Dutch version of the joke: 'Performances through manipulation.' For the French, it was *Plein de Manipulation de Dopage*. In English, it was transliterated to *Pills, Drugs and Medicine*. Events at the 1991 Tour would enshrine PDM's notoriety, as would the trickle of doping confessions from former riders a decade and more later, but even when Kelly and Earley signed with the Dutch team in 1989, its reputation preceded it.

Kelly's old Sem teammate Jock Boyer was press officer at PDM during his time there, as well as a business partner of the general manager, Manfred Krikke. He maintains that PDM's ill repute stemmed primarily from Gert-Jan Theunisse's positive test for testosterone at the 1988 Tour, and that it was no better or no worse than any other team in the peloton at that time. 'I don't buy into all that,' Boyer says of the Pills, Drugs and Medicine moniker. 'I think a lot of it came from the issues with Gert-Jan Theunisse, and I actually believe he was innocent, that his testosterone level was abnormally high. What individual riders did, I don't know. But I really don't think it was happening as a team, I did not see that. I think the 1991 Tour de France case kind of tainted the whole team.'

The revelation in 2013 by Dutch newspaper *Volksrant* that seven out of eight of PDM's team for the 1988 Tour – the year before Kelly and Earley joined – had been administered banned substances, information hewn directly from the notebook of soigneur Bertus Fok, offers a rather powerful counterargument. American Andy Bishop emerged as the odd man out, and he subsequently told *Cyclingnews* that his refusal to take testosterone had precipitated his departure at the end of 1989. 'In the first year, they did not force or suggest any doping on me,' Bishop said. 'It wasn't until 1989 that there was a very strong suggestion that I take testosterone. I didn't and then I didn't go to any more big races.'

Bishop's account of the use of testosterone at PDM tallies with that of his compatriot Greg LeMond, who spent an unhappy, injury-hit season with the team in 1988. A year later, his attorney Ron Stanko claimed that PDM's stance on doping had encouraged him to leave. 'Their approach to the whole subject of hormones is like something from Mars. Their philosophy is that anything natural is permissible, even if it is acquired through artificial means,' Stanko told the *Los Angeles Times*. 'He never knew from one day to the next whether they would slip him something.'

Paranoia seemed the norm at PDM. During the 1989 Tour, the team unsuccessfully lobbied for a third sealed sample to be collected at doping control. 'We need that third bottle of urine in case one of our riders is found positive, then we could allow our own doctors to do a counter-analysis in a different laboratory to the one in Paris,' Boyer's predecessor Harrie Jansen told *De Stem*.

In 1989, the PDM team doctor was Peter Janssen, who would, incidentally, publish a book in 2009, *Bloedvorm*, in which he argued that EPO, when properly dosed, was 'an extremely safe medicine', though he also insisted that the product had not been used by cyclists in the Netherlands and Belgium in the late 1980s. In 1990, Janssen's place was taken by a fellow Dutchman, Wim Sanders. 'I don't know if that was Jan Gisbers's decision or Manfred Krikke's decision, but they obviously made a very bad choice,' says Boyer.

In the winter of 1997, after an investigation of Sanders's tax affairs demonstrated, among other things, that he had purchased 178 ampoules of Eprex, the brand name for EPO, between 1990 and 1995, Krikke uttered the words that would become the epitaph of the PDM team. 'The one rule imposed by the PDM directors was there were to be no drug affairs, rather than no drug taking,' he told the VNU newspaper group.

'Within this direction, we experimented with products that were just within the edge of legality.'

One such product was Intralipid, an emulsion of fatty acids, most commonly used as a means of intravenous nutrition for those unable to eat solid food. Prior to the Tour, Sanders informed Kelly, Earley and the rest of the PDM riders that Intralipid would be added to their regimen of injections during the race as a means of boosting recovery, with the substance due to be administered every fourth day. On the evening of Bastille Day, after the finish of stage 9, each of PDM's nine riders reported in turn to Dr Sanders's room in the Hotel du Cheval d'Or in Rennes, where they each received an intravenous injection. Interviewed in 1993, the Dutch rider Jean-Paul van Poppel said the process took no longer than a minute, but Kelly has described sitting for about half an hour as Sanders administered the product, before going downstairs to dine with the team. While Boyer describes it as an infusion, Kelly and Earley both term it an injection.

'The doctor would have explained what it was, that it was to help recovery and that it wasn't a doping product,' Earley says. 'It's more of a nutritional product than a doping product. It wasn't unusual. Injections were common, but drips weren't, and Intralipid was by injection.'

Earley endured a fitful night's sleep and woke up feeling ill. His roommate Kelly was in a similar state, and at the breakfast table, all their teammates reported near-identical symptoms: pounding headaches, aching bones and chills, but no nausea and no soaring temperatures. Nico Verhoeven was too ill to start the day's stage and stayed in bed. Uwe Raab made it as far as the start line before turning back to the hotel. Van Poppel and Earley lasted around an hour into the stage. Falk Boden was dropped by the peloton and reached Quimper well outside the time limit.

'I was just really weak. I had no strength whatsoever. We started falling ill straightaway, within a few hours of the injection. I think it was realised pretty quickly what had happened when everybody was feeling feverish,' Earley says. 'It was like food poisoning, in that the symptoms were similar.'

The four survivors – Kelly, Erik Breukink, Raul Alcala and Jos van Aert – were ashen-faced as they climbed aboard the PDM bus at the stage finish, while the Tour's press pack assembled outside. The PDM Affair was born, and the team's failure to provide a coherent explanation for the mystery illness in the hours and days that followed only exacerbated the issue. The following morning, the lobby of Hotel Le Griffon was a bigger draw than the *village départ* in the charming heart of Vieux Quimper. A track-suited Kelly and his teammates boarded the bus, not to go to the start, but to drive all the way to Eindhoven for medical tests. Verhoeven was already in hospital there. The entire PDM team had left the Tour.

'I would not have been able to start today as I had a temperature of 39.5,' Kelly told the *Irish Independent*, a statement contradicted by his account in *Hunger* in 2013, when he wrote, 'I was sweaty and warm but I didn't have a temperature.' Then again, there were plenty of mixed messages emerging from the PDM camp that morning. On Channel 4, Phil Liggett reported that Jan Gisbers had claimed that he, too, had been stricken by the same illness, but this was patently untrue. The malady was limited only to the nine riders injected by Sanders, and none of the staff was affected. Boyer found himself in the positon of having to disseminate information in the vaguest possible terms to a press room that already harboured suspicions about PDM.

In February 1990, the PDM rider Johannes Draaijer had died in his sleep at the age of 26 after suffering a heart attack. Although the link has never been proven, the Dutchman's death quickly came to be associated in media reports with the arrival of a new doping product, erythropoietin, better known as EPO. Interviewed by the *New York Times* during the Tour Dupont in May 1991, Gisbers claimed that he had not heard of anybody in cycling using the drug. Earley maintains now that Draaijer's death was due to an underlying heart condition rather than doping. 'As far as I'm aware, that's all it was. It's not an unusual occurrence,' he says. When Paul Kimmage called him for comment for a feature on Draaijer in 2014, Earley preferred not to contribute. 'I kind of respect the way that he decided, "Look I've been through a lot of shit here, I'm getting out of it now and I'm not talking about it." I kind of respect that in a way,' Kimmage says. 'But it was still a massive disappointment to me.'

Not surprisingly, given the team's reputation, the explanations of Gisbers, Krikke et al. at the 1991 Tour were met with scepticism. 'Acute PDM-itis', read a suitably sarcastic heading in *L'Équipe*, far from alone in raising the prospect of doping. PDM's hypothesis of food poisoning, meanwhile, was met with indignation by the Hotel du Cheval d'Or, whose spokeswoman pointed out the riders had eaten precisely the same food as the team management.

In Ireland, most accounts focused on Kelly's resilience in completing a day's racing despite his illness, as though it were simply another folkloristic feat of strength to be catalogued alongside Mamore and the Clonmel time trial. David Walsh was in Namibia with the touring Irish rugby team, but he reached Kelly by phone for a sympathetic piece in the following week's *Sunday Independent*, where the doping hypothesis was dropped as quickly as it was picked up. Too hot to handle. Paul Kimmage was on the Tour for the *Sunday Tribune*, and though he dealt with the doping question in more depth, he was, just two years removed from the peloton, reluctant to condemn the use of needles by his former colleagues. 'Now this may be uncomfortable to a lot of dreamers out there but doctors (and witchdoctors) do stick needles in most of the competitors' bums,' Kimmage wrote. 'And there is absolutely nothing wrong with this because needles *do not* equal doping!'

Behind closed doors, the PDM riders had already identified Sanders as the culprit, despite his protestations of innocence, yet almost a month passed before the team publicly offered Intralipid as its explanation for the mystery illness. Krikke said the supplement had been administered three times during the race, but either had not been stored at the correct temperature or had been administered with unsterilised needles, leading to a bacterial infection. Sanders's services were quietly dispensed with later in the year, though only after some heated internal discussion.

'To this day, I still don't know exactly what happened. I know Dr Sanders was pretty incompetent and I believe he did not follow protocol with the needles,' Boyer says. 'Whether it was benign or something else I don't know, and I never was told to this day, but definitely something was contaminated and it got everybody sick. When it's an infusion, it gets in pretty quickly, because it's in your blood.'

'Intralipid is a supplement we were given in injection form and it wasn't stored at the correct temperature. The team tried to mask it over but that wasn't the way to do it,' Kelly says. 'There's nothing… We were taking it. We admitted to that.'

PDM's obfuscation meant that the initial whiff of doping about the case developed into a stench that would never dissipate, not even when the team went public with the Intralipid line. 'The Intralipid Affair was exactly that: it was Intralipid that had gone off,' Earley says. Yet even if one accepts that it was simply a case of a contaminated food supplement, it raised further, disturbing concerns: cycling's longstanding relationship with the syringe was leading it to some very dark places.

Sam Abt of the *International Herald Tribune* consulted Sean Kelly's biographer on the issue. Unsurprisingly, David Walsh defended the rider and, by extension, his team. 'If it comes out of a syringe, the public thinks it probably has to be dope,' he told Abt. 'Whatever it looks like, many teams prefer injections to pills or syrup because injections work faster.'

Abt also phoned up Earley, who was by now back home in Stoke and had returned to racing at the Wincanton Classic. He asked the Dubliner whether he had any concerns about following PDM's medical policy in the future. There was a pregnant pause on the line. 'I have no idea,' Earley told Abt. 'I'm not a doctor. I can't say I won't listen to the doctor. What would you do?'

20

THE LAST HURRAH

Eddy Schepers and Patrick Valcke were gone, but Stephen Roche still had a confidant by his side when he linked up with Tonton Tapis in 1991: his brother. Eight years his junior, Laurence Roche began cycling with Orwell Wheelers in 1980, the year Roche rode for ACBB and went to the Moscow Olympics. Laurence vowed to follow the same timeline, and he indeed raced for ACBB in 1988, though he failed to make the five-man squad for the Seoul Olympics. 'I'd beaten Gérard Rué in a sprint in a pro-am race in France, and I thought that was my ticket to the Olympics,' Laurence Roche says. It wasn't to be. Wins at home apparently carried more weight than performances abroad.

If the Roche name had seemed a hindrance as much as a help in Ireland, it only opened doors on the Continent. Laurence began talks with Carrera in April 1988, after just two months on the French amateur scene, and he turned professional with them the following year. 'I'd won some races, but they saw I had pedigree because of who I was too,' Roche says. He based himself in San Felice on Lake Garda, but was frustrated to be treated with kid gloves by Carrera and raced only sparingly in his two seasons on the team. 'I could have done with being thrown in at the deep end,' he says. 'I was pleading with them to let me race.'

Barely a year after his brother's departure from Carrera, Laurence's arrival caused a minor stir. 'Bontempi was a little bit hostile at first, just with little smart remarks,' he says. Roberto Visentini had left the team by then, but there was much mirth among the Italians on Carrera when they encountered him on a training ride near Lake Garda. 'It was a bit tense, but I didn't speak Italian at the time and he had no French so it's not like we could get into an argument,' Roche says. 'We did speak at races later on, but just about the weather and things. We never mentioned Stephen.' Mercifully, there were friendly faces, too, like Kelly's old teammate Acácio da Silva, and Claudio Chiappucci, the emerging star of the Italian *gruppo* with a penchant for performing WWF moves in his hotel room. 'Ultimate Warrior was the big guy at the time in WrestleMania, and Chiappucci would be there in front of the mirror doing this impression of him. It was gas,' he says.

On signing for Tonton Tapis in 1991, Laurence Roche moved north to Paris to be close to Stephen, and they trained together through the spring. As well as lacking Carrera's quality, the team, sponsored by a carpet concern (literally, 'Uncle Carpet'), had none of its sartorial elegance. With the Gulf War dominating the news cycle, some wags on the team couldn't resist likening the logo on the jersey, a moustachioed man with a rolled-up carpet on his shoulder, to Saddam Hussein holding a rocket launcher.

Roche's early victories at Critérium International and Semana Catalana secured a Tour invitation, but four years on from the yellow jersey, he had little say in the composition of the line-up, which was to be split roughly between Tonton Tapis's Belgian and French wings. Laurence earned selection only thanks to a strong showing at the Dauphiné Libéré, and at 23 years of age, he travelled to the *Grand Départ* in Lyon as only the sixth Irishman to participate in the Tour. A bout of tendonitis had hampered Stephen's preparation, but, as at Histor, the Tonton Tapis contingent set out convincing themselves they had a podium contender in their ranks.

Taking 104th place in the prologue in Lyon quickly laid bare that misconception, and 24 hours later, Stephen Roche's Tour was already over after what his admirer CJ Haughey might have termed a grotesque, unbelievable, bizarre and unprecedented team time trial, where he arrived seven minutes late to the start and finished outside the time limit. His teammates tried to stall and wait, but quickly realised that they, too, risked elimination. 'We all just sat there on the start line at first, but the director told us we had to ride or we'd be going home,' Laurence Roche says. When Stephen finally arrived, he was told he couldn't go on. He went on, rode the 35-kilometre course alone, and crossed the line 14 minutes down on the stage. He was eliminated from the Tour.

The entire Tonton Tapis team, as it turned out, had been under the impression that their start time was eight minutes later than it really was, yet all bar Stephen Roche had reported with ample time to spare. He was nowhere to be found, apparently warming up alone. In the immediate aftermath, Roche deflected some blame towards the team manager, Roger

De Vlaeminck, but the Belgian was nonplussed: 'I'm not Roche's daddy. He has his own wristwatch.' Roche was fined a month's salary and any prospect of extending with Tonton Tapis ended there, amid insinuations he had deliberately contrived the situation to mask his poor condition.

'That nearly finished me altogether. I couldn't accept that the journalists I'd been so good to all my career could suggest I was faking these problems to finish outside the time limit. That hurt me a lot. I nearly hung up my wheels,' says Roche, who also claims the widely reported explanation – that he couldn't be found because he had left the warm-up area to use the bathroom – was a fabrication. 'I got the wrong start time, and they made it look I'd gone away for a piss, which was crazy.' That is rather contradicted, mind, by the excuse Roche offered at the time. 'Because of stress, I got stomach cramps during the warm-up and I had to relieve myself,' he told the *Irish Independent*. He elaborated further for Gary Imlach of Channel 4: 'They put out an announcement for me, but I had some cramps in my stomach and I had to go into a house for a visit.'

Laurence Roche, meanwhile, was left to fend for himself in his debut Tour. Within a week, following PDM's withdrawal, he was the only Irishman in the race. 'That was a big blow, because Martin and Sean were great. You'd have great craic with them, and they'd look out for you,' Laurence Roche says. He pressed on. His worst day came on the first mountain stage to Jaca, when he decided to copy the American Andy Hampsten's gear selection to cope with the opening climb of the Soudet. Only when they lined up for the start did Roche realise he and Hampsten had been talking about different passes. Hideously over-geared, Roche was the first rider dropped. 'I got left behind. The autobus hadn't even been formed, and I had to chase and chase and chase, just to catch up to the bus,' he says. 'It was a savage stage. But after that, I was able to manage it.'

Most Irish journalists, there to cover Kelly and Roche, had gone home by that point, and Laurence Roche's considerable achievement of becoming only the sixth Irishman to finish the Tour received only cursory coverage. He battled gamely to reach Paris in 153rd place, and even spent seven laps off the front on the Champs-Élysées on the final day. It was to be the high point of his career. Unable to find a contract for 1992, he returned to live in Dublin. 'A lot of teams were folding or cutting back. It was very difficult,' Roche says. The small Chazal team, where riders could pay their way by finding a sponsor, offered a chance, but despite appeals to Irish backers and the Federation of Irish Cyclists, he was unable to rustle up the £10,000 required. In time, he took a job with Smurfit and studied for a business degree.

Another race, another hotel. It could be anywhere, but this evening it is La Coruña in north-western Spain, the night before the Tour of Galicia. Kelly and Earley, flaked out on their beds, idle away the time before dinner by absent-mindedly flipping through the channels. A month on from the Intralipid debacle, the return to normality is almost complete. The phone trills. Kelly turns down the sound as Earley picks up. He passes the receiver to Kelly. It's Linda. The news is bad. No athlete performs in a vacuum, but for the best part of 15 years, Kelly's personal life had never once seemed to impinge on his professional one. All year round, across every season and all terrains, Kelly was ready. Fitness or morale was never an issue. It was as though he had hit pause on much of the outside world while he focused on his work within the moving citadel of professional cycling. Now life and its attendant sorrows had breached the walls.

Joe Kelly died on the evening of 11 August 1991, when he was struck by a car as he cycled the final miles of the Comeragh 100 leisure ride, which was ending in Carrick-on-Suir. He had just joined the main road after climbing Seskin Hill, a favoured training climb of his younger brother, when he was hit by the car and killed instantly at the age of 39. His death was a front-page story across the Irish newspapers the following morning. By then, Sean had caught the first flight to Ireland. Joe was survived by his wife Helen, who had been waiting at the finish to take his photograph as he crossed the line, and their three-month-old daughter. Over a thousand people attended the funeral at St Molleran's Church three days later.

Barely a week afterwards, Kelly was back in the peloton, preparing for the World Championships in Stuttgart, but bereft of motivation. He rode anonymously in Germany, abandoning the race midway through, and was still struggling to summon any semblance of form by the time the Nissan Classic rolled around in late September. As well as mourning his brother, Kelly was riding for his future. He hadn't won a race in 16 months and PDM's contract offer for 1992 marked a huge reduction on his terms for the preceding three years.

'In the beginning, it was difficult to focus but then you just say to yourself, "Well I think my brother Joe would prefer to see me going on,"' Kelly says. 'And then you just slowly try to refocus yourself and try to get something out of the year. It was a really bad year but you just keep the head down and keep working and try to get a result out of it.'

The turning point came on a rain-soaked Saturday in Cork, one of those suddenly dark afternoons when winter encroaches on autumn without so much as a whisper. On the road between Ballyhooly and Fermoy, Kelly forged clear in the company of Sean Yates. Over four ascents of St Patrick's Hill, they stretched their lead out to 44 seconds. At the finish, the yellow jersey fell to Kelly, the stage honours to Yates. A day later, Kelly rode into Dublin to win his fourth and final Nissan Classic.

Contemporary reports alluded to the recent bereavement, but from Kelly, there were no dedications, no gestures pointing at the sky. It wasn't his style. In all walks of life, people experienced tragedy and loss. They suffered, they grieved, and then they went back to work and tried to carry on as best they could. Kelly was one of them. 'Everybody's different,' he says. 'Some people feel they might make some sort of an issue about it. I think the way to do it is on the bike.'

The Nissan victory seemed but a temporary respite in a trying year when Kelly showed up in Milan for his final major rendezvous of 1991, the Tour of Lombardy. On the eve of the event, he was expected at the race headquarters at the Fiera di Monza to accept an award from the AIJC, the international association of cycling journalists, but instead he remained in the Leonardo da Vinci hotel to receive what *Il Corriere della Sera* described as 'a series of injections' to his left knee, which he had injured in a training crash in midweek.

That setback, allied to his lacklustre season, meant that Kelly wasn't rated as a favourite, but the season-ending classic, cycling's last chance saloon, has always lent itself to men who feel they have nothing left to lose. After joining a break of six on the descent of the Madonna del Ghisallo, Kelly's forcing on the climb of Lissolo burnt off dangerman Franco Ballerini. In a gloomy industrial estate in Monza, the two-up sprint against Martial Gayant proved a formality. In the grand tradition of the Italian cycling press, Kelly was asked to whom his win was dedicated. It was, he said quietly, for Joe.

The Lombardy win marked a literal upturn in Kelly's fortunes. Widely held to be in steady decline during his time at PDM, his market value had depreciated accordingly. Now there was a sudden spike in demand for his services. PDM mulled over improving their offer, pending the arrival of a co-sponsor, and Dutch squad TVM expressed interest, but in the week before Christmas, Kelly confirmed that he had chosen the third way, and signed for the Spanish outfit Festina. Earley, meanwhile, had already agreed a deal to stay put at PDM.

Despite his Stakhanovite reputation, the consensus as Kelly approached his 36th birthday was that the Tour of Lombardy had been a mere aberration, an unexpected day of grace as he raged against the dying of the light. His twin children, Nigel and Stacy, had been born in 1990, and his stated intention was to be retired and living in Ireland by the time they were old enough to start school. This Festina deal, the last major payday of his career, was widely assumed to be his pension plan. And yet, rather than deteriorating, some of the old powers seemed restored as Kelly began his 1992 campaign, his 16th in the professional peloton. He won the Trofeo Luis Puig and a stage of the Tour of Valencia in February, his earliest victories since the halcyon days of the mid-1980s.

All the same, Kelly wasn't counted among the long list of favourites for Milan-San Remo, but something stirred within him as he lined up for *La Classicissima*. Perhaps it was simply muscle memory. The rituals were all so familiar. Lining up early on a Saturday morning with Milan's *centro storico* gently snoozing. Pedalling through the frigid air of the Plain of Lombardy and Piedmont. Climbing from Masone over the Turchino Pass and dropping towards the warmer temperatures of the Ligurian coast. The road trips along the headlands of the Riviera like the words of a song. Up and over the Capo Mele, Capo Berta, Capo Cervo and Cipressa, Kelly ran through the scales and realised he could still carry a tune.

On the Poggio, however, Moreno Argentin, the old foe from Villach, was hitting notes that no one else could reach, and he broke clear. His rivals had heard it all before. Argentin, conducted by one Dr Michele Ferrari, had won the last three stages of Tirreno-Adriatico seemingly at will. Yet one of his pre-race statements had struck a chord with Kelly. 'If Milan-San Remo finished on top of the Poggio, I'd feel pretty certain of winning. I don't know why, but I haven't been descending well lately,' Argentin said.

Argentin held a winning advantage at the summit, but he trickled down the other side like cement. Kelly reached the top 15 seconds down amid the remnants of a group that assumed it was racing for 2nd place. Argentin's Ariostea teammate Rolf Sørensen was blocking for him at the front, but Kelly squeezed past him at the second opportunity, and began clawing back ground on the leader. Kelly has insisted since that he didn't take any undue risks on the way down, but it didn't seem that way from the helicopter shots, which showed him using every available inch of the road on each of the hairpin bends.

As the road flattened out in the outskirts of San Remo, Kelly could see his prey, and he caught a shocked Argentin as they entered the final kilometre, much like the Italian had swooped upon Roche at Liège-Bastogne-Liège six years earlier. Kelly was in the enviable position of being able to afford to lose. He refused Argentin's entreaties to take a turn on the front, and then streaked past him in the sprint on the Via Roma to claim the ninth monument classic of his career.

'I hadn't been performing anything like I had in my big years but with experience you can go away and prepare quietly,' Kelly says of his late Italian wins. 'That's what I did for Lombardy and Milan-San Remo. I knew I was coming on from the way I felt in the weeks beforehand, so I just decided to keep under the radar on the day. That's how I did it in both.'

The photographs immortalising the win on the Via Roma are marred somewhat by the bulbous white helmet atop his head, but Kelly was never overly concerned by aesthetics. Of greater interest was the handsome bonus promised by Brancale if he won a classic wearing their product. The improbable Italian coda to Kelly's career wasn't only about legacy.

Stephen Roche was damaged goods in the winter of 1991. Few teams were willing to take a punt on a 31-year-old Irishman with a troublesome knee and back, occasional weight issues, and a penchant for polemic. 'I had the Roche personality as well: we can be a bit argumentative and headstrong,' Laurence says. There had been the occasional false dawn since 1987, but his decline had been consistent and appeared terminal. After finishing out the season insipidly with Tonton Tapis, Roche raced on the track in November at the Grenoble Six, hoping to dredge up a contract for 1992, but without success. He sounded out Carrera, and Davide Boifava threw him a line.

'It was a big satisfaction when he told me he wanted to come back, and I did everything I could to make it happen,' Boifava says. In Roche's telling, Carrera initiated contact and pleaded with him to join. 'Davide Boifava rang me up and said, "Stephen, you can't finish up like this,"' Roche says. 'After I signed, I told him not to call me until January for the team presentation, and he said OK.' Roche's salary and influence, in any case, had diminished since his previous spell on the team. 'Stephen tried to get me on Carrera but they were already full when he tried to get in there himself,' Laurence Roche says. 'At the time, a certain percentage of the team had to be Italian, so when they took on Stephen, they had to take on another Italian to make that quota. Stephen said he wanted me, but they hadn't the money to take on four people.'

The lie of the land had changed at Carrera. In 1987, Chiappucci had been a humble *gregario*, but the wannabe Ultimate Warrior had since established himself as team leader by twice placing on the podium of the Tour and winning Milan-San Remo in 1991 with an improbable solo break. Even before his surprising ascent, Chiappucci had always been imbued with a certain confidence, and had asked Roche for not one, but two signed pink jerseys during the 1987 Giro, even though he had sided with Visentini at Sappada. Given his previous dealings with Italian co-leaders, one might have anticipated tensions as Roche settled into the unfamiliar role of deluxe domestique at Carrera in 1992, but directeur sportif Beppe Martinelli recalls no teething troubles. 'Not at all, he knew exactly where he was at,' Martinelli says. 'He had a lot of freedom, but he knew he was at the end of his career and things had changed.'

Without the pressure to win races or lead a team, Roche enjoyed a low-key but consistent start to the campaign. Perhaps Kelly's Indian summer had not gone unnoticed. Roche seemed to rediscover himself in haste as the spring drew on. 'I haven't cycled as well for over two years and I know I am getting stronger,' he said after placing 8th in Tirreno-Adriatico, adding of Chiappucci: 'I will work for him, no problem. But when I get the good legs, the really good legs...' Roche proceeded to finish 14th overall in his debut Vuelta a España, and though he arrived at the Tour ostensibly in the service of Chiappucci, he allowed himself to daydream publicly of finishing in the top five and challenging for the leader's jersey. On the evidence of the preceding five years, it seemed a rather fanciful ambition, yet in the opening two weeks of that Tour, Roche seemed a man transfigured.

Roche took 2nd in Valkenburg after an attacking display in week 1, and although he, like everyone else, was battered by Miguel Indurain in the Luxembourg time trial, he recovered to go on the offensive once more on the road to Saint-Gervais in the company of Pedro Delgado, and was even briefly the virtual race leader. At day's end, Roche lay 3rd overall, only 30 seconds behind Indurain and four minutes ahead of Chiappucci. His wholly unexpected resurrection was the talk of the Tour, and

Roche revelled in the attention by playing up his chances of overall victory even though he knew Indurain was unassailable. 'I felt I could match Indurain's time trials if I was my normal self, but I wasn't because of my back. I was riding on one and a half legs,' Roche says.

The surprise podium challenge collapsed in the high Alps, where Chiappucci shook Indurain with an implausible lone raid to Sestriere. Roche briefly slipped out of the top 10 overall, but his effervescence returned in the final week in the Massif Central. On stage 16, Roche escaped from the peloton on the Col de la Croix-Morand, picked off the remnants of an earlier break and disappeared into the envelope of low cloud at the summit, not to be seen again until the finish at La Bourboule, 30 kilometres later. Turning the pedals with disarming facility, Roche opened a winning gap and defended his lead on the mist-shrouded haul to the finish. Visibility was down to just a few metres in the closing kilometres, and Roche's sudden emergence from the gloom at the finish provided an easy lead for the *salle de presse*. 'Normally this year was preparation for next year, but I've found form sooner than I thought,' Roche said at the finish, though in truth, there was already a valedictory air about the win, and the entire 1992 Tour, which he finished in 9th place overall.

'La Bourboule was the day my career finished. I won the stage and I hung my head over the bars and said to the journalists, "This is it, it's over,"' Roche says now. 'It was very important to end it that way, because people might have been left with the bad taste that I was someone who wasn't doing things properly.'

And yet Roche still reported for duty for one more year in 1993, taking 9th in the Giro, before lining up for a farewell Tour, where he claimed he could form a two-pronged offensive with Chiappucci. At a Carrera training camp in St Moritz ahead of the race, David Walsh found Roche in contemplative mood for a *Sunday Independent* feature. 'Money is the only reason for carrying on. I don't think it is a good enough reason,' Roche told him of his impending retirement. 'The glory, the honour: that's all bullshit.'

All the same, Roche was determined to enjoy every accolade a former Tour winner might expect as he took his final bow. He reached Paris in 13th place overall, and stoked the ire of Indurain's Banesto team by nipping ahead of them to lead the race onto the Champs-Élysées, an honour he felt was his due. Speaking on the eve of his last race before retirement, the World Championships in Oslo, Roche sniffed at how his contemporary Laurent Fignon had exited cycling that same summer without any pomp or ceremony. 'A lot of people have said to me that of the good guys stopping this year, you're the only one stopping like a champion should,' Roche told *Cycle Sport*.

Barely two years previously, Roche had seemed destined to retire in far more ignominious circumstances than Fignon, but his remarkable final act at Carrera had altered the tenor of his entire career. It had been a startling transformation, and David Walsh grappled for an explanation. 'Roche's rehabilitation began from the moment he and Valcke separated,' he wrote in his pre-Tour piece. In time, he would come to doubt that theory.

'I wasn't there, so I can't talk about it,' Patrick Valcke says carefully of Roche's late-career fillip. 'As all the Anglo-Saxons say, "No comment."'

►☉◄

Kelly and Earley were in the same jersey once again in 1993, when Festina expanded to incorporate two defunct teams, PDM and RMO. It meant that erstwhile PDM boss Jan Gisbers was part of the Festina management staff, while Willy Voet, a soigneur at RMO for the previous three years, was back at Kelly's side. Yet for all the apparent conviviality, tensions soon manifested themselves between the French and Dutch factions, managed by Bruno Roussel and Gisbers, respectively. On a vast roster of 31 riders, which included a young Richard Virenque, the Irish pair soon found themselves cast as yesterday's men.

Perhaps the greatest measure of the esteem in which Earley was held in the peloton was the fact that he was selected to ride the Tour in each of his first eight seasons as a professional. At Fagor, Kas and PDM, he was a man who could be relied upon to get the job done with a minimum of fuss. After a difficult spring in 1993, including an abandon at the Vuelta, however, Earley spent July at home for the first time in his career. Rather than view it as a slight, Earley heeded the message. He had progressed steadily, reached a peak in the summer of 1989 and now, at 31 years of age, was experiencing the ineluctable decline.

'It wasn't a heartbreak,' Earley says. 'It was another sign. If you're not selected for the Tour, it means you're not going right. I'd been a pro for so long, and been selected every year because generally I was pretty good for the team, but I know my performance wasn't that good that year.'

Several riders who shone in the 1980s, among them LeMond and Fignon, later suggested that their natural downward trajectories in the early 1990s were accelerated by the profusion of new and more potent forms of doping – namely, EPO – in cycling in the early 1990s. Earley downplays the correlation. 'I know I was struggling where I wasn't struggling before. Whether that's the aging process or what, I don't know,' he says. 'Personally, I think I raced too much when I was younger. I was at a point where I wasn't recovering as well as I was. I could see I wasn't performing at the same level. Whether that was me trailing off or everyone else going quicker, I don't know.'

Earley made no attempt to find a berth on a Continental team at the end of the season, preferring instead to switch to the British-based Raleigh squad, where he would focus primarily on mountain biking. Since the mid-1980s, Earley had been living in Hilderstone, near Stoke, but often spent weeks between races back in his old room in Fontainebleau or with Kelly in Vilvoorde. Riding a UK-based programme meant being able to spend longer periods at home with his family, while the reduced time commitment of a mountain bike rider suited his new schedule, as he began studying to be a physical therapist in 1994. He continued racing until 1996, closing the circle by competing in the Atlanta Olympics in the mountain bike event, 12 years on from his exploits with Kimmage and McQuaid in Los Angeles, and then switched his focus to sports therapy.

'By the end, I'd had enough of travelling and living out of a suitcase and it felt like the time was right,' he says. 'Part of the attraction of mountain biking was that I was able to study and do more sports therapy and adapt to the next phase. You spend less time training, but it was also a fresh challenge training-wise, and I'd always had an interest in that. I was using heartrate monitors in the mid-'80s. I didn't really know what to do with the information but I always had the interest.'

For Kelly, meanwhile, being deemed surplus to requirements for the Tour provoked a deeper existential crisis. His spring campaign, hampered by illness and crashes, had been underwhelming, and he was 37 years old, but he was still Sean Kelly. The power struggle between Gisbers and Roussel has seen the Frenchman win out, and he had no place for Kelly in a Tour team built around the former RMO men Virenque and Pascal Lino. The news, though hardly unexpected, came as a profound disappointment. Kelly had ridden his 14th Tour in 1992 without realising it was his last. As ever, he found a sympathetic ear in David Walsh. 'Because I have done nothing this year, I don't want to say publicly what I think of Roussel,' Kelly told the *Sunday Independent*. 'But there is still some way to go before the season and I think I can do something. When I do, I will then say what I think of him. And he wouldn't want to come too close to me.'

Kelly's hunger and focus, however, were beginning to waver. 'In the last two years of my career, you'd have a plan to go training for so many hours and then you end up coming back an hour early or not training as hard,' he admits. Fourth place at Paris-Tours was as good as it got over the remaining months of the campaign, which increasingly seemed as though it had been his last, even if a formal announcement of retirement was not forthcoming. When Kelly won a mountain bike race in Clonmel in late November, however, he intimated that he was still in the market for a team. By the time he won his umpteenth Hamper Race in Carrick at Christmas, Kelly was giving serious thought to following Earley into mountain biking in 1994.

Kelly eventually signed a short-term contract with a new French squad, Catavana, managed by his former Sem teammate Guy Gallopin, and joined Marc and Yvon Madiot. The deal was only confirmed in early March, just in time for Paris-Nice. 'I had a plan to get out at the end of '93 but then I was approached by a new team and I said I'd do half the season,' Kelly says. 'And that's what I did.' He rode his final Paris-Roubaix that April, abandoning quietly after the Arenberg Forest, while his one notable result came in his final major race for Catavana, the Dauphiné Libéré. In a sprint finish on stage 4 to Échirolles, Kelly found himself doing battle with Greg LeMond. For a moment, they were young again, but then the Frenchman Emmanuel Magnien streaked by to claim the stage win, while Kelly placed 2nd. The time had come.

On the Sunday before Christmas 1994, Kelly was feted in Carrick-on-Suir with a special edition of the Hamper Race. President Mary Robinson attended a banquet on the eve of the race, Eddy Merckx, Laurent Fignon, Claude Criquielion and Roger De Vlaeminck were among the visiting stars, and Kelly's Irish contemporaries all lined out on the day, including Kimmage. 'I was the black sheep, but I wasn't treated like it,' he says. Seemingly every amateur rider in Ireland also took part – 'Everybody had a go off the pros,' Earley recalls – and the win, inevitably, went to Kelly. Like the Nissan Classic nine years earlier, the script had to be respected.

And yet if the Carrick-on-Suir celebration was a fitting homage from the Irish cycling community to its greatest rider, Kelly's final professional race six months earlier was perhaps a more accurate reflection of cycling's standing in Ireland by the mid-1990s. Through the previous decade, as the number of

Irish professionals grew, there had been occasional murmurings of holding a professional national championship, but it came to nothing. The maiden such race eventually took place on 26 June 1994 on the Isle of Man, during the Manx International, which also incorporated the British national championships. Kelly, Earley and the northerner Joe Barr raced in the same peloton as the British riders, with the best-placed among them to be crowned Ireland's first-ever professional national champion. 'There was a jersey and there was a sprint at the end, and I think we were both in the front group,' says Earley, whose 5th place in the main event gave him his first national title since he was a junior. It was scarcely granted a paragraph in most newspapers, focused as they were on the Irish football team's World Cup campaign in America. For Irish cycling, the party was over.

21

CHÂTEAU DE DUBLIN

The great symbol of the Irish cycling boom was never likely to survive its bust. Nissan ceased sponsorship of the Nissan Classic when its contract expired after the 1992 edition of the race, and with Kelly and Roche fading out of the picture, there was only one way of ensuring its survival. 'A local hero is necessary,' Jim McArdle wrote in the *Irish Times* after Phil Anderson had won a low-key race. The trouble, of course, was that there was no such star on the horizon. Irish cycling's gilded era produced five Tour finishers, but when Kelly hung up his wheels in 1994, it left Ireland with no professional rider on the Continent, a state of affairs that would endure for the remainder of the decade.

'We tried to get a new sponsor for 1993, but it didn't come because Kelly and Roche were at the end of their careers, and because the race was too closely associated with the name Nissan,' Pat McQuaid says. 'A new sponsor taking over would have needed a really good business reason to do it.' None was forthcoming.

At grassroots level, too, the years of plenty of the 1980s were followed by a fallow period in the 1990s. Just shy of 3,000 riders held racing licences in Ireland when the federations formally unified in 1987, a figure which rose to 4,220 by 1989, but then dropped below 2,000 by the late 1990s. Although young Irish riders continued to travel to the Continent to race, none would survive the first winnowing process at amateur level. Conor Henry, a stagiaire with TVM in 1992, the same year he won the Milk Race, was the only one to come close. Mark Scanlon's junior world title in 1998, meanwhile, felt like the work of a once-in-a-generation talent rather than the product of any overarching development strategy. Back in Ireland, the flow of juvenile riders into the sport slowed to a trickle in the 1990s. It was unfortunate, too, that Kelly and Roche's most nondescript Tour appearances coincided with the summer of the Irish soccer team's exploits at Italia 90. Cycling quickly receded from the mainstream.

While the main figures of Irish cycling's golden decade agree that an opportunity was squandered, pinpointing precisely what could have been done differently is less obvious. 'I think we all thought it was going to be a snowball effect. An opportunity was missed, but you can't pick the federation out and put all the blame on them,' says Kelly. For Kimmage and Earley, cycling's inherent hardships meant it was always going to be problematic to keep youngsters in the sport, even when Kelly and Roche were in their pomp. 'Maybe it was too hard for the kids who got into it and tried it, and there weren't the structures in place to hang onto them,' Kimmage says. 'But I don't honestly know what the federation could have done to change it. I don't know if you could have sold cycling to the mass population then.'

Roche, on the other hand, apportions at least some of the responsibility to the federation's management of amateur cycling in Ireland. 'Everybody was putting on a green shirt as a rider or manager even if they had no experience. It went pear-shaped because there was no structure or organisation to the federation,' he says. Frank Quinn, whose *Irish Cycling Review* ceased in 1995 as the bike industry dropped off, believes the federation should have actively courted non-competitive riders at the time, as it has since done over the past decade, to sustain the sport through the inevitable post-Kelly lull. 'It was a false bubble, but when we had the farewell for Kelly, there were something like 1,000 cyclists out that day and the federation should have embraced that. But they told me: "We're a racing association,"' he says.

Pat McQuaid, meanwhile, complains that the federation viewed the Nissan Classic with detachment rather than actively using it to market the sport in Ireland. 'They wanted their money from me, £1,000 a day or whatever it was. They were happy to get the fee and be invited to the finish, but they didn't sit down themselves and look to ensure that we get a lot of youngsters into the sport from it,' McQuaid says. His own departure from the role of national team coach in 1985 hardly lent itself to a close working relationship with the federation.

One brief stint as international director for the newly unified Federation of Irish Cyclists in 1989 aside, McQuaid focused primarily on organising professional bike races through the late 1980s and early 1990s. As well as continuing their work on the Tour of Britain and Nissan Classic, McQuaid and Rushton branched into the Asian market, organising events including the Tour of the Philippines and the Tour de Langkawi in Malaysia.

All the while, he ran a bike shop, and was far from the only McQuaid working in the cycling industry at the time. 'There's 10 members of the McQuaid family and at one stage, seven and a half of us were making our living full-time in cycling,' says Kieron McQuaid, who worked as a bicycle wholesaler. 'John and Oliver both had bike shops. Siobhan in South Africa and Noelle in the USA had nothing to do with it. Then Jim was a policeman in Whitehall and had a bike shop in Swords as well, so that's the half. Paul was running a cycle holidays business. My sister Anne was publishing *Winning Magazine* and Darach was working for her. And that was all before Pat got involved in any way with the UCI.'

Pat McQuaid first ran for UCI office in 1993, when he narrowly failed to be elected to the UCI board of management, but his links with the governing body were longstanding even at that juncture. Although he held no administrative role in the ICF, McQuaid had attended the UCI Congress each year since the mid-1980s, initially to lobby for the Nissan Classic's slot on the calendar. 'We'd organise an Irish breakfast for all the delegates at UCI Congress and the management committee. We'd have Irish coffees and smoked salmon, the Irish Food Board would send it over,' McQuaid says. 'When I was organising the Nissan over those years, I got to know quite a lot of people in the political world. I was there in a private capacity, not as a delegate, but Irish cycling wasn't even sending anyone to Congress at the time.'

After McQuaid missed out on election to the UCI board in 1993, he was taken aside by a couple of existing members and told his time would come in four years' time. In the meantime, it didn't harm McQuaid's credentials that he was elected president of the Federation of Irish Cyclists in 1995. 'I think I would have supported him when he went for the presidency of the federation here,' Kimmage says. 'But then once he got a whiff of power, he knew what he was doing...'

McQuaid returned to the UCI Congress in 1997 and duly gained election to the board. His candidacy had been heavily supported by UCI president Hein Verbruggen, and the Dutchman then immediately elevated his ally to the board's most prestigious role. McQuaid was appointed head of the road commission, which overlooked all levels of the sport bar professional cycling. He was on the inside.

Sports politics was growing on McQuaid. In 1996, he had run – unsuccessfully – for vice-president of the Olympic Council of Ireland, having previously served as part of a think tank set up by Dublin mayor Gay Mitchell to explore the feasability of mounting a bid to host the Olympic Games. While that whimsical idea never gained any traction, the pipedream did indirectly lead to the arrival of another major sporting event on Irish shores.

'At the time, I happened to be involved in bringing the Tour de France to the UK for two days in 1994, and I knew it could come to Ireland too, but it would have to be for the start, where they'd come in at their leisure the week before and then get out quickly,' McQuaid says. It helped that McQuaid had history with the Tour de France organisation. Technical director Jean-François Pescheux had, like McQuaid, broken the boycott to ride at the Rapport Toer in 1976, while the Tour's race director Jean-Marie Leblanc and press officer Philippe Sudres visited the Nissan Classic each year for what, to all intents and purposes, amounted to an end-of-season piss-up.

'I'd get a phone call the week before from Sudres saying, "Myself and Jean-Marie are coming, can you organise a car for us?" and I'd say, "No problem,"' McQuaid says. 'We'd see them the night before the race started in Dublin, then we wouldn't see them for 24 hours. Then they'd be back on the race and then they'd go away again for 24 hours. They'd be telling me stories about how they ended up on Achill Island or some mad pub where they spent the night drinking pints of Guinness.'

At a meeting in Andorra during the 1993 Tour, Leblanc gave McQuaid his benediction: provided the logistics – and, more important, the fee of £2 million – were in place, the Tour could start from Ireland. McQuaid and Rushton's company, now called L'Evenement, set about drumming up support for the project in Ireland. France's hosting of the World Cup meant that 1998 was a suitable year for a foreign *Grand Départ*, and it also coincided neatly with the 200th anniversary of the 1798 Rebellion. Despite a rather brazen attempt from then Minister for Tourism Enda Kenny to route the Tour into his constituency via Killary Harbour, a more practical three-day schedule was eventually agreed, which saw the race start in Dublin and travel to France via Cork two days later. In April 1997, the Irish *Grand Départ* was officially confirmed for the following year.

After a decade or more of treating a child's game with the attendant solemnity of a vocation, retirement is rarely a simple readjustment for the professional cyclist, especially successful ones. Many, suspecting that they don't have the skills to make it on the outside, do everything in their power to stay in cycling, seeking work as managers, mechanics, masseurs or drivers. Others find stepping off the carousel to be a relief. All realise in time that there are few certainties once the cheering stops.

On the advice of Frank Quinn, Kelly seemed to treat his retirement as if he were a member of an uncontacted tribe emerging from the depths of the Amazonian rainforest. The first two years or so after hanging up his wheels were spent in a quarantine of sorts, as though developing the antibodies to survive in his new environment. He continued to ride his bike most days, and his principal occupation was building his new house outside Carrick-on-Suir. 'I said, "Don't rush into anything. Pull back, see what you want to do and then be comfortable when you make the choice,"' Quinn says. 'He was just down in Carrick, not driving fast cars around the place or anything. He just stood back from cycling, and in retrospect it was a very good decision.'

'It's something unknown, how you're going to adapt, until you actually do it, but I had no problem at all,' Kelly says. 'When I got out from cycling, I got away from it. For the first couple of years, I didn't go to the races at all. I needed that time to clear my head.'

Roche was a more restless retiree. After claiming that he didn't want to 'go through the motions' by racing deep into his 30s, he possibly felt compelled to fill his post-cycling life with activity to justify that decision. After riding on a reduced salary in those final years, perhaps he simply needed to fill those days more than he let on. One of Roche's first business ventures would prove the most enduring, a Majorca-based cycling holiday company established with Claude Escalon that continues to this day.

Others were less felicitous. Given his charm and his command of languages, public relations seemed a natural path for Roche to follow, but, initially at least, he rebelled against it. He invested money and time in Eurodatacar, a car security system, moving back to Dublin to oversee its unsuccessful Irish launch. 'I wanted to prove that I had the potential to do more than just sell hot air,' Roche had said as he prepared to take the plunge. By 1995, he was performing promotional work for the Coeur de Lion cheese company on the Tour de France, selecting the most aggressive rider on each stage. Roche also continued for a time to compete in rallying events, now without the estranged Valcke. Going nowhere fast seemed a heavy-handed but apt metaphor for his post-cycling life.

As early as the weekend of Kelly's farewell event in Carrick-on-Suir in December 1994, Roche confessed to the *Irish Independent* that he had fallen into something of a depression after hanging up his wheels, but that admission of vulnerability was followed by a show of spikiness. Praise for Kelly for sacrificing his chances at the 1987 Worlds, Roche complained, was misguided. 'It angers me when I hear that. I mean when you see the work I did that day, I did everything for Sean that day and still had the strength to win,' he said. 'There's no doubt that in results, he did an awful lot better out of me than I did out of him.' It read like resentment of Kelly's popularity and beatific status as a man of the people, but it was equally a statement of Roche's lingering dissatisfaction at his own reception in his home country, which would begin to manifest itself ever more clearly in retirement.

Events at the *Grand Départ* of the 1998 Tour would hardly help to redress the balance. Roche, who was by then established as David Duffield's co-commentator on Eurosport's cycling coverage, was invited to co-host the pre-race presentation with RTÉ's Mary Kennedy in Dublin Castle, rechristened Château de Dublin by the Tour organisation for the occasion. At that point, Roche had been living in Dublin for over two years. The spell coincided initially with a separation from Lydia, though she joined him in Ireland in the summer of 1996, bringing their children Nicolas and Christel with her. Their third child, Alexis, was born in 1998. They had already decided to move the family back to France in the year after the *Grand Départ*, partly for the children's education but also because Roche's promotional services were in greater demand there than in his own country. 'I thought there would be a sort of ambassador's role with the tourist board after the Tour de France. I thought Ireland as a producer of cheese might be looking to use me to promote Irish cheese in Europe,' Roche says. The erstwhile Galtee cheese kid's prior endorsement of a French brand constituted a conflict of interests. 'I said, "If an Irish cheese company gives me penny for penny what Coeur de Lion are giving me, I'll change tomorrow," but nobody came on board with that, so I continued on my own.'

With no Irish riders in the Tour peloton, RTÉ did not broadcast the entire team presentation on the night before the race, but rather a shortened version as part of a special edition of its *Nationwide* magazine programme. As well as having Roche introduce selected stars of the peloton on stage, the programme featured a pre-recorded interview in which he plugged his Majorca training camps and discussed the differences between life in Ireland and France, specifically for teenagers. 'When you see so many kids on the street corners, so many delinquents and especially the drink, it does frighten me,' Roche said of his native city.

Kelly was seated in the crowd at Dublin Castle, and already dismayed that his contribution to Ireland's Tour history, as well as those of Elliott, Earley and Kimmage, had been relegated to a mere footnote in what now seemed to be a Stephen Roche Joint. When the interview, complete with Roche's ad hoc commentary on Ireland's social ills, was played on the big screen, he stood up and walked out.

For casual observers in Ireland, the unexpected melodrama of Kelly and Roche's very public falling-out was of more interest than a bike race that didn't feature any Irish riders. 'I was upset at what was on the clip. It was not the occasion to put it out,' Kelly said the following day. Aggrieved by the mere 90 seconds RTÉ had afforded him during the presentation, he refused to grant any interviews to the state broadcaster for the remainder of the Tour's visit. This was particularly embarrassing for RTÉ on stage 2, which feted Kelly by passing through Carrick-on-Suir en route from Enniscorthy to Cork. Kelly was driven through the town centre ahead of the race in a vintage car, and then sat alongside Minister of Sport Jim McDaid in a makeshift grandstand as the peloton came by. 'I'm very, very disappointed and I'm very hurt,' Kelly said, an unusually candid admission for a man whose default setting was country reserve.

After being hauled over the coals in the written press over the weekend, Roche appeared on RTÉ's *Liveline* radio show in a bid to undo the damage, insisting that the context around his remarks had been edited out of the *Nationwide* interview. His attempt at a mea culpa backfired, mainly because he never actually provided one. 'I was asked to retract what I said, and I said, "Prove to me I'm wrong; otherwise it's staying."' Roche says now. 'Of course, when I was looking for a job with the tourist board, it wasn't really ideal.' Perhaps as grave a misjudgement came when Roche looked to justify why he had received so much airtime in comparison to Kelly. He pointed out that he had retained closer links with professional cycling, but added what sounded like a needless jab at Kelly. 'Sean's been at home taking it easy,' he said.

Public affection for Kelly and Roche, distributed relatively evenly in 1987, seemed to shift decisively towards Kelly in their retirement. 'As the years went on, you got a sense there was a much greater *grá* for Kelly because of his personality,' Kimmage says. 'People had a greater affinity to Kelly's laid-back, humble style.' In 2009, for instance, Kelly placed sixth in a public poll conducted by RTÉ to select Ireland's greatest-ever sportsperson, and would surely have finished higher had Roche – who failed to make the top 10 – not drawn part of the cycling vote. 'I've no hang-up about not being the golden kid in Ireland,' Roche says. 'But sometimes you see reports about the athlete of the century and they might come up with a dog trainer or something, and you say, OK where is the comparison there? I feel that my achievement is one of the best in Irish history.'

Events at the 1998 *Grand Départ* only seemed to exacerbate the tacit binary view of Kelly and Roche in Ireland. Kelly married a Carrick-on-Suir woman; Roche married a Frenchwoman. Kelly kept his Carrick accent; Roche picked up a French twang. Kelly moved home to Carrick and drove a tractor; Roche stayed in France and drove fast cars. In short, Kelly was perceived in some quarters as being somehow more 'Irish' in personality than Roche. In truth, Kelly and Roche simply represented two different sides of the Irish emigrant experience. Kelly had moved to the Continent to make his fortune and come home. Roche had moved to the Continent and built a new life. Each was as valid as the next.

Even so, coverage of the Kelly–Roche spat seemed to be tinged with an underlying resentment that Roche had deemed France a more agreeable place to live than Ireland, and his own inference that he had never been adequately compensated or acclaimed in his home country only exacerbated matters. Kelly would never have misread the temperature of the room in the same way. In the circumstances, the manufactured outrage of a *Sunday Independent* columnist was only to be expected – 'Perhaps it was easier for Roche to blame Ireland again for his woes' – but the indirect yet obvious admonishment of Roche by British publication *Cycling Weekly* carried rather more weight: 'Kelly, let's face it, is an iconic figure in Irish cycling, one who has always stayed close to his roots, who wasn't about to move out of the country, and who has never managed to annoy anyone in the 20 years since he started out as a professional.'

The furore died down once the Tour left Cork Harbour and headed for France, and though the tensions between Kelly and Roche lingered for longer than they had after the 1987 Paris-Nice, say, relations quietly normalised. Typically, Roche's 2012 autobiography offers a lengthy account of the quarrel, including how he and Linda Kelly didn't speak for a decade afterwards, while Kelly's offering the following year doesn't so much as mention the episode. 'It was RTÉ who were calling the shots with the programme,' Kelly says now, with the air of a man who would rather let bygones be bygones. 'I think there should have been a pretty much equal exposure for us and the other guys as well – certainly Martin Earley, because he won a stage of the Tour and the Giro – so I think it was an unfair deal.'

Kelly wouldn't have to wait long to get his share of television exposure. That very summer, Eurosport invited him to come on board as a co-commentator. In time, he would replace Roche in the booth, and after almost two decades in the role, Kelly's flat vowels and cogent analysis are as much a staple of Eurosport's coverage as the late Duffield's flights of fancy were in yesteryear. In some ways, the 1998 Tour marked Kelly's formal entry into his very active post-racing life.

It was also, of course, a watershed of another kind. In the build-up to the race, a Festina soigneur was stopped at the Franco-Belgian border, and police arrested him when they found he was carrying 234 doses of EPO in his car, as well as vials of human growth hormone, ampoules of Synacthen and capsules of epitestosterone. His destination, Dublin. His name, Willy Voet.

22

THE BOOK OF EVIDENCE

Kelly has always stayed at the Leonardo da Vinci in Milan. Okay hotel for a creature of habit. It is Thursday afternoon and six teams have checked in. Riders, mechanics, masseurs, managers, sponsors. Cycling's full circus.

In the restaurant you pick out the faces. Men who were once part of Kelly's entourage. Titi, a masseur, who was with him on the Tour of Switzerland, missed the birth of his second son so he could rub Kelly's legs. Ducrot, once Kelly's soigneur, who wished to learn English. A serious man who hankered for a more important place at the table.

Then there was Willy, the Belgian soigneur Kelly liked. At another table Christian Rumeau, the directeur sportif who held Kelly when he shook with the disappointment of crashing out in the '87 Tour.

Titi, Ducrot, Willy, Rumeau. Back in the mid-eighties they were important men. Journalists sought their company, dropped a few casual questions, hoping to catch some little anecdote. We all did it. Something to bring light to stories on Kelly.

Now they work with different teams. Ordinary men again. Props that travel with the circus. How many Kelly stories are they still telling? Lots, you can be sure.

– David Walsh, *Sunday Independent*, 22 March 1992

B y the spring of 1999, Willy had a surname, and he had some darker tones to add to his Sean Kelly stories. After his arrest in July 1998, Willy Voet spent 16 days in a prison cell while the Tour de France was engulfed by what came to be known as the Festina Affair. Team manager Bruno Roussel and team doctor Erik Rijkaert joined Voet in custody as details of Festina's systematic doping programme emerged, and the squad was ejected from the Tour at the end of the opening week, with French favourite Richard Virenque tearfully denying any wrongdoing. He persisted in the same vein until the matter went to trial in Lille in November 2000, before finally confessing. By then, most of the sordid details were already public knowledge following the publication of Voet's exposé *Massacre à la chaine* in May 1999.

The scandal-ridden 1998 Tour – on two separate occasions, the peloton went on strike in protest at police searches – marked a turning point, though not, sadly, for cycling itself. With some exceptions, business seemed to resume as usual in the peloton after the race, albeit more furtively than before. There was a change, however, in public perception. For decades, press and fans alike had willingly suspended disbelief, ignoring cycling's doping culture. After Festina, there was a readiness to look under rocks and hear tell of doping that had not really existed at the time of *Rough Ride*'s publication. The second edition, printed to coincide with the 1998 Tour, could hardly have been more timely.

The publication of Voet's book in 1999 proved more troubling for Kelly than Kimmage's text ever had. As well as recounting the soigneur's arrest and incarceration, and shedding light on the doping programme in place at Festina, Voet also dusted off some anecdotes from his 20-odd years in professional cycling, including his time as a soigneur on Jean de Gribaldy's team. Kelly featured in several. They could hardly be described as flattering.

Although Kelly had left Flandria by the time Voet joined as a soigneur in 1979, the Belgian cycling milieu is a small one. Voet lived just seven kilometres from Vilvoorde, and Kelly regularly availed of his services as a masseur during his time at Splendor, paying a day rate. Voet went on to have spells with the Marc Zeep Centrale and Daf Trucks teams, but the rider–soigneur relationship was formalised in 1982, when both men returned to the de Gribaldy stable at Sem.

'It was with Sem-France Loire that I gained my reputation as a *soigneur*. More precisely, it was with Sean Kelly,' Voet wrote in *Massacre à la chaine*. In those days, a soigneur's reputation wasn't earned simply by rubbing legs and filling water bottles. If Voet's stock rose with each Kelly victory, it was because of the part he played, to borrow the old cycling euphemism, in *preparing* the Irishman for action.

Voet matter-of-factly implicates Kelly on three occasions in *Massacre à la chaine*. The first anecdote comes from the eve of 'a Tour of Lombardy in the 1980s', most likely 1983. Kelly was behind the wheel of a packed team car as the riders returned to their hotel from the team presentation. Voet, his lowly soigneur, was crammed into the boot. 'He was never slow when it came to winding people up,' Voet wrote. 'To amuse the other riders, he began swerving all over the place and slamming on the brakes. The more I yelled, the more wildly he drove, until I ended up smashing my head on the car roof.'

After a row at the hotel, a sullen Voet wordlessly massaged Kelly that evening. 'And when the time came to minister to his other needs, notably the cortisone injection, I got a bottle ready with a very bad grace and threw it down on the bedside table. 'There's your shit. Goodnight.' He had to fend for himself which didn't seem to trouble him in the slightest,' Voet wrote. The following afternoon, Kelly sprinted to win the Tour of Lombardy. 'We fell into each other's arms and cried like a pair of kids,' Voet wrote.

The second Kelly tale recounted by Voet is the story of his disastrous day in the yellow jersey at the 1983 Tour, which the Belgian attributed to an injection of Synachten Retard on the eve of the stage to Bagnères-de-Luchon. The third related to Kelly's positive test for Stimul at the 1984 Paris-Brussels. According to Voet, Kelly had been suffering from bronchitis ahead of the race and was treated with ephedrine, which cleared up his illness but had the glaring drawback of being a detectable, banned substance. 'At the end of the race, he had to go for the drug test. There was nothing to worry about. We hid a flask of urine – kindly donated by a mechanic – in his shorts and the rider managed to dodge round the control,' Voet wrote. By this telling, Kelly had at least been truthful in saying he hadn't taken Stimul. 'To stay awake at the wheel of the car, the mechanic had charged up a bit but had forgotten,' Voet wrote. 'The rider was disqualified and since then that mechanic has always been careful before donating anything.'

In France, media interest on the book was centred on the revelations about the doping programme at Festina and the quirks of Virenque's personality, although in an interview with *L'Équipe*, Voet was asked if he was concerned about the damage the book might do to Kelly's reputation. 'Above all, I don't want to smash the legend of Kelly,' Voet said. 'He was a champion.'

Word of the book's contents had reached Ireland even before publication, thanks to the extracts printed in *Paris Match*. On the weekend before *Massacre à la chaine* hit the bookstores, the *Sunday Independent* ran a story on the front page, which carried a short statement from Kelly: 'I will not be making any comment until I get more information on the full contents of the book.' The author of the piece was Paul Kimmage, who had left the *Tribune*. The following week, Kimmage travelled to Paris for the book's launch, where he interviewed Voet. On his return to Ireland, he drove to Carrick-on-Suir and presented Kelly with a copy. 'I went down to him with the book and said, "Listen, you need to address this." Vinny the brother was with him, and he got very upset,' Kimmage says. 'I said, "Listen, open your fucking eyes." I said, "Will you talk about this?" And he wouldn't do it. And I thought, that's not good enough now.'

In an echo of his response to *A Rough Ride*, Kelly made a vague pledge to read the book before commenting, but Kimmage was well versed in that playbook. He even referenced it in a column he wrote that same week, entitled, 'Why silence is no longer good enough'. When *A Rough Ride* was published in 1990, Kimmage wrote, he was grateful for Kelly's refusal to comment: 'Rightly or wrongly, I interpreted this silence as support.' Now, Kimmage argued, circumstances had changed. Cycling's doping culture was in the open and there was a chance to tackle it, even if the tone of his piece was pessimistic: 'There have been no resignations at the helm of the UCI or the Societé du Tour de France. It will be almost business as usual come the Tour in July.'

It was business as usual for Kelly, too. He never did tell the *Sunday Independent* whether he had read Willy Voet's book, far less comment on its contents. The storm passed. When the book was finally published in English two years later, translated by William Fotheringham as *Breaking the Chain*, the three anecdotes implicating Kelly remained, but his name had been expunged in each instance. Although Kelly made no legal attempt to block its publication, Random House in London decided independently to redact his name from the offending passages, mindful of Britain's strict libel laws.

In Kelly's autobiography *Hunger*, ghostwritten by British journalist Lionel Birnie and published in the summer of 2013, Willy Voet's name is never even mentioned. It is as though the Belgian soigneur had never existed. Kelly's ephemeral spell in yellow at the 1983 Tour is described simply as 'one of my worst days on the bike'. His positive test at the 1984 Paris-Brussels is blamed on a vague accusation that the testers had failed to follow protocol, and he claims that when the B-sample was examined, 'there was a tiny amount of urine in the jar, far less than the minimum required'.

The winter prior to *Hunger*'s publication, David Walsh had written of standing with Kimmage at the start of that Paris-Brussels and hearing pills rattling in Kelly's pocket. In February 2013, at a reception in Dublin to mark the arrival of the Giro d'Italia the following year, a reporter asked Kelly if Walsh's account was accurate. Kelly hesitantly said he didn't recall the precise episode, but that any rattling pills would have been legal products, such as caffeine. An hour later, the reporter's mobile phone buzzed. It was Kelly, asking that his remarks be taken off the record. On reflection, he had no comment to make. Later that year, Kelly eventually went on the record with the same explanation on the *Second Captains* podcast, saying 'having something in your back pocket wouldn't be out of the ordinary.'

Interviewed for this book in December 2016, Kelly rejected the allegations outlined by Voet in *Massacre à la chaine*. 'Well that was, as I said, totally incorrect. Willy Voet was just writing his book,' Kelly said. 'He wanted to write his book and of course he wanted names, and he wanted something also to make his book sell. It was all about promoting his book.'

Kelly's obvious discomfort at discussing doping is no surprise to anyone who has followed his work as a co-commentator on Eurosport. As a race analyst, he is unparalleled. His knowledge is formidable, but worn lightly, and dispensed with a fluency that belies his old reputation as the quiet man. And yet, on the rare occasions on-air conversation turns to doping, Kelly's default response is familiar. Silence.

'You can't talk about things until somebody is guilty. Every time there's been a problem and somebody was guilty – proven – then I've talked about it,' Kelly says. 'But otherwise I don't start talking about hearsay. That's my way.'

It always has been. Kelly is a television star, a successful businessman and, since 2006, has run his own professional cycling team, An Post-Chain Reaction. It's hard to argue that silence hasn't served him well.

►⊙◄

The post-*Rough Ride* détente between Paul Kimmage and Stephen Roche was not a lasting one. When Michelle Smith emerged from obscurity to win three swimming golds at the 1996 Olympics, Kimmage's was among the dissenting voices in the Irish press, but flipping on the radio one afternoon, he heard an old acquaintance disputing his work. 'Roche was there on Joe Duffy, and he was on about Kimmage, and how this is disgraceful,' Kimmage says. 'I'm thinking what the fuck is this? I absolutely fucking nearly flipped. I was going to kill him.' Smith was later sanctioned for manipulating an anti-doping sample in 1998, but that same year Roche stoked Kimmage's ire still further with his reaction to the second edition of *Rough Ride*. 'He has to wake up some time and realise what he's doing to sport in general,' Roche complained to Sam Abt. 'Yes, it's OK to wake everybody up to the danger of drugs, I do agree, but at the same time there's a limit as to what you can say. He's said it once, OK, but he keeps saying it again.'

It came as a surprise, then, when Roche phoned Kimmage up and suggested they meet for peace talks. They differ on the date and the location – Roche says they met in the Berkeley Court Hotel in the winter of 1998, Kimmage reckons it was the Burlington in 1999 – but both agree on the timbre of the conversation and its outcome. 'By that time I realised that I did overreact about Paul's book, so I said I'd arrange to see him and say sorry,' Roche says. The apology soon segued into a lecture. 'I said, "Don't tell parents not to put their kids in cycling because if your parents hadn't put you into the sport, where would you be today? What would your life be today? Just be balanced in your articles."'

'He said, "Let's make up, let's shake hands,"' Kimmage recalls. 'And I said, "No, I'm not shaking hands." And I remember Jim Glennon, the rugby man, was in the hotel. He saw this and was intrigued by what was going on. But I wouldn't shake his hand and I left. A few weeks later, I got a call about the Conconi connection and the blood doping. And then I thought, "Ah, this is what it's about, getting me onside for this." And I thought, "You bastard."'

In the final week of 1999, Italian newspaper *La Repubblica* broke the news that police in Ferrara had raided the offices of Professor Francesco Conconi as part of an anti-doping investigation, and uncovered computer files that showed he and his assistants, the former Carrera doctor Giovanni Grazzi and the former Gewiss doctor Ilario Casoni, had treated 23 athletes with EPO in 1992 and 1993. It was a particularly egregious case. Conconi was a poacher posing as a gamekeeper. Appointed to the UCI's medical commission in 1993 and rector of the University of Ferrara in 1998, Conconi had received funding from the International Olympic Committee to devise a test for the then undetectable EPO in the early 1990s. At a conference in Lillehammer in 1993, he announced that he had administered EPO to 23 amateur athletes over a period of two years as part of his research, but in truth, only one of the athletes was an amateur: Conconi himself. The others were professional athletes, including cyclists, canoeists and cross-country skiers. Among the cyclists named by *La Repubblica* were former world champions Maurizio Fondriest and Gianni Bugno, Carrera riders Guido Bontempi, Claudio Chiappucci – and Stephen Roche.

Now it was Kimmage picking up the phone to call Roche, seeking comment for the *Sunday Independent*. Unlike Kelly, Roche was never likely to choose silence as a mode of defence. He told Kimmage that Grazzi had assured him it was all a misunderstanding. Roche added that he had met Conconi just once, in 1986, when he first joined Carrera, to undergo a VO2 max test in Ferrara. Conconi gave Roche 'a training programme based on his work with Moser', which he claimed didn't suit his own needs. During his second spell at Carrera, Roche said he had worked primarily with Müller-Wohlfahrt, who had advised him on 'different things such as amino acids, minerals and that kind of stuff'. Asked if he had used EPO, Roche said: 'All I can say is I have had a very, very clean career.'

The story refused to die, not least because Roche was incapable of letting it blow over. He was booked as a guest on the *Late Late Show*, now presented by Pat Kenny, to offer his version of events to the nation. David Walsh, who had added more damning detail to the story in the *Sunday Times*, where he now worked, was invited to appear on the show, ostensibly to provide balance. 'It wasn't really what I wanted but it was better than walking away,' Roche says. Though Walsh had a longer association with Kelly, he was ghost writer for each of the two autobiographical books Roche published in 1988, and they had grown quite close. 'I would always have found Kelly the more interesting,' Walsh says. 'I think it was because he said less but it meant more. Everything he said seemed to have weight, whereas Stephen was just like a fountain.'

Having batted on Kelly's behalf after the Intralipid affair in 1991, it was perhaps surprising that Walsh was so firm in his condemnation of Roche now, but the lie of the land had changed since Michelle Smith and Festina. The conversion was completed at the 1999 Tour, where Walsh was prominent in questioning the validity of Lance Armstrong's success. 'I always had a suspicion that there was plenty going on but I didn't have much of an inquiring nature because I didn't really want to know,' Walsh says of his early writing on Roche and Kelly. 'I think it was what Samuel Taylor Coleridge called the willing suspension of disbelief. But when the Roche stuff came out, the Conconi stuff, I just thought that was so definitive. You couldn't sit on the fence on that one.'

Walsh travelled to Italy when the news broke and gained access to sections of the documentation that implicated Roche, whose name was listed alongside a number of aliases, including Rocchi, Roncati and Righi. Conconi's purported test for EPO was based on measuring the rate of erythropoiesis in the blood by recording the transferrin receptor concentration. According to Conconi himself, a concentration above 3.1 was indicative of EPO usage. On 4 and 13 June 1993 – during the Giro d'Italia, where he placed 9th – Roche recorded values of 5.5 under the aliases Rocchi and Roncati. A source close to the case told Walsh that Roche's haematocrit – the proportion of oxygen-carrying red corpuscles in the blood – had reached 50.2 per cent. Since 1997, the UCI had, in the absence of a ratified EPO test, introduced a haematocrit limit of 50 per cent. Furthermore, the letter 'S' for Sì appeared periodically alongside Roche's aliases. Walsh's source told him this was to indicate when he had been treated with EPO.

Roche and Walsh's 50-minute *Late Late Show* appearance was structured like an episode of Jerry Springer, and almost as farcical. Roche came out alone for 15 minutes of gentle questioning in front of a broadly sympathetic audience, before Walsh was permitted to join him. 'I was the bad guy,' Walsh says. In his opening gambit, Roche clumsily decried 'the sensationalism that's become part of our modern-day life, whether it be in politics, the Church or in sport', and then denied he had ever used EPO. When Walsh sat down beside him and outlined the information he had seen in the Conconi documents, Roche produced a colour-coded chart of his ferritin levels that clouded rather than clarified the issue. Roche's muddled claim that his blood samples had been 'used in experiments', hence the distorted values, only added to the confusion.

Kenny later would chide Walsh for 'convicting somebody with a headline' and the obvious pro-Roche tilt was confirmed when he invited one Dr Bill Tormey to speak from the audience. Tormey, a Fine Gael councillor and pathologist at Beaumont Hospital, didn't allow complete ignorance of the case itself to prevent him from playing out the part of 'appeal court judge' and 'clearing' Roche of wrongdoing. 'He was a total plant. They knew he was coming, they knew what he was going to say,' Walsh says. Roche's parents, Larry and Bunny, were also seated in the audience, and towards the end of the segment, they spoke emotively in his defence. 'We have kids being asked if they're taking drugs because they're winning, because of David Walsh and Paul [Kimmage],' Larry Roche complained.

Walsh's key question – 'Why would Professor Conconi go to such lengths to make it look like Stephen Roche had used drugs?' – went unanswered, however, and for all the hostility towards his stance in the studio, it got a better hearing elsewhere. As he left Montrose, he was told RTÉ had received 400 phone calls, with opinion split down the middle as to Roche's guilt. 'That to me felt like the most brilliant result,' Walsh says. 'I thought the Irish public had a very different take on it than Pat Kenny had.'

Having attempted to depict himself as a latter-day Josef K., Roche also came away claiming victory, and still evinces no regrets about dealing with the accusations so publicly rather than maintaining a studied silence like Kelly. 'I think it got a better result,' he says. 'People who saw the interview would have understood that the values were totally untrue. I think in hindsight, it didn't look good or bad. It just explained certain things more in detail. It might have cleared up some things in people's minds, and people who don't want to believe it won't believe it anyway.'

The judgement of the court of public opinion can be nebulous, but Judge Franca Oliva delivered a clear verdict after the Conconi investigation went to trial in Ferrara. The tectonic speed of the Italian legal system ensured that the statute of limitations had passed by the time the trial finally ended in November 2003, meaning that from a technical standpoint, Conconi, Grazzi and Casoni were acquitted. In a damning 44-page reasoned decision published in March 2004, however, Oliva made it abundantly clear that Conconi, Grazzi and Casoni were indeed guilty of fraudulently enhancing the performances of athletes under their supervision.

'The accused have, for several years and with systematic continuity, aided and abetted the athletes named in the court indictment in their consumption of erythropoietin, supporting them and de facto encouraging them in that consumption with a reassuring series of checks on the state of their health, with exams, analysis and tests designed to assess and maximise the impact of that consumption with regard to sports performances,' Oliva wrote. 'Therefore, on a point of law, the crime as originally charged against the defendants still subsists.'

Oliva concluded that Roche was one of five Carrera riders to be administered with EPO by Grazzi between January and July 1993, citing the evidence contained in files labelled 'ERP' and 'EPO'. During his defence, Grazzi confirmed that the five individuals listed in the 'ERP' file were Carrera riders, and the codenames were deduced as belonging to Claudio Chiappucci, Mario Chiesa, Guido Bontempi, Rolf Sørensen and Roche. Grazzi claimed that the numbers listed in a column headed 'quantity' referred to doses of Esapent, an omega-3 acid, and that the acronym 'ERP' stood for 'Esapent Research Protocol'. The prosecution argued that this was a cover. When they cross-referenced the information from the 'ERP' file with that of the different aliases in the 'EPO' file, the dates of the supposed treatment with Esapent coincided precisely with dates in the 'EPO' file where treatment with EPO was indicated.

'One cannot but arrive at the conclusion that Dr Grazzi was effectively involved in the direct dispensing of EPO to Bontempi, Chiappucci, Chiesa, Roche and Sørensen,' Oliva wrote in her reasoned decision.

Neither Roche nor any of the athletes were defendants in the case, and he complains that he was never asked to provide evidence. 'I was never interviewed, never a phone call,' he says. Quoted in *Ireland on Sunday* in January 2000, Roche made the scientifically improbable claim that the distorted blood values were caused by EPO being added to his blood samples after they had been taken from his body. He quickly revised the comment, simply saying his blood was manipulated in the laboratory, a stance he maintains to this day. 'There was blood tampering there, but afterwards,' he says. 'It wasn't Stephen Roche's blood straight from his body because the results were so up and down.'

Dr Giovanni Grazzi, who remains in the employ of the University of Ferrara, declined to be interviewed on the case for this book, saying he was 'busy', but did respond to (some) questions sent to him by email, including an outline of the explanation he gave Roche about his blood samples: 'The blood samples were left to sediment. Then a sample of the supernatant liquid was removed in order to measure various parameters. The underlying cells were thus concentrated, and not only did the red blood cell count rise, but also that of the white blood cells (which with EPO does not increase).'

As well as the documentary evidence outlined in the trial, there is a problem of perception for Roche. His return to Carrera in 1992 and 1993, during the period covered by the Ferrara trial, coincided with a marked upturn in his level of performance, particularly in three-week races. Circumstantial though it may be, his late-career renaissance also coincided with cycling's era of excess, the years when EPO use was becoming increasingly prevalent in the professional peloton.

'But what did I do? Compare it to what I did before,' Roche says of his performances in his final two seasons. 'I went to Carrera to help Chiappucci, so I had no pressure at all. No pressure at all. I went back to Carrera because there was no pressure. I went back to ride my bike. So why get involved in hard drugs? For what?'

Carrera was also Roche's team in 1987 and Grazzi was the team doctor. The Conconi trial may have dealt only with his second spell on the team, but it raises further, uncomfortable questions about his year of years: most obviously, if, as Judge Franca Oliva affirmed, Grazzi was doping Roche in 1993, then why not in 1987?

Grazzi declined to answer questions relating to Conconi's level of involvement with the Carrera team, and whether blood transfusions were carried out on Carrera riders in the 1980s. '[These questions] regard things that have nothing to do with the Carrera team of the 1980s,' Grazzi wrote. 'No further comment.'

Roche is all too aware that the Ferrara verdict impinges on his entire legacy as a cyclist. His career and the validity of his earlier achievements are inescapably called into question by the evidence pertaining to his final six months in the peloton.

'It doesn't matter what I say. People want me to say "I did it." They'd love to hear me saying that. And then some people mightn't even believe you, so what's the point in going on about it,' Roche says. 'There's nothing I can prove. What I can say is, to this day, almost 40 years on, I'm still the youngest rider to have won the Rás. Does that mean I learned very early? I'm still the youngest rider to win Paris-Nice as a neo-professional. I must have learned really, really fast. Don't just say I won the Tour de France after seven years as a pro because of all the stuff I was taking. Go back and look at where I came from and say, maybe Stephen had talent, and accept that maybe I was a talented guy.'

Ultimately, Kelly and Roche's responses to the doping allegations levelled against them were in keeping with the tenor of how they had comported themselves throughout their careers.

Over the years, Kelly often jokingly recalled the early counsel he received from de Gribaldy about dealing with the press: 'If you give them three words, they'll make 25 out of them.' When the Voet book was published, he took that lighthearted advice very seriously indeed. Roche's *Late Late Show* appearance, by contrast, gave the impression of a man who had never heard the old political adage, 'If you're explaining, you're losing.' Or as Walsh puts it: 'Stephen has always thought that he's brighter than he is and plays at being brighter than he is, and Kelly plays at being dumber than he is.'

It is difficult to assess what damage, if any, the association with doping has done to the legacies of Kelly and Roche. Within the world of cycling, certainly, it seemed to do precious little harm. Kelly is the voice of cycling on a television channel that touts itself as the 'home of cycling'. In the spring of 2017, Roche emulated Bernard Hinault as an ambassador for Tour de France organiser ASO.

But then cycling has always been inclined to look the other way when it comes to the sins of its champions. In time, doping offences come to be dismissed as indiscretions rather than underlined as transgressions. Eddy Merckx is generally regarded as the greatest cyclist of all time despite three positive tests during his career, not least because it is impossible to propose a demonstrably clean alternative. From generation to generation, so many of cycling's stars have either held similar rap sheets or, in the era before drug testing, made no secret of their recourse to doping. And so, despite Voet's book and his positive tests, Kelly still figures among the greatest-ever classics riders, and Roche's 1987 season, despite Conconi, remains among the most extraordinary in cycling history.

Kelly and Roche arrived into this culture when they landed in the peloton in the late 1970s and early 1980s. They didn't create it; it was already in place, and it remained after they left. At Kelly's first Tour in 1977, his team leader was thrown off the race for attempting to cheat a doping control while wearing the yellow jersey. At Roche's first Tour in 1983, a doctor associated with his team publicly advocated doping. Their final victories came as EPO was taking root in the peloton. In such a climate, it is harder to opt out than it is to opt in. By 1987, Kelly and Roche were the two best cyclists in the world. Few of their peers, if any, seemed to feel they had cheated their way there.

'During my time with them as a pro, I really fucking admired them,' Kimmage says. 'I knew they were doping but that didn't matter. I just thought, "This is the job. They do it, they've made their choice. It isn't their fault."'

The impact on Kelly and Roche's reputations in Ireland is perhaps more nuanced. Unlike Michelle Smith, their careers were already over before the legitimacy of their performances was questioned, which limited the damage. Damning as the revelations from Voet and Ferrara were, there was sufficient wriggle room for Kelly and Roche to cling to protestations of innocence, however unconvincing. Nowadays, a Kelly or Roche appearance on a mainstream radio show will typically elicit at least one doping question from the host, but the issue does not define their public profiles. Nostalgia, too, lends a soft focus. Over the past decade, as leisure cycling has flourished in Ireland, some of the more popular sportives on the calendar carry Kelly and Roche's names. The great men smilingly press flesh and pose for pictures as they pedal among middle-aged cyclists who were only children when the athletes graced Cidona adverts and Galtee tea towels.

'Despite what's gone on and what's been said, I still think my achievements are highly regarded back in Ireland,' Roche says. 'The real genuine person doesn't associate the David Walsh article with my career. It's there and they acknowledge it, but I don't think they really say he won because he was doping.'

Doping is an inextricable part of the story of Kelly and Roche's careers, but it hasn't obscured the rest of the narrative, in their home country and elsewhere. Walsh, the man whose journalistic pursuit of Lance Armstrong was made into a Hollywood movie, neatly summarises the cognitive dissonance as he ponders the Kelly revelations. 'You'd wonder: does it diminish your regard for him? A little bit, but not completely.'

23

CORRIDORS OF POWER

Pat McQuaid's tenure as president of the UCI began as it meant to go on. He was elected at the 2005 World Championships in Madrid as the anointed successor of Hein Verbruggen, but during the campaign, a fellow UCI Management Committee member, Sylvia Schenk of Germany, complained to the IOC ethics committee that McQuaid had been in the paid employ of the UCI since the previous February, a breach of the governing body's constitution. Verbruggen and McQuaid insisted that he had simply been paid allowances. As a failsafe, Verbruggen even formally entered the campaign lest McQuaid be prevented from running, but he stepped aside when the IOC ruled in the Irishman's favour. 'Maybe we'll have an Irish approach,' McQuaid said when asked how his presidency would differ from Verbruggen's. 'Maybe we'll do the negotiations in the bar instead of in the office.'

He may have been more genial than his predecessor, but in eight years as UCI president, McQuaid could never shake the impression that he was a proxy for Verbruggen, who had been in the position since 1991 and had overseen cycling's calamitously inadequate response to the doping problem. He was the man, after all, who appointed Francesco Conconi to the UCI's medical committee. Verbruggen went on to become chairman of the coordination commission for the Beijing Olympics but remained the UCI's honorary president and a regular visitor to its headquarters in Aigle, Switzerland. 'It was never planned. I came along, not by design, but by chance, when Verbruggen was stepping down,' McQuaid says. 'The European confederation decided they would support me to become president.'

McQuaid took over the reins in turbulent times. Doping scandals overshadowed the 2006 and 2007 Tours de France. Although McQuaid oversaw the implementation of the biological passport, an anti-doping measure designed to monitor riders' blood values throughout the season, the crises bled from doping to sports politics. Relations between the UCI and Tour de France organisers ASO, already tense, escalated into naked conflict during McQuaid's presidency. For 2008, ASO, Giro organiser RCS and Vuelta organiser Unipublic removed their portfolio of races from the UCI's season-long competition, the ProTour. The Tour de France is by far the biggest race and most lucrative brand in cycling, and the standoff was perilous for the UCI, but just when there seemed to be no ready solution to the impasse, a *deus ex machina* appeared.

In September 2008, Lance Armstrong announced that he was coming out of retirement and targeting an eighth Tour win. If the Tour was bigger than cycling, then Armstrong was bigger than the Tour. He had, after all, once reportedly considered trying to buy it. Barely a month later, the UCI and ASO thrashed out a compromise.

'Sitting here now, I wish he'd stayed away,' McQuaid says of Armstrong. He didn't feel that way at the time, however, even though there was a hint of a confession about the way Armstrong couched his desire to return during a phone call to McQuaid in the summer of 2008. 'He didn't say it in an admissive way, but it could have been on reflection a bit of an admission. He indicated to me that the peloton was cleaner and that he could kick ass. The impression I got was that he wanted to ride the Tour clean and see what he could do. He knew himself he'd won seven Tours with doping and now he found the doping landscape had changed.'

Despite the inference, McQuaid was most accommodating to Armstrong's return. As he had not been in the drug-testing pool for the requisite six months, Armstrong was not eligible to race in the Tour Down Under in January 2009, but McQuaid rubber-stamped an exemption in early October 2008. That same week, Armstrong agreed to compete in the Tour of Ireland in August 2009, the event having been revived in 2007 by Alan Rushton and McQuaid's youngest brother, Darach. It was the only race Armstrong competed in after the Tour de France, and, unlike the Tour Down Under, where he received an appearance fee estimated at $1 million, he raced in Ireland for free, before appearing at a global cancer summit in Dublin. It had all the appearance of a quid pro quo.

'They were two completely separate things altogether,' McQuaid insists. 'Darach's always been a lot closer to Lance than I was. He tweeted him, he knew him. Armstrong said they were going to have a cancer conference in Europe the following year, didn't know where, but it was looking like Rome. Darach said, "Why not Ireland?" That process started, Darach was working on it. That was all totally separate to me. There's no link.'

Armstrong came to Ireland in August 2009 for what proved to be the final edition of the revamped race, going through the motions before pulling out at the base of St Patrick's Hill on the final day. McQuaid, meanwhile, was re-elected unopposed as UCI president the following month in Mendrisio. It must have seemed as though Armstrong's comeback had been most propitious. The feeling wouldn't last.

In May 2010, Floyd Landis eviscerated the Armstrong myth by pressing 'send' on a series of emails detailing the doping programme in place on his US Postal Service team. Over the next 18 months, US Food and Drug Administration agent Jeff Novitzky gathered testimony to prepare a case of federal fraud against Armstrong. When that case was closed abruptly in February 2012, he passed his evidence on to the US Anti-Doping Agency (USADA), who handed Armstrong a life ban eight months later. Although the UCI had vehemently disputed USADA's jurisdiction over the case, on 22 October 2012 McQuaid called a press conference in Geneva and upheld their decision, confirming that Armstrong would be stripped of his seven Tour wins. 'Lance Armstrong has no place in cycling,' McQuaid intoned gravely in his opening statement.

But tough talk is cheap after the fact. Having held the door open for Armstrong's return four years earlier, and then seemingly shown himself hostile to the investigation into him, the tenability of McQuaid's position as UCI president was in question.

One of those opposing McQuaid was Paul Kimmage, who had published an interview with Landis in the *Sunday Times* in February 2011, and then released the full transcript on the NY Velocity website. In January 2012, shortly after he had been made redundant by the *Sunday Times*, Kimmage learned that he was being sued for defamation by the UCI, McQuaid and Verbruggen due to his Landis piece and to comments made in a *L'Équipe* interview suggesting that the UCI had covered for Armstrong. 'It's just a total fuck job that did not need to happen,' says Landis, who was himself subject to a writ from the same three parties. 'But with me, it was different. Fuck it, I'm an American, come and get me…' While the case against Landis petered out, Kimmage received a subpoena in September 2012.

'Somebody had to call a halt to it. Somebody had to call his bluff and get him to be careful in what he writes and says,' McQuaid says. 'If as a journalist you want to write certain things you have to back it up with evidence. There was no evidence.'

It made for disastrous public relations for McQuaid and the UCI, yet still they waded on. An online fund established to finance the unemployed Kimmage's legal battle eventually raised almost $100,000 (though one of the fund's handlers would later syphon off $64,000) as he became a cause célèbre. In suing the individual rather than the publication, it was hard to dispel the sense that McQuaid was playing the man rather than the ball. 'If I made a mistake, it was suing a journalist, because the media supports the media. But on the principle of it, I felt very strongly for the people working around me, that they were being called corrupt,' recalls McQuaid. He says that he can't pinpoint precisely when the mutual enmity between him and Kimmage began in earnest.

'I don't really know where it started to be honest with you, other than I didn't praise him and clap him on the back when his book came out. My view was that Kimmage had an engine which was a certain size. When he turned pro, he didn't have the engine to go to a higher level and he blamed everybody else – because they were leaving him on a hill, they were doping. Quite a few of them may have been, but not all of them were. But he said they all were. That was the basis of his book and everything he did. I didn't agree with that.'

'I remember RTÉ doing some *Primetime* pieces on the state of pro cycling and McQuaid would always be brought on spouting shite. There was also a debate about doping in sport with a panel on the *Late Late Show* in '97 or '98, and McQuaid was in the audience and I had a go at him. That was the dynamic,' Kimmage says. 'He was Verbruggen's puppet. Pat's opening his mouth but it's Verbruggen's voice coming out. Everything he ever did was what Verbruggen wanted. It was classic Verbruggen. It was always reactive and never proactive.'

By early 2013, McQuaid's bid for a third term as UCI president was beginning to feel increasingly like a local row. Two of his most prominent critics were fellow countrymen, Kimmage and David Walsh. Though it was Landis's whistleblowing and Novitzky's subpoena power that eventually undid Armstrong, the longevity of Walsh's pursuit meant he was enjoying considerable celebrity in the wake of Armstrong's downfall. With the White Whale harpooned, attention turned to the governing body that had allowed him to prosper in the first place. 'The ideal president coming in should have been representing everything that Hein Verbruggen wasn't as opposed to being a disciple, almost the appointed successor. That was a problem,' Walsh says of McQuaid.

The head of British Cycling, Brian Cookson, announced his intention to run against McQuaid in June, though, as a member of the UCI Management Committee, he was hardly running on a mandate of change. Even so, his challenge to McQuaid was endorsed to varying degrees by figures such as Kimmage, Walsh and Greg LeMond – and, more important, was backed financially by the Russian oligarch Oleg Makarov, president of the European Cycling Union. McQuaid, by contrast, seemed to be struggling to find voices of authority to stump on his behalf, but two old friends dutifully expressed their support for his position: Kelly and Roche. They were hardly neutral observers. Both men had been nominated to UCI committees during McQuaid's presidency; Kelly sat on the road commission, while Roche was part of the Professional Cycling Council.

'First of all, there was that loyalty there from the earlier days,' Kelly admits. 'But I also know that it wasn't a good time to be president, and they were going for his head. But was there anybody there who could do better? I don't think so. And since it's changed, has it got better? I don't think it's got much better.'

Roche had some previous experience in presidential campaigns, and a history of backing establishment candidates: during the 2007 French presidential election, he appeared in a spot on behalf of Nicolas Sarkozy. He rejects the idea that he stumped for McQuaid out of friendship or self-interest, claiming he might have withdrawn his public support had a more inspiring candidate than Cookson come forward. 'But when I saw who was up against Pat, there was no way,' Roche says. 'They didn't sack the president, they sacked Pat McQuaid. Maybe he didn't always take the best decisions, he was ducking and diving, but he made decisions to try to keep the business floating and attract sponsors.'

In private, however, Roche was not blind to McQuaid's failings, most notably his close alignment with Verbruggen. 'It was difficult to do because of how much Verbruggen had done to get him in there, but I felt that after a couple of years, Pat should have been able to sit down with Verbruggen and say, "Listen Hein, I appreciate everything you've done for me over the years but you have to move your office. You cannot stay in the back room of my office," ' Roche says.

Kimmage, however, disputes the idea that McQuaid's sole failing was meekness. 'Oh, he's not weak. He was greedy. Pat Hickey, John Delaney, Pat McQuaid, they're all cut from the same cloth. It's not about sport. They don't give a fuck about sport. It's all about power and privilege for them, and that's it,' Kimmage says. 'And that's another aspect to my relationship with Kelly and Roche. They backed McQuaid. At a time when I was being sued by him and the UCI, they were rowing in with McQuaid.'

In time, Kimmage would also fall out with David Walsh, a very public divorce that seemed to have its genesis in Kimmage's departure from the *Sunday Times*, and came to a head when Walsh spent the 2013 season shadowing the Sky team of Bradley Wiggins and Chris Froome. In a rerun of his rapport with Kelly and Roche, Walsh would even go on to ghostwrite Froome's autobiography in 2014. When Walsh vouched publicly and, as it turned out, very prematurely for the bona fides of Team Sky, Kimmage saw it as a betrayal of ideals. In 2010, Sky manager Dave Brailsford had reneged on an offer to have Kimmage, then at the *Sunday Times*, follow the team at the Tour. 'These cunts – Sky, Brailsford, lying bastard – they fucked me over big time, and this is my best fucking friend getting into bed with them and validating them,' Kimmage says. 'I was so angry.' Walsh has declined to discuss the falling-out in public.

The respective sentiments of Kelly, Roche, Kimmage and Walsh had, in truth, only a notional effect on an electorate made up entirely of UCI delegates, but in the early summer of 2013, it briefly appeared as though Irish opinion could still have a material impact on McQuaid's election bid. He needed to be nominated by his federation to stand for election, and, as in 2005 and 2009, he sought the support of Cycling Ireland. The board voted 5–1 in favour of nominating McQuaid, but the lone dissenter, Anto Moran, highlighted a procedural error, and successfully called for an emergency general meeting to vote on the matter.

On 15 June, after an hour-long and often impassioned debate, delegates at the EGM voted 91–74 against nominating McQuaid for the presidency of the UCI. It was a stunning defeat for McQuaid and, indeed, for the board of Cycling Ireland. It also seemed to speak of a new kind of split in Irish cycling. A recurring lament from McQuaid supporters was that the demographic voting against him was composed predominantly of young and recent members of Cycling Ireland, who were involved in leisure riding rather than in competitive racing. That rather overlooks the fact, however, that among the weightiest and most considered voices arguing against McQuaid were longstanding and active members such as the Cycling Ireland doctor, Conor McGrane. Another intriguing element of the debate is that the opinions of Kelly and Roche – admittedly less forcibly and volubly expressed than those of Kimmage, for instance – seemed to carry precious little weight.

'I suffered the most masterful display of begrudgery,' McQuaid says, continuing:

> That hurt me badly at the time. I was angry. I don't think the EGM was necessary. I think the board should have stuck to their guns. It wasn't as if they were electing me as president of the UCI; they were nominating me, that's all. But social media got to them, they pushed very hard. The people who had been involved in cycling all their lives supported me. The ones who were speaking out against me were the new young groups that had come in and joined clubs for insurance reasons; most of them don't even race.

McQuaid's concurrent attempt to secure a nomination from the federation in Switzerland, his place of residence, fell through the following August, but thanks to a creative reading of the UCI constitution, he eventually arrived at the election in Florence backed by the Moroccan and Thai federations, of which he was an honorary member. It was all for nothing. McQuaid lost the election to Cookson, by 24 votes to 18.

McQuaid smiles wanly at the idea that his defeat in Ireland, or the opinion of cycling fans generally, had any impact on the outcome, citing instead the influence of Makarov's backing for Cookson. As FIFA, the IOC et al. regularly demonstrate, sports politics exists in a vacuum, and its power brokers seem inured to public opinion. On the night before the election, five delegates from McQuaid's core vote switched their preference to Cookson. 'That's what buggered me in the end,' McQuaid says. 'It wasn't all the social media or the Paul Kimmages.'

►⊙◄

Thirty-six years on from Leipzig came another trip into the absurd for Kimmage and McQuaid, this time in Vevey, Switzerland. In April 2016, they sat on opposite sides of a small courtroom for the hearing of Hein Verbruggen versus Paul Kimmage. On his election, Cookson had swiftly removed the UCI from the suit against Kimmage. Five months later, McQuaid also opted to withdraw from the case, but, as was his wont, Verbruggen fought the matter to the bitter end. McQuaid, once his protégé, was his star witness. A month later, the court would rule in favour of Verbruggen, ordering Kimmage to pay damages of 12,000 Swiss francs as well as various legal costs.

In the lead-up to the hearing, McQuaid, now living in France, had let slip in an interview with *L'Équipe* that he was planning to write an autobiography. Kimmage couldn't resist bringing it up when they encountered one another at the entrance to courtroom. 'Pat, I hear you're writing a book. You'd better get your facts right or you'll be back in here with me,' Kimmage said. McQuaid responded in kind: 'Don't worry, you'll figure in it.'

McQuaid struggles to recall the last time they spoke at any length, but places it to prior to the publication of *A Rough Ride*.

'I probably haven't had a good conversation with him since before that,' he says. Kimmage remembers a brief meeting at the launch of Pat Daly's authoritative history of the Rás in the winter of 2003. As a journalist, he had never interviewed McQuaid.

In the courtroom, McQuaid was called as one of five witnesses on behalf of Verbruggen, and he performed his duty for his mentor. Kimmage was bemused when McQuaid listed his profession as 'PE teacher': he had not, after all, been inside a classroom in more than 30 years, not since he left teaching to focus on building the Nissan Classic. 'The judge just asked factual questions of me, really. I was only there for five or 10 minutes,' McQuaid says. 'Did I think Mr Kimmage was over the top in writing what he wrote? I said a journalist should be objective and write both sides of the story, but Mr Kimmage never wrote the other side of the story; he wrote his opinion.'

'He essentially gives a statement and then he has to sit down with the interpreter and make sure everything he's said has been properly recorded,' Kimmage says. 'He signs off on that and then walks past, and he taps Verbruggen on the back as he goes out, and I'm thinking, "You fucking bastard." He goes out and I don't see him again.'

Not quite. The following morning, they sat on opposite sides of the departure lounge in Geneva airport, waiting in frosty silence for the same flight to Dublin. A small world.

EPILOGUE

It was not quite summer, and not quite daylight, but despite the sleepiness of the season and the hour, there were people and there was life along the seafront strip of Playa de Muro. As the clock ticked on towards seven o'clock, the sky's hues lightened in instalments to powder blue. Beneath the lifting gloom, a couple of thousand cyclists swapped small talk in the chill dawn air as they waited for the start of the 2014 edition of the Mallorca 312 mass participation event.

Deference was paid to the invited *galacticos*, who lined up on the front row. Men like Miguel Indurain, Oscar Freire and Fernando Escartin may have come for the appearance fee, but they were happy to stay for the privilege of dusting off some old war stories, struggling up a couple of climbs together and then, when it was all over, marvelling quietly at how quickly the years had gone by.

Among their number was Sean Kelly. There is something of Clint Eastwood about the way he has aged. As a young man, his long, stoic face always looked older and more battle-hardened than his passport suggested. Now, on the cusp of 60, he bears his years lightly, and smiles more in a morning than he was seen to do in two decades as a rider. He might go on for ever. Cyclist, commentator, team manager, businessman. He's crammed a lot in already.

Alongside Kelly, Stephen Roche is more corpulent, and heavier of bearing, but a closer look at the cheeks and the eyes is enough to confirm the identity. The days since retirement have not always been kind, but the smile, though sometimes uneasy, is always affixed. Those early years after hanging up his bike were spent trying to salvage his marriage to Lydia. After the divorce, their youngest son, Florian, endured and overcame leukaemia. Roche's second wife, Sophie, recovered from cancer. In 2011, Roche spent a night in a police cell after prospective business partners turned out to be fraudsters. The sharks of the peloton must have seemed toothless by comparison.

An old comrade was lined up a few rows back. Paul Kimmage is more feted for his work as a journalist than he ever was as a cyclist, but, like his compatriots, he is defined by those seasons in the peloton. Few illusions survive intact when a child's dream doubles as a man's job.

Roche and Kimmage studiously ignored one another, but for all his toughness on a bike, Kelly was never much given to confrontation off it. He made a beeline for Kimmage and engaged in small talk. Perhaps there was a hint of quiet devilment, too, when he called out to alert Roche to Kimmage's presence. Nothing to be done.

'Kelly sees me and says, "Ah, there's Kimmage, how are you?" He'd just talk away,' Kimmage says. 'And then Kelly's there saying, "Hey, Stephen, look who's here," and Roche just looks across. There was a stop an hour later and Roche was there and I just walked by him. I've had no contact with him and I don't desire to have any contact with him. And it's the same with Kelly now. I wasn't going over to him, he came over talking to me. And I'd say his view of me has soured since then, because I'm not letting him off on anything now.'

When Kimmage left cycling for journalism, he decorated his home office with framed photographs of each of Irish cycling's Fab Four. One by one, they came down off the wall. Roche went after the breaking of the post-*Rough Ride* peace. Kelly was gone after his backing of McQuaid in 2013. Earley lasted as far as 2014, when Kimmage was writing of Johannes Draaijer.

The Men of Villach have never held a reunion. They haven't even all been in the same place at once since the start of the 1998 Tour de France. Their lives intertwined intensely in the 1980s, but they were bound together by circumstance more than by friendship. Once their careers ended, the ties loosened. The schedules of Kelly and Roche, both still working in the cycling industry, mean they still meet quite regularly, at bike races, trade shows and training camps. Earley, happily withdrawn from cycling, speaks occasionally with Kelly, but never with Roche or Kimmage. 'You just don't cross paths really,' he says.

Not even posterity, it seems, can bring them together. When Cycling Ireland inaugurated its Hall of Fame in 2013, Kelly, Roche and Pat McQuaid were among the first 20 inductees, but, absurdly, there was no place for Earley and Kimmage, nor, indeed, for Laurence Roche.

There has, of course, been a steady stream of Irish success once the long fallow period that followed their retirement eventually passed, with Ciarán Power and Morgan Fox's entry into the professional peloton in 2000. Roche's nephew Dan Martin has shone brightest, winning Liège-Bastogne-Liège, the Tour of Lombardy and a stage of the Tour de France. Nicolas Roche, Stephen's son, has enjoyed a fine professional career, and Mark Scanlon, Philip Deignan and Sam Bennett have all competed and won at the highest level. On the track, Martyn Irvine won the scratch race world title in 2013, a year after Caroline Ryan had won Ireland's first medal since Harry Reynolds. On the road, more young riders, including Ryan Mullen and Eddie Dunbar, winner of the amateur Tour of Flanders in 2017, are emerging. Unlike the early 1990s, the future holds promise.

And yet nothing, it seems, will ever match the achievements and the popularity of the golden generation of the 1980s. How could it, when not even the main players themselves can fully comprehend how it happened? To have two riders of the calibre of Kelly and Roche emerge independently of one another within the space of four years seems a most astonishing accident of history, as though Tupelo had produced a second Elvis Presley shortly after the first. It defies logical explanation.

'I think it was just chance,' says Earley in the arrivals hall at East Midlands airport, where he sometimes has to be prodded into reminiscence, as if he doesn't quite understand what all the fuss is about. 'It was all a long time ago,' he smiles.

Kelly puffs out his cheeks in a hotel lobby in Calpe. 'Well, it was amazing,' he offers eventually. His story alone is one of the most extraordinary Irish lives, from a shy boy in a lonely farmhouse in Curraghduff to world number one. Almost as remarkably, the remorseless winner seemed to make no enemies along the way. He bookends a dissection of his rivalry with Eric Vanderaerden with a casual revelation: 'Sure, his son Massimo is on the team now.' In Rheims in 1985, nobody would ever have believed that Vanderaerden would one day entrust his son into the care of Kelly.

Across a day in Majorca, Roche apologetically leaps from his seat on several occasions to take phone calls, to greet guests to his training camp, to sort out contracts. In between, he offers a romantic rationale for Irish cycling's gilded age. 'The genes of

Irish people are incredible for sport,' he says. 'And we learned to enjoy cycling before becoming cyclists.'

Were it not for Roche, one wonders whether Earley and Kimmage would have made the grade. Kelly, further removed in age and in background, must have seemed almost as distant as Shay Elliott, but Roche was one of them, more accessible. 'Roche had a much greater bearing on us, because we'd grown up with him,' Kimmage says in the café of the National Library of Ireland on Kildare Street. 'He made the gap a bit narrower for myself and Martin. I don't know if it would have happened for us really, without Roche.'

Kimmage is a difficult read for eavesdroppers. He swears and blinds when he's enthusiastic, and he swears and blinds when he's annoyed. After a morning of turning the air blue, he shakes his head at the very public second acts of so many figures from Irish cycling's golden generation. Perhaps there is an explanation of sorts there. For better and for worse, the men were driven. They never stopped climbing.

At the time of Lance Armstrong's downfall, the man feted for pursuing him was from Kilkenny, the UCI president was from Glasnevin, his staunchest critic was from Coolock, and cycling's most popular television commentator was from Carrick-on-Suir. More than a quarter of a century after the glory days, they were still, in their own ways, at the centre of the sport.

'In a word, it's fucked up, isn't it?' Kimmage says. 'That is fucking bizarre. How do you explain that? How do you fucking explain that? What does it say about us?'

SELECT BIBLIOGRAPHY

Astorqui, Fernando with Gómez Peña, Jesús. *Mi Vuelta*, El Correo, Bilbao, 2017.

Bacon, Ellis and Birnie, Lionel eds. *The Cycling Anthology, volume 4*. Yellow Jersey Press, London, 2014.

Bergonzi, Pier and Trifari, Elio, eds. *Un secolo di passioni. Giro d'Italia 1909–2009*, Rizzoli, Milan, 2009.

Blondin, Antoine. *Tours de France. Chroniques de 'L'Équipe' 1954–1982*, La Table Ronde, Paris, 2001.

Bordas, Philippe. *Forcenés*, Fayard, Paris, 2008.

Carrey, Pierre. *Le Tour de France à dévorer*, DirectVelo, Paris, 2016.

Chany, Pierre and Cazeneuve, Thierry. *La fabuleuse histoire du Tour de France*, Editions de la Martinière, Paris, 2011.

Colombo, Paolo and Lanotte, Gioachino. *La corsa del secolo. Cent'anni di storia italiana attraverso il Giro*, Mondadori, Milan, 2009.

Cossins, Peter. *The Monuments: The Grit and the Glory of Cycling's Greatest One-Day Races*, Bloomsbury, London, 2015.

Daly, Tom. *The Rás: The Story of Ireland's Unique Bike Race*, Collins Press, Dublin, 2002.

Donati, Alessandro. *Lo sport del doping. Chi lo subisce, chi lo combatte*, Edizioni Gruppo Abele, Turin, 2013.

Ejnés, Gérard and Schaller, Gérard eds. *Tour de France: 100 ans, 1903–2003*, SNC L'Équipe, Paris, 2002.

Fignon, Laurent. *Nous étions jeunes et insouciants*, Grasset, Paris, 2009.

Fotheringham, Alasdair. *Reckless*, Bloomsbury, London, 2014.

Fotheringham, Alasdair. *The End of the Road*, Bloomsbury, London, 2016.

Fotheringham, William. *Racing Hard*, Faber and Faber, London, 2013.

Fotheringham, William. *The Badger: Bernard Hinault and the Fall and Rise of French Cycling*. Yellow Jersey Press, London, 2015.

Géminiani, Raphaël with Vespini, Jean-Paul. *Mes quatre vérités*, Jacob Duvernet, Paris, 2010.

Guimard, Cyrille. *Dans les secrets du Tour de France*, J'ai lu, Paris, 2013.

Guinness, Rupert. *The Foreign Legion*, A & C Black, London, 1993.

Healy, Graham with Allchin, Richard. *Shay Elliott. The Life and Death of Ireland's First Yellow Jersey*, Mousehold Press, Norwich, 2011.

Kelly, Sean with Birnie, Lionel. *Hunger*, Peloton Publishing, St Albans, 2013.

Kimmage, Paul. *A Rough Ride*, Stanley Paul, London, 1990.

Maertens, Freddy, translated by Hawkins, Steve. *Fall from Grace*. Ronde Publications, London, 1993.

Rendell, Matt. *The Death of Marco Pantani*, Orion, London, 2006.

Roche, Stephen with Cossins, Peter. *Born to Ride*, Yellow Jersey Press, London, 2012.

Roche, Stephen. *My Road to Victory*, Stanley Paul, London, 1987.

Roche, Stephen with Walsh, David. *The Agony and the Ecstasy*, Stanley Paul, London, 1988.

Various authors. *Cols mythiques du Tour de France*, L'Équipe, Paris, 2005.

Voet, Willy, translated by Fotheringham, William. *Breaking the Chain*, Yellow Jersey Press, London, 2001.

Voet, Willy. *Massacre à la Chaîne*, Éditions Calmann-Lévy, Paris, 1999.

Walsh, David. *Inside the Tour de France*, Hutchinson, London, 1994.

Walsh, David. *Kelly*, Grafton Books, London, 1986.

Walsh, David. *Seven Deadly Sins*, Simon & Schuster, London, 2012.

Watson, Graham. *The Tour de France and its Heroes*, Hutchinson, London, 1990.

Whittle, Jeremy. *Bad Blood: The Secret Life of the Tour de France*, Yellow Jersey Press, London, 2008.

Whittle, Jeremy. *Yellow Fever: The Dark Heart of the Tour de France*, Headline Book Publishing, London, 1999.

Yates, Sean. *It's All About the Bike*, Bantam Press, London, 2013.

Newspapers and magazines

BiciSport

Cycle Sport

Cycling Weekly

Il Corriere della Sera

International Herald Tribune

Ireland on Sunday

Irish Examiner

Irish Independent

Irish Press

Irish Times

L'Équipe

La Gazzetta dello Sport

La Repubblica

La Stampa

Le Monde

Libération

International Herald Tribune

Mundo Deportivo

Munster Express

Procycling

Sunday Independent

Sunday Press

Sunday Times

Sunday Tribune

The Kerryman

Tuttobici

Vélo Magazine

Websites

Cyclingnews.com

Cyclisme-dopage.com

Dopeology.org

Jeandegribaldy.com

Stickybottle.com

Tuttobiciweb.it

Veloveritas.co.uk